🐾 Praise for 8 State Hurricane Kate

"8 State Hurricane Kate is a great true story which will appeal to dog owners and their best friends... A story of the indomitable spirits of human and canine combined, it's a brightening tale for dog lovers and those seeking a story of overcoming one of the worst natural American disasters in recent history." —*Midwest Book Review*

"..8 State Hurricane Kate deserves to be near the top of every one's "must read" list... Jenny Pavlovic's story should inspire everyone to do a little bit more, to try a little bit harder, and to believe in our abilities to get things done." —Jeff Dorson, *Founder, Executive Director, Humane Society of Louisiana*

"A heartfelt recap... a story of one woman's experience of stepping out of her comfort zone and into a disaster zone, and then stepping out again with... a dog that she was able to lift out of harm's way...8 State Hurricane Kate is a book for anyone who has adopted a pet and ever wonders where he or she really came from. It's a book for anyone who couldn't go to help animals after Katrina, but wished they could." —Kelli Ohrtman *of Best Friends Animal Society in the Star Tribune Pet Central Blog*

"8 State Hurricane Kate... exemplifies the tremendous spirit of the people of the Gulf Coast, of the animals caught up in the maelstrom, and of the individuals who couldn't stand by and watch it happen without doing something to help." —Amy Maher, *Board Chair, Noah's Wish*

"An inspiring and challenging book that explodes with passion and primordial wisdom." —Sharon Azar, *Guideposts Magazine,* Weekly blogger for www.guidepostsmag.com, *Founder of WOOF! (Wagging On and On Forever!), rescuing NYC dogs*

"Jenny's passion for animals flows freely and gracefully throughout this book, and her deep connection with Kate is a strong testament to what's possible when our hearts are completely open." —Sage (Stacy) Lewis, *Author of JAVA: The True Story of a Shelter Dog Who Rescued a Woman*

"A story that captures your heart... an exploration of the ties between humans and animals, grief and recovery, and the spiritual side of lending a hand to those in need." —K. Melissa Tooley, *in Urban Dog Magazine and The Australian Cattle Dog Quarterly*

"...an insider's story that provides a real look at the devastation that was Katrina. Read it and share it with the dog lovers in your life... an inspiring, well-written story." —Lori Martinek, *Branding Expert, Speaker and Author of Be the Bulb! (Herlife Publishing 2009)*

"A touching and motivational story that helps to spread the message that we will continue to teach the world that animals matter." —Gail Monick, *Katrina Volunteer, Noah's Wish,* www.noahswish.info

"A moving story about the relationship between a dog and a human who experience an adventure that will touch your heart and soul." —Donna Chicone, *Host of the TV Dog Show*

🐾 From Readers... 🐾

"A deep book that takes the reader to the depths of despair and brings back hope. Buy it, read it and give another copy to a friend. " —Eileen Bertie, Arizona

"A book you will never forget. This true story takes you through all the wonderful highs and devastating lows of rescue work and reminds you to love with your all - because that is how animals love you back." —J.R. Greer, Texas

"A moving emotional and spiritual journey... Kate is the symbol for the power of Spirit in times of great adversity." —Dana Lisa Young, Georgia

"This is one of the most inspirational books I have ever read. I am telling everyone I know about it... There are so many passages... that go straight to the heart." —Lynn Peaslee, Florida

"For the true love of animals... This book is so well written that you can feel the experience as best one can without actually having gone through it. I highly recommend it to anyone who loves dogs." —Debra L. Okamura, Hawaii

"I just wanted to say thank you....This book is something I believe all dog lovers should read! I...ended up reading the whole story yesterday. I just couldn't put it down..." —Melissa Osborne, Ohio

8 State

Hurricane Kate

the Journey
and Legacy *of*
a Katrina Cattle Dog

jenny pavlovic, Ph.D.

In Memory Of

...Al and Duke, Shannon, and the many others who
didn't survive Hurricane Katrina and her aftermath.

...Dr. Stan Waters for his generosity to Kate and me.
I'll do my best to pay it forward.

8 State Hurricane Kate
Copyright © 2008 Jenny Pavlovic, Ph. D.
www.8StateKate.net
Afton, Minnesota, United States of America

Second Edition
ISBN: 1-4382-1649-1
EAN-13: 97-81438-21649-2

Library of Congress Control Number: 2008905570

Cover & Interior Design by Gregory Rohm

Printed in the United States of America

*This book is available at special discounts when purchased in quantities for use in fundraising.
For details, please contact the author at njennyr@8StateKate.net.*

Dedication

This Book is Dedicated to...

...Christa, Jace, Bruce and the other Katrina survivors who will never be the same,

...Those who were left behind,

...The concerned and dedicated people who traveled to the Gulf Coast to help,

...The network of caring people who helped Kate and me, and who help animals every day,

...Nike, Pippi, Alex, Zena, Rusty, Rainbow, Marble, Cayenne, and my boys Bandit and Chase who have taught me so much and bring me joy.

Most of all, this book is dedicated to Kate, for what she has meant to all of us. Kate, you are not forgotten.

ಌ ❤ ಚ

Thank you to...

...my family and friends for your love and support, even when you think I'm crazy! MK, that includes you.

...Di, Eileen, Susan, Sarah, Nickie, Roxane, Stacy, Bazza, KC Jim, Georgia, Amanda, and Mom for their input and encouragement during the creation of this book, and to Connie who strongly urged me to write this story.

Thank you to...

I'm especially grateful to my editor Nickie for her patience and the intrepid hours she spent taking a rough draft and shaping it into the book you see today, to Di for her countless hours building and maintaining Kate's website (all the way from Cairns, Australia!), to Sarah for being a true friend and for all the animals she has saved from an untimely, ugly death (including my lovebug Chase), and to Eileen for her dedication to cattle dog rescue, and for always being there.

Thank you also to John Nemo who taught me how to make this book a reality, and to Gregory Rohm who beautifully brought it to life.

Acknowledgements

I'm very grateful to the following people and organizations for their financial and/or emotional support during this journey. Kate and I would not have made it without you and I can never thank you enough. Sometimes it really does take a village!

Australian Cattle Dog Rescue, Inc., especially Deb Ray

Becky C of Hastings, Minnesota

The "C" Family of Baton Rouge, Louisiana

Guidant Corporation

Hertz Rent-A-Car

Holiday Inn of Lincoln, Illinois

Lisa of PAWS-a-tively Pet Care, Newport, Minnesota

Mary Getten, Orcas Island, Washington

Minnetonka Animal Hospital, Minnetonka, Minnesota

Northwest Airlines

Stillwater Veterinary Clinic, Stillwater, Minnesota

    (Dr. Waters, Dr. Winter, and Dr. Thorson)

T-Mobile

Wellness Matters, Lake Elmo, Minnesota

ACD-L Friends:

Alex H, Angie F, Armanda S, Barry S, Becky L, Carol G, Cheyenne M, Christine W, Dana F, Dana P, Deb R, Debby E, Debra W, Diane S, Doug M, Eileen L, Jim J, Kathleen H, Kathy B, Luis S, Nickie P, Nicole C, Rodrica T, Susan P, Tina T, Trish C

Acknowledgements

Friends from All Breed Obedience in Woodbury, Minnesota:

Amy, Ann, Bobbi, Deb and Michael, Donell, Donna, Janna, Libbe, Rebecca, and Sharon

Minnesota Friends:

Bob L, Bridget L, Eric and Jenny S, Leslie C

Fellow Volunteers from the Lamar-Dixon Expo Center:

Beryl B (Rescue A Golden Minnesota), Cindy J (Virginia), Connie E (Pasado's Safe Haven, Washington), Jaye W (Missouri), Lori S (Wisconsin), Nancy T (Louisiana), Sarah D (Lost Fantasy Stables and Animal Rescue, Virginia), Monica O and Veronica O, (Homeward Bound Rescue, Texas)

Website Support:

Di Edwards, Eric Smith, Janna Hora, and Sarah Dutton

Table of Contents

Foreword

by Sarah Dutton, Katrina Animal Rescuer

Sometimes the strangest things drive you to act in a way you could never expect… completely changing your life from that point on. That's what happened to me and that's how I met Jenny and Kate.

I watched in horror as newscasts showed Hurricane Katrina bearing down on New Orleans. New pictures of the widespread devastation surfaced each day. What concerned me most were the thousands of animals who suffered because a bureaucratic system showed no mercy for their lives. The animals were not allowed to be evacuated with their owners, but were left instead to die in the flooded streets or starve to death from lack of food. I knew that I couldn't stay home and watch this tragedy unfold. I had to go to New Orleans to help.

When my group pulled through the gates of the Lamar-Dixon Expo Center in Gonzales, Louisiana, the parking lot was full of cars. The sheer number of animals was staggering, with over 1,400 animals on the grounds and more coming in every hour. Rescue teams were in the city, working against the clock to pull animals to safety. Many of the animals were suffering from severe dehydration and starvation, and had chemical burns on their feet and bodies from being trapped in the contaminated floodwaters. Many were so terrified of human contact that they shook when you approached them or cowered in the backs of their cages, refusing to come out.

My traveling companions and I were put to work in Barn 5. We bathed dogs to remove the oily residue from their tender skin, cleaned cages, walked dogs, and fed dogs that hadn't eaten for days. We took dogs to the vetting area to be vaccinated, microchipped for future identification, and catalogued for the Petfinder website, so they could hopefully be reunited with their families. Once vetted, the dogs were prepared for export to animal shelters around the country. This made room at Lamar-Dixon for more newly-rescued dogs.

The heat in the barns was unbearable for both the dogs and the humans. Some volunteers didn't stay long due to the heat, the smells, and the overwhelming feeling of not knowing what to do next or how to make order out of this chaos. The constant barking was enough to put your nerves on edge. If you weren't confident in your abilities as a dog handler, some of the dogs were too much to handle. Many were pits or pit mixes and some had been fighting dogs prior to the storm. Most volunteers didn't feel comfortable handling these dogs, so I was often called on to walk them while others cleaned their pens.

I met many volunteers at Lamar-Dixon and I don't even remember most of their names. Jenny was the first one who made an impact on me by her dedication to what she was doing and her desire to make the dogs as comfortable as possible. I watched Jenny work nonstop in the heat, bringing food and water to the dogs, rounding up dog walkers, cleaning dirty cages, and going on food-finding missions for both the people and dogs. I was very impressed. Jenny, my traveling companion Cindy and I became friends. We saved food for each other so we could eat in the evenings, when we sat and talked about what had happened during the day.

Jenny introduced me to an old cattle dog and told me she wanted to foster her. This poor dog was a wreck…hot…scared…beat up…like many others in the barns. We talked about getting permission from the higher powers to take the dogs out of the heat. I watched as Jenny jumped through many hoops to get permission to foster Kate. The day Jenny loaded Kate into her rented SUV, I said a prayer that their drive home would be safe and that Kate would go on to live a wonderful life. Thanks to Jenny, she did.

Hurricane Katrina taught me many things. I learned that I'm much stronger than I thought and that I can make a difference…that love is stronger than anything else, but love can't always save us…that friends come to you from the most unlikely places, and that a true friend will always be there for you day or night…that many people do not view their pets as part of their family (which makes me sad)…that nightmares can drive you on when you want to quit…and that a broken heart doesn't always heal the way you thought it would.

I tell everyone to remember because that's what keeps us going through good and bad times. Remember those who were lost: Kate, Me-Moo, Shannon, and Al. Remember those who remain: Bruce, Tootsie Roll, Gonzo, Little Man, Carolyn and Paul. Remember the lessons we learned. Remember and never forget.

May the blessings of the animals be with you always,

Sarah Dutton
Katrina Animal Rescuer
Founder and President of *Lost Fantasy Stables and Animal Rescue*
Ceres, Virginia

Prelude

When I was four years old, we lived in an apartment and could not have pets. I was found walking a neighbor girl on her hands and knees, with a jump rope looped around her neck. She barked and carried on just like a real dog, playing her role perfectly. She enjoyed being a dog, and I enjoyed having a "dog", but it was awkward because her father was my dad's boss!

When I was twelve, a puppy appeared on our front porch one morning. He was lost and scared and we took him in. But Mom said it was only long enough to find his real owners, period! We couldn't have a dog because my sister was allergic. A few days later, we found the dog's "real" owners, some kids who had won him at the fair. They already had a dog and couldn't keep him. By then, we realized that my sister was not allergic to him and he became my dog.

My first *real* dog found me when I was a kid and dogs have been finding me ever since.

ဆ ♥ ◌

Throughout this book, first names are used to protect people's privacy.

The word "who" is intentionally used with respect to animals. Although this may not be officially grammatically correct, it is correct in my book.

"I am only one, but still I am one. I cannot do everything, but still I can do something. And because I cannot do everything, I will not refuse to do the something that I can do."

Edward Everett Hale

"A problem is a backwards opportunity."

fortune cookie

Chapter 1
Mobilizing

I didn't go down there to get a dog. I didn't know what was going to happen, I just had to be there to help. But there she was, an old blue cattle dog, down for the count and running out of options. I noticed her right away because I had cattle dogs at home. She had been rescued from a rooftop with no collar, ID, tattoo, or microchip to tell where she was from. She had been left behind at least once already and I couldn't let that happen again. One thing simply led to another.

I've often been asked why I went to Louisiana after Hurricane Katrina, and why I am so involved in animal rescue now. Here is my story.

We all knew that Hurricane Katrina was coming. Even in Minnesota, Public Radio gave daily updates well in advance of landfall. Katrina was expected to be huge. She was heading right for the Gulf Coast, and people were advised to evacuate.

Monday, August 29th, 2005

When Katrina hit, it was hell along the coasts of Louisiana, Mississippi and Alabama. Lower Plaquemines Parish (southeast of New Orleans) received heavy rain and the full force of Katrina's 150 mile-per-hour winds. On the Mississippi coast, the storm surge left a waterline more than 28 feet high. In New Orleans, the relief of surviving the hurricane ended abruptly when the levees failed and all hell broke loose. The water flooded in, submerging 80 percent of the city, with some areas flooded to a depth of 20 feet.

Tuesday, August 30th

I received an e-mail message requesting donations to support animal rescue efforts along the Gulf Coast. I sent a donation to The Humane Society of the United States (HSUS). But it wasn't until almost a week later, following the hurricane and then the flood, that I realized just how desperate the situation was.

Saturday, September 3rd

Over Labor Day weekend I watched the disaster footage on TV. People were stranded on rooftops crying out for help, wading in waist deep water carrying small children, and searching for lost loved ones. I was appalled by the footage showing long-winded government officials in Louisiana, trying to save face. I wondered—if so many people were in trouble, what in the world was happening to the animals?

Tuesday, September 6th

My employer offered one week of paid time to anyone who volunteered to go down to help. The steady stream of e-mails describing the animals' predicaments kept coming, including pleas for people to help rescue and care for the thousands of animals left behind. The animals were locked in sweltering houses, chained in flooded backyards, swimming in the streets, stranded on car roofs, homeless and hopeless unless somebody got there to rescue them. I started seriously considering going to the Gulf Coast.

Wednesday, September 7th

To support the rescue efforts, I sent a donation to the Red Cross. Although my employer matched this donation, sending money did not seem to be enough.

The HSUS sent me a thank-you e-mail for my donation, signed by the president and CEO. Little did I know that I would soon come face-to-face with him in the heat of the battle!

A Minnesota animal shelter alerted people that they were forming a rescue group to leave on September 14th for Waveland, Mississippi. They chose Waveland after hearing from a reporter who was alone there, trying to help dozens of injured and emaciated dogs and cats roaming the area. No animal rescue groups were working there yet. The Waveland shelter was closed, and the wandering animals had no food or water. The Minnesota shelter requested donations of cash and supplies, and volunteers to go rescue and care for stranded animals.

Thursday, September 8th

Wow—this was more than a week after the hurricane! An e-mail arrived describing how the HSUS had initially been blocked from entering the most devastated areas in Louisiana and Mississippi and was now racing against the clock to save abandoned animals. It said: *What we are finding is truly heartbreaking – animals trapped in flooded houses, caregivers wandering the streets desperately searching for their beloved pets, and nearly destroyed animal shelters where the surviving animals have spent days keeping their heads above water in their cages.*

Friday, September 9th

I received another, more urgent plea for immediate help. Time was running out for the animals needing rescue. Help was needed to care for the thousands of already rescued animals that were housed in temporary shelters in Gonzales, Louisiana and Tylertown, Mississippi. The plea went out to boat owners, animal care and control professionals, owners of large trucks, natives who knew the streets of New Orleans, and anyone else who could help. People were needed to bring supplies, build temporary shelters, transport rescued animals, and reassure and care for rescued pets. The rescue groups in Gonzales and Tylertown were desperately short of people and warned that anyone coming to help must be sure that they could look after themselves and had enough gasoline to return home.

The situation was not under control more than ten days after the hurricane! All of my life I have cared for animals —gerbils, ponies, dogs, and cats. I was born to do this. The TV coverage worried me though...the looting, the shooting, the police officers abandoning their posts, people stranded at the Superdome and the convention center, desperate people in a desperate situation. Who in their right mind would go to the Gulf Coast now?

I had visited New Orleans a few times and had just been there for a conference in May. A colleague and I stayed at the beautifully restored Le Pavillon Hotel, attended a meeting at the convention center, and enjoyed the legendary New Orleans food and hospitality. We walked the streets near the convention center and in the French Quarter. I purchased an amber necklace from a small store in the Riverwalk Marketplace. Was the store still there?

Help was desperately needed. The people and animals were in such deep trouble, I thought that somebody should do something! Then it occurred to me, if I didn't go, why would I expect anyone else to? The wheels started turning.

I had just transferred to a new job on September first and didn't have much vacation time. I didn't know my new supervisor well, but was pleased to learn that he supported me to take a week of paid time to volunteer. He also told me about craigslist (www.craigslist.org), an online classified ad site where people were communicating about the Gulf Coast area. This turned out to be a blessing.

I contacted the local Minnesota animal shelter and volunteered to go with them. But they already had enough people for their September 14th trip. Abandoned animals needed help and the clock was ticking. I tried to find someone to drive down with me. I thought about packing my truck with supplies, strapping my aluminum canoe on top, and borrowing or renting a trailer to haul supplies. I asked co-workers, friends from dog activities, everyone I knew who had animals. Although people generously offered to donate funds and supplies, I couldn't find one single person to go with me. Meanwhile, more desperate pleas for help showed up every day.

One message said that about 150 dogs were stranded on the roof of the American Can Company, a converted warehouse in mid-city New Orleans. Could that be the sort of situation where I might help? I was afraid to go into New Orleans until law enforcement had it under control. What about health risks? I'd had a tetanus shot, but what other infectious diseases might I encounter? Still, I thought that maybe I could take the canoe to help evacuate animals.

Saturday, September 11th

A new plea for help from Tylertown pushed me to act. They asked for a long list of supplies and said that while rescuing animals, they had found a young girl who had been missed by the FEMA rescue efforts. They asked people to come help and included the following warning: *Tylertown is in southern rural Mississippi, and like much of the rest of that area has no running water or landline telephones, but conditions seem to be improving. So... you have to treat any decision to go down and help like an extreme camping expedition. You must be totally self-sufficient. Bring all your own supplies, including medicines and enough gas to get home again.*

I asked all the people I knew who had pets and worked with animals, but nobody could go with me. I couldn't believe it. As my urge to go help became stronger, I started to wonder if I was hanging around with the wrong people! Perhaps the only way to meet people who would actually go down there was to just go.

Sunday, September 12th

Plan B started to come together. If I flew, I could spend more time helping animals and less time traveling. The best plan seemed to be to fly to Memphis, Tennessee or Jackson, Mississippi, rent a vehicle, buy supplies and go from there. Then I heard that gas and water could be purchased near Baton Rouge, about eighty miles northwest of New Orleans.

A friend e-mailed that volunteers from Pasado's Safe Haven were caring for rescued animals at the Lamar-Dixon Expo Center in Gonzales, Louisiana, between Baton Rouge and New Orleans. Pasado's Safe Haven is an animal welfare organization based in Washington State. I contacted Pasado's and they invited me to meet their volunteers at Lamar-Dixon.

I also considered going to Tylertown, but thought I'd be safer on my own if I drove the shorter distance from Baton Rouge to Gonzales. I booked a plane ticket to Baton Rouge and reserved a rental car. Then I received an offer that I couldn't refuse.

On craigslist, I saw a post from a Baton Rouge man who had volunteered at Lamar-Dixon. I e-mailed Cliff and asked what I should take along. It was tough to know because the needs changed daily. Our correspondence resulted in Cliff offering me a room in his family's air-conditioned home, about ten miles from Lamar-Dixon. Cliff's son Patrick generously gave me the use of his room for the week. One more piece of my journey had fallen into place.

The only stumbling block left for me was fear. I was 44 years old. If I didn't do this, when would I ever get involved? And how would I ever forgive myself if I didn't take the chance?

Before I knew it, I had travel plans, was gathering supplies for the trip, and had found friends to care for my pets while I was gone. Others offered donations and assistance. My friend and co-worker Leslie offered to distribute e-mails for me when I called her with updates. My neighbor Bob offered a ride to the airport and free shipping of supplies via his UPS business. Turns out I *was* hanging around with the right people. They generously supported the effort even though they weren't able to go along.

Friends donated cash, towels, collars, leashes, bowls, and other pet supplies. I bought knee-high rubber boots, tarps, rope, tie-wraps, bungee cords, trail mix, office supplies, paper plates and bowls, hand sanitizer, Kleenex, other supplies, maps and a small journal. When I told the salesman at T-Mobile about my trip, he gave me a free cell phone charger for my car. I dug out a New Orleans map from the May conference and found a small pen—from Le Pavillon Hotel—that fit perfectly in my new journal.

I packed colostrum to support my immune system, colloidal silver to protect against viruses, bacteria, and fungus, pascalite clay for bug bites and puncture wounds, and Rescue Remedy for myself and for the animals. I also took liquid soap donated by my doctor, and surgical masks and rubber gloves provided by a veterinarian friend.

Friday, September 16th

The night before I left, I was up very late packing as much gear as I could take on the airplane. My living room floor was spread with supplies. How would I carry them all? I sorted the supplies into what would be needed right away and what could be shipped. Cliff, in Baton Rouge, provided last minute advice on what to bring and gave me directions to his house. I got to bed very late and woke up in the middle of the night, wondering what I was getting myself into and what I would find in Louisiana.

Saturday, September 17th

My neighbor Bob drove me to the Minneapolis-St. Paul airport. I was on my way to Louisiana, traveling solo, wondering what would happen next.

Supplies in my living room the night before I left

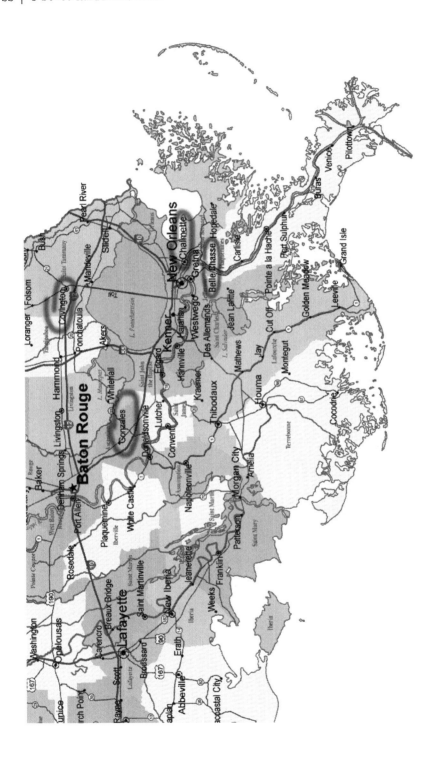

> *"Fearlessness may be a gift but perhaps more precious is the courage acquired through endeavor, courage that comes from cultivating the habit of refusing to let fear dictate one's actions..."*
> Aung San Suu Kyi

> *"Be fearless"*
> Dove® Chocolate wrapper

Chapter 2
Lamar-Dixon, Gonzales, Louisiana

Saturday, September 17th to Thursday, September 22nd

Bob offered moral support on the way to the airport. He advised me to focus on what I could do, so I wouldn't be overwhelmed by all that I couldn't do. His wise words later echoed in my mind when I was sweating it out at Lamar-Dixon.

People at the airport all seemed to be going on vacation. It felt strange to see so many people going about their business when an enormous crisis was occurring in another part of our country. Northwest Airlines allowed me four large bags because I was traveling to do rescue work. It was a lot to haul, but the supplies would be needed. I was only able to check two bags at the curb and had to lug the other two into the airport. Bob generously boxed up the remaining donations and shipped them to Cliff's house in Baton Rouge.

At the airport, I stopped to buy a travel pillow and noticed a refrigerator magnet that said, "Leap and the net will appear". Would I find a net at the bottom of this cliff I was jumping from? I also bought the book <u>Between a Rock and a Hard Place</u>, by Aron Ralston. It's his story of being alone in the wilderness when his arm became wedged between two rocks. Whatever I was getting myself into, his story could give me some perspective!

Sleep didn't come easily on the plane. My brain was going too fast. Instead I read my dog first aid book and made notes in my journal. I wrote, "Leap and the net will appear", "Everything will be all right", and "I hope I can be calm enough to be effective."

I'm not a city girl by any means. I've been on many wilderness trips and enjoy adventure. I had the Swiss army knife, the cargo pants, the hiking boots, the ball cap, and the basic first aid kit. Still, I sat in the Memphis airport on my layover wondering once again what I would find in Louisiana.

In Memphis, I began to see signs of the trauma caused by Katrina. The weather monitor showed a big red blob, a rainstorm covering the New Orleans area. The CNN monitor showed an endless stream of pictures of missing people, many of them children. Three Red Cross workers who had been on my plane from Minneapolis were also on the flight to Baton Rouge. They didn't know where they would be assigned once they got to Louisiana, but at least they weren't going alone!

I called my friend Mark and we discussed the most recent TV episode of *Survivor* and what I might find in Baton Rouge. Mark had become a big *Survivor* fan and I thought that perhaps the show had some useful lessons for my Louisiana trip.

I wore my black T-shirt showing Jackson, the rescued horse. The shirt says, "It takes just one person to change the world for the better". Black might not be the best choice for a shirt to wear in Louisiana, but I needed the inspiration. I also wore my Native American blue bear fetish on a chain around my neck. The bear is a symbol for courage.

On the flight to Baton Rouge, I sat next to Pamela, a professor and associate dean at Louisiana State University (LSU). We talked about the animal rescue efforts at the LSU triage center just after Katrina. Pamela had been there when they were overloaded with animals needing help, before the Lamar-Dixon and Tylertown temporary shelters had been set up. She gave me driving directions for the 30-mile trip from the airport to Gonzales.

The human tragedy was never far from my thoughts. Some of the people on the plane were returning for the first time to find out what was left of their homes. They had evacuated before Katrina and didn't know what they would find or whether their homes were still there.

I arrived at the Baton Rouge airport in the afternoon and waited in the rental car line for about two hours, despite having a reservation. The only vehicle left was a Ford Excursion, which was much larger than I'm used to, and a gas guzzler. But I was lucky to get a vehicle at all. It was evening by the time I left the airport, and I headed straight to Lamar-Dixon.

I drove down the interstate highway in a downpour—that red blob I had seen on the TV weather map. The drive offered one more delay, a traffic accident. I was relieved when I finally saw the gates of Lamar-Dixon, as evening darkness descended.

Lamar-Dixon is an exposition center, like what we call the fairgrounds here in Minnesota. It had been converted to a facility where rescued animals were taken to be vetted and cared for. When I told the guards at the front gate that I was there to care for the animals, they let me in and directed me to the barns at the back of the grounds. Lamar-Dixon was completely fenced, and the barns were surrounded by a separate chain link fence with another entry gate. Inside that gate was the white tent where volunteers signed in, filled out forms, and learned how the place was organized. Escaping the downpour under this tent, I met Deb and Heather, a mother and daughter who had just arrived from Seattle. We later worked together cleaning crates and feeding, watering, and walking dogs.

Deb and Heather were the first of many I met who could not have forgiven themselves if they had not interrupted their busy lives to go. We were all astounded by what we had seen in the news. We knew that there was no safety net for the animals, so we went to become that net.

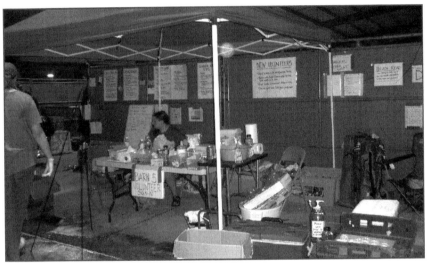

Front of Barn 5 at night

At Barn 5, I looked for people in Pasado's Safe Haven T-shirts. The first person I met there was Connie, a very generous woman from the Seattle area who has done a lot for the animals. Although she was nearing retirement age, much younger people had a tough time keeping up with her. Connie remains a true friend today.

The scene inside Barn 5 was overwhelming at first. Picture an open-air barn. In front was a card table with a couple of chairs, office supplies, forms, and a row of signs with instructions and daily updates, including weather forecasts and the latest news from the health department. There were also snacks, bins with supplies, and coolers with water and Gatorade. Down the length of each aisle, on both sides, were rows and rows of dog

Bonnie (Missouri), unknown, Lori, seated (Wisconsin),
and Connie (Washington) in front of Barn 5

crates, all full. The barn housed big dogs, little dogs, hundreds of all kinds of dogs.

It was hot and muggy, and had been raining for a while. The dogs had been cooped up due to the rain. They needed to have their cages cleaned and to be walked, fed and watered. Barn 5 had six aisles, A for intake, B-C and D-E for holding dogs until their families came to claim them or transport was available, and F for the "dangerous" dogs that only skilled handlers worked with.

The noise was incredible. Huge barn fans sounded like small airplanes, drowning out smaller box fans. Volunteers had positioned the fans to get air flowing to all of the dogs, with an encompassing white noise effect compounded by all the dogs barking.

In the center of the barn were bins of dry dog food, canned food, can openers, dog treats and a water station. At the back of the barn were restrooms, dog wash stations, and bins of dog collars and leashes, towels, and other donated supplies. Behind the barn, next to stacks of unused dog crates, volunteers washed soiled crate pans. Down the road to the right was the exercise area, where dogs were walked and poop was scooped. Further along were more barns (including another dog barn), food and first aid tents, ice freezers, the HSUS trailer, campers, and a very large, official animal rescue tractor trailer.

Barn 5

We new arrivals were advised to get oriented and return early the next morning to get to work. I had worked so hard to get there that I wanted to contribute right away. Every hour was precious, since I would have to get back to my job all too soon. But it had been a long, exhausting day and the days ahead wouldn't be any easier. The photos I took of the barn that night were the last I had time to take for a while.

Late that night, I drove to Cliff's house, where I met the whole family for the first time: dad Cliff, mom Cindy, daughters Shelby and Addison, son Patrick, and the family dogs, Cassie, Cody, and Bailey. The family showed me to my room and offered me access to their kitchen. Their hospitality was fantastic. I was one of the luckiest volunteers at Lamar-Dixon! At their house I took a long shower late every night, enjoyed the peace and quiet, plugged in my cell phone, slept in a nice bed, and recharged myself for the

Barn 5

In front of Barn 5—about the only place to sit!

Dog wash station in back of Barn 5

next day. Cindy even laundered my smelly, sweaty clothes that week. Later I heard the stories of volunteers who had stayed in the crowded FEMA tents at Lamar-Dixon and had not even been allowed a daily shower.

Early Sunday morning, a blast of heat and humidity fogged my glasses as I left the house. I put my hair in a ponytail and stuffed it up under my baseball cap. On the way to Lamar-Dixon, I passed a dead beagle along the side of the highway. Sadly, I passed him every time I made that trip. We were so busy trying to care for the living that there was no time yet to tend to the dead.

I arrived at Lamar-Dixon early to start caring for the dogs in Barn 5. The first task was to read the updates posted in front of the barn. Then I began working in aisle D-E, where I would spend most of my time. A woman from Florida showed my new friends Deb and Heather and me her systematic way of working. I'm glad she got us organized that first day because the next day she was gone and we were suddenly the 'experts'.

We quickly learned that it was best to work in pairs or groups of three. One or two people walked dogs while one or two others cleaned and disinfected the crates and prepared food and clean water. Each dog had a log sheet and photo in a plastic sleeve on top of the crate. We recorded when the dog had been walked, fed, vetted, and pottied. The records were not always complete and sometimes it was hard to concentrate and remember everything.

Temperatures at Lamar-Dixon were in the 90s or 100s every day, with the heat index well over 100. The humidity was overwhelming and could not be escaped. Dehydration and heat exhaustion were always looming over us. As people became dehydrated, they felt dizzy (especially when bending over), lost energy, and found it difficult to concentrate.

On my first full day working in Barn 5, I met a woman who had been hospitalized for dehydration the day before. We were encouraged to drink water almost continuously, and electrolytes regularly. Even so, I became pretty dehydrated that day. I realized that I needed to be careful or I would be no good to anyone. It was tough to drink all the water my body needed. I didn't want to stop working to get water, so I carried water bottles in the pockets of my cargo pants and took a sip every few minutes.

The first dog I walked was a shepherd mix. He was not leash-trained and perhaps had never been on a leash. I used a slip lead to keep the dog from backing out of his collar, but he bounced up and down, fought with the leash, and chewed through it before we reached the exercise area. I quickly grabbed him and a passer-by gave me a new leash, then ran to get a spare.

The dog was a challenge and I realized that I would do better to spend more time cleaning crates than walking dogs. An old back injury was very sensitive to being yanked. The repetitive bending to clean crates was tiresome and sometimes made me dizzy, but at least I could control my movement and set my pace. I wouldn't be useful for long if I continued to walk cooped-up, stressed-out dogs that weren't leash-trained. Fortunately, most people who volunteered wanted to walk dogs, not clean cages, so they were happy to have me do the cleaning.

Deb, Heather and I found a comfortable rhythm of walking dogs and cleaning cages. I learned to keep a watering can, paper towels, and other supplies with me to save steps and increase efficiency. We needed to conserve effort to last the entire day. It was maddening to turn around, find that another volunteer had grabbed "my stuff" and have to gather supplies again. We tried to teach other volunteers to work together systematically, but this was a challenge since each day brought new volunteers.

Entering the barn overwhelmed the senses. A wave of dog smell, along with odors of sweat, urine, and feces, washed over us from the countless dogs in crates along both sides of aisle D-E. Huge fans moved the air and helped mitigate the heat. At first the steady hum of the fans, along with the cacophony of continuous barking, made us cover our ears with our hands.

We were tempted to take the dogs from the soiled crates first, but quickly learned that it was best to proceed from one end of the aisle to the other, making sure that no dog was missed. Besides, if we went to the soiled crates first, it was likely that the clean crates would also be soiled by the time we got to them. There simply weren't enough volunteers. We did the best we could, but it was painful to know that it was never enough.

Even record-keeping was difficult. Dehydration made it more likely that someone would forget to complete a dog's log sheet. We wanted to make sure that none of the dogs were missed. We were so sad for all that they had been through already and that we couldn't do more for each one. But there were always others waiting. Each dog was walked and fed twice per day—every 12 hours or so.

Each day I arrived around 7:00 a.m. and began walking dogs and cleaning cages. Even that early in the day, it was hot and very humid. We tried to walk as many dogs as possible before the worst heat of the day, but there weren't enough of us. Many volunteers were exhausted from the day before and had a tough time rolling out of bed early. Sometimes we weren't even able to get all of the dogs out and walked by noon.

The barns were very noisy during the day, with dogs barking continuously. They all needed something—food, water, a potty break, to get out of a puddle or pile that they hadn't been able to hold in any longer. It was very tough to work continuously and not be able to get to all of them in time. We would have liked to just sit and comfort them, but we needed to keep going. We were doing our best to meet their basic needs. I tried to see each dog as an individual in a sea of dogs, to look at each one and give her a comforting pat when it was her turn to go outside.

Many of the dogs had patches of hair missing, with skin discolored from chemical burns. Some dogs were so thin that they must have been underweight before the storm, and likely had been strays. Some had the scars and wounds of fighting dogs. Others appeared to be in relatively good shape and seemed to have come from loving homes. How had they ended up here? Was anyone out there looking for them?

Between noon and 2:00 p.m., whenever all the dogs had finally been taken out, we took a break in the heat of the day. On a good day, food was delivered and we had lunch. Otherwise, I grabbed snacks from the Excursion. I had come prepared to live out of the Excursion if necessary, but was glad that I didn't have to. During the mid-day, we reorganized the barn, swept the aisles, re-stocked supplies, and made sure that all the dogs had water. Sometimes I sat under a tree behind the barn and had a good cry. Later we were back walking dogs, cleaning cages, and providing more food and water until late into the night.

One night behind Barn 5, I met a New York City firefighter who had just arrived with his comrades. He asked me how the barns and system operated. Seeing so many rescued animals overwhelmed him. He was so moved by the tragedy, he had tears in his eyes. He told me that he had four dogs at home and that he and his buddies had brought their firefighting equipment to go into the city to rescue animals. So many people had been kind to them after 9-11 that they wanted to give something back. This was the kind of person I had hoped to meet—someone who couldn't ignore the devastation, and would go out of his way to help. I don't know his name and I didn't see him again after that night. I imagine he spent the rest of his time in the city, carrying animals to safety.

I wish I'd had my camera when I met the firefighter. The first couple of days were so busy that I rarely took a break, and didn't have my camera along. Later, I started carrying the camera in a fanny pack, hoping to catch a photo of the rare reunion of a lost pet with its family. It seemed disrespectful to take photos of the dogs when they were in need, and rude to stop working to take photos when so many were waiting for help.

And yet, there were people in clean HSUS shirts who only ventured into the barns for a 'photo op'. They would take a picture and then leave, never getting dirty, never even touching an animal. How could anyone see all that need and not stop to help?

I only saw a few reunions of people with their pets during the week I was there. People who were searching for their pets checked in at the white tent and were escorted through the barns to look through the rows of dogs. It was tough to be helpful when someone came by and asked if I had seen a "brown dog". I thought, well, yeah, I've probably seen hundreds of them! But I helped them look.

To find their dog, people had to get there on the right day and look through all the barn aisles. The dogs were first put in the intake aisle, then moved to other aisles, and then shipped out, so it was hard to keep track of an individual dog. The paperwork with each dog had a photo attached, if it had not been damaged or chewed up. When we arrived in the morning, many of the dogs that had been in our aisle the night before had been moved to another aisle or exported to another shelter during the night, and new dogs had taken their place. Even if I had perhaps seen someone's dog the day before, I might not be able to find it again.

During that week, people had to be lucky enough to arrive during the two or three day window that their dog was at Lamar-Dixon, before he was exported. Even three weeks after the hurricane, many rescued dogs arrived every day. Some were quickly exported to shelters across the country to make room for more. I can't say for sure how many dogs went through Lamar-Dixon that week, but it was more than a thousand, probably thousands. The dogs left by the planeload, as more rescued animals were brought in from the New Orleans area each day.

Reunions were rare, so we were all very excited to see one man reunited with his two dogs. People gathered around and celebrated with him, crying and smiling at the same time. He had been forced to evacuate without his dogs, so he put them in a rowboat with food and water and sheltered part of the boat with a tarp. Rescuers found the dogs and they were brought to Lamar-Dixon. This man was very lucky to arrive on the right day to find them. He was overjoyed to see them and so glad that the rowboat had saved their lives. We were all very grateful for that reunion; it helped keep us going.

One afternoon I was cleaning cages when another man and his family came by looking for their three dogs. They found one of their dogs near where I was working and the man came over, took my face in both of his hands, and planted a kiss on my cheek. He was so excited to find his dog and was so grateful for my efforts. On the street, this rough-looking guy might have scared me. But we cried tears of joy together when he found his dog. Then, with mixed emotions, the family returned to the search for the other two dogs.

That was one of the hardest things about working at Lamar-Dixon. I saw so many lost animals, and people desperately searching for their pets. I will never know how things turned out for most of them. There are so many broken threads.

I saw two men reunited with their pit bulls. It was clear that they were excited to find each other, and they obviously belonged together. The men had huge grins, and the two dogs jumped up and down in excitement, even though it was very hot. They were gracious enough to pose for photos.

When I looked at the photos later, I was disappointed to notice that the male dog wasn't neutered and I doubt that the female was spayed. We saw so many unaltered dogs that it was discouraging at times. With so many homeless pets across the country being euthanized every day, we don't need unplanned litters.

I also witnessed the cruelest sort of heartbreak. A family came in to look for their lost cat. They had their dog with them and it was too hot to leave him in the car. Someone offered to care for the dog while they searched the cat area. When they returned, they couldn't find their dog, and they were devastated! Somehow the dog became mixed in with the hundreds of unclaimed dogs and they had to start looking for him. I don't know whether they found him again...another broken thread.

∞ ♥ ∟

One of the greatest gifts that I received in Louisiana was new friends. It was an honor to work alongside people like Jaye from Missouri. Jaye stood out in her pink sh*t shovelin' Barbie outfit.

Jaye (Missouri) by the import area in front of Barn 5

When I first saw Jaye at Lamar-Dixon, I thought she was perhaps a crazy person. But as I got to know her, I realized that she is a very wise woman with a great sense of humor. She tried to cheer us up as we set about the grueling task of caring for Katrina's animal victims. Jaye described Lamar-Dixon in her blog:

When I heard about Katrina, I suddenly found myself on the road to Gonzales, Louisiana. I had found animal rescue locations from reading online referrals to "staging areas" where animals were being brought out of New Orleans. I spent two weeks at the Lamar-Dixon Exposition Center feeding, cleaning, walking, and processing dogs who had been brought out of the destroyed areas.

As rescue workers, we slept in tents, sometimes ate food delivered in Styrofoam boxes (if we ate), endured 100+ heat, dust, toxins, and trucks that sprayed for bugs every night. We worked from 6:00 a.m. until near midnight every day. We were denied adequate shower facilities, though there were some showers available in the back of a livestock barn for the evacuees who lived in an air-conditioned YMCA building on the premises. The Red Cross was afraid we'd "contaminate" the shower area with animal feces, although there was tons of bleach available on pallets at the site. I was threatened with military arrest by soldiers hired to work on the grounds as 'security' when I tried to use the showers very late one night.

I loved the work, frankly. I love working hard and nonstop, I love digging into my deepest parts and finding that much and more that I can call up in the way of strength, endurance, and 'meaning' in life. I didn't feel anything except a sense of wanting to keep going, to keep working, to keep giving what I could. I felt also that it was never enough. I felt that there were so many dogs in need, so much that needed to be done, and so few volunteers to cover the enormity of the tasks, and yet each day was one more series of successes.

The analyses of the Katrina disaster have the advantage of hindsight. We saw the individuals at the Super Dome and we asked why. We read the truth about the levees and we wondered how these were acceptable. We've analyzed to death the events leading to Katrina, and post-mortemed the results. Among these analyses, finger-pointing, the blaming, rebuilding, endless discussions....the Event itself feels lost.

Katrina was/is about something so real. It was suddenly about meeting every instant's need with a response that was not about Self. Katrina was about seeing a Whole, breaking it down to tiny pieces, and trying to attack each moment by addressing that tiny piece. It became so intricate, so delicate, and each tiny element built back to the Whole.

My work there was a metaphor for life. Had I stopped to assess the total picture, I would have been completely overwhelmed with the enormity. In a sense, everyone there was 'nobody.' We were dependent on each other. There were those who thought they were in charge, but anarchy in its finest sense reigned over the disaster and saved many animals and humans who would not have survived.

When I arrived there, I was set upon by members of HSUS who threatened to have me removed because I was not "following orders." I had brought along grooming equipment and had set about shaving a dog who was covered in mats, overheated, and in very bad shape. I was told to quit what I was doing because it was not a priority. I argued with them and tried to 'reason' with them.

This was my first and most important lesson about survival of my Self, my abilities, what I had to give, and what needed to be accomplished. I realized that these individuals needed to give orders, to feel 'in charge', to command, and to wield authority. I realized there were probably 100 of us who were very experienced at what we were doing, what needed to be done, and what we thought were priorities, who are used to being the authority in charge. And there were at least 1,000 dogs, the same number of cats, as well as horses, and other livestock in fewer numbers, that all had to be cared for. None of us were expendable at that point, and the last thing we needed were continual ego conflicts.

I think many of the volunteers came to the same conclusion, each of us silently and at times sullenly, but we knew the immediacy of what had to be done. I myself understood after Day 1 of my tenure, that the best response was a soldier-like "Yes, sir" a nod, and the appearance of compliance. This settled their authoritarian needs, they moved on to other areas, and I continued with the projects I felt needed my attention, ignoring their directives unless I felt they had a perspective that made sense.

The issue was not whether I was doing something wrong or right. There was no wrong or right at that point. We did what needed to be done. There were some volunteers who were very kind-hearted and well-meaning but who had little experience handling large volumes of dogs/cats. They needed guidance and advice, but commanding and discouraging them was counter-productive in that situation. I felt there was a task for everyone that showed up. One woman spent the day just finding ice for each of the dogs' water bowls in the heat of the day.

It was incredibly distressing seeing dogs sitting in their feces, old dogs who looked sad, dirty dogs, puppies with skin irritations, dogs barking incessantly, dogs just sitting with blank looks, and dogs so thin and dirty they seemed hopeless. The first day for each volunteer was emotional overload. If we could put them on a task and help them through the first day, it was miraculous how they grasped and adapted to the environment within a day of coming on board.

The dogs were walked once a day. There were never enough volunteers for more than that. But we evolved a system of cleaning crate trays, serving food, water, and care that worked. More dogs began getting two walks a day. I saw volunteers who spent the day giving special time and love to dogs who seemed "lost" emotionally. I found as I talked with different people that each of us had adopted our own 'special' dog that we looked after and loved. Those dogs began looking for us and knowing we would come.

The Katrina disaster was not about what was done or not done to prevent Nature's control over our lives. Katrina was about our ability to respond to the tiny little tasks, for each of us to pick up one little thread and follow it, weave it into the Whole. Our responses wove a fabric of strength, of adaptability, of courage.

It's hard for me to understand what people expect from "the government" after disasters. We lose everything. That's what a disaster is. It's our job to dig down, find the bottom of our strength and courage and pull ourselves up out of rubble. The loss was huge when viewed in its totality, but each individual has to find her/his inner core. It's easier maybe to look outside ourselves for some tangible help and it's great if it can be found. But I wish for us to not expect that the government fixes everything for us.

Jaye described so eloquently much of my own experience at Lamar-Dixon, including the efforts to placate the "authorities", yet do what we felt needed to be done.

ॐ ♥ ୨

I was just getting into the rhythm of working the long days at Lamar-Dixon when I met Kate.

"Three things it is best to avoid:
a strange dog, a flood,
and a man who thinks he is wise."
Welsh proverb

Chapter 3

Meeting Kate

Sunday, September 18th

Late on Sunday night, after my first full day of caring for dogs at Lamar-Dixon, Connie dragged me over to aisle A to nab some dog rustlers. The fear was that people were stealing pit bulls for dog fighting, a cruel and gruesome spectator "sport". The new chain link fence around the animal barns had been built to prevent dog rustlers from getting in. Before the fence was installed, dogs had gone missing and there was still great concern for them.

When Connie grabs you by the arm to help find dog rustlers, you can't say no, even if you're wondering what in the world you'll do if you find some. Fortunately, it was a false alarm. As I turned to go back to aisle D-E where I had been working, I spotted an Australian Cattle Dog! I hadn't seen any cattle dogs there yet and noticed her right away because I had cattle dogs at home. She was an older blue girl, a bit thick through the middle, a bit worn around the edges, but with a keen intelligence in her eyes. Her teeth were worn down and she was worn out. She didn't have one whole tooth left in her mouth. Connie had been the first person to sign the log sheet, noting, "canned food only—bad teeth." The log sheet said "9-17. 6:45, new arrival." This girl had arrived at about the same time that I had on Saturday evening. It didn't feel like a coincidence.

The dappled blue cattle dog was burly like a teddy bear. Her expressive brown eyes drew me in. She had a red head with a white blaze, which on cattle dogs is called a Bentley. She was a mix of colors, with the edges of a black mask in front of her ears, tan points on her chest, red speckled legs, and a beautiful white tail with blue-gray markings. She had a wear mark under the hair on one side of her neck, like a mark left by a chain collar. Her forehead was missing a patch of hair and her red ears were riddled with bug bites, with a ragged edge where part of one ear was missing. The damage could have been from the storm and its aftermath, or perhaps it was her usual condition.

The cattle dog, looking for a way out

She had paperwork from the Louisiana SPCA, number 0001-1442. The box next to "rescued animal" was checked. It said, "scanned—no chip." Address of incident: "17th St – Canal – P/UP on roof top by rescue." "Male" was circled and later crossed out, then "Female" was circled. "Primary breed: Aussie" crossed out, with "Blue heeler/Australian cattle dog" written in. "Primary color: Bk Secondary color: Tan/merle. Markings/comments: No ID." She had a pink tape around her neck with ID number 0001-1442, but apparently had no collar when rescued.

She had no tags, microchip, or identification to tell us who she was or where she had come from. Was anyone was looking for this girl? Where was she from, and how had she ended up at Lamar-Dixon? I wondered about her all night.

Monday, September 19th

The next morning I took a few moments to check on the cattle dog before beginning work in aisle D-E. There I met Nancy from east of Baton Rouge, about 25 miles away. Nancy also had a fondness for cattle dogs and

was keeping an eye on the blue girl, but she had to return to work the following day. We both felt a special need to get the old girl out of the heat and into a home where someone could care for her. Nancy had written, "Vol will adopt," with her name as the volunteer, and local phone numbers on the log sheet. I put my name on the sheet too, noting that I was there at Lamar-Dixon, would be willing to foster this dog, and knew of a local home where she could stay.

Nancy with the cattle dog

At first I didn't walk the cattle dog or spend much time getting to know her. I was afraid to get attached to the dog and not have any way to really help her. It would hurt too much to give her hope and then fail her. It would also hurt to come in one morning and find out that she was gone – "exported." But I couldn't help but keep an eye out for her.

"Exports" took place in the middle of the night. When dogs were ready to be shipped out to sponsoring shelters around the country, they were moved to aisle D-E, taken for vetting in the afternoon, and moved to the airport later that night. Planes carrying dogs had to fly at night when it was cooler and the airports weren't as busy. The aisles of the dog barn were never empty though. By the next morning, other rescued dogs had arrived to fill the empty crates.

The old cattle dog wasn't pulled right away for export. She stayed in aisle C of Barn 5 long enough for me to figure out the export system. A shelter wouldn't be likely to select her as being adoptable due to her age and her bad teeth. I was concerned that she wouldn't survive a flight. If nobody claimed her and a shelter didn't take her, her future looked bleak. This dog needed someone to watch over her to make sure that she would be okay.

As I grew more committed to this dog's well-being, I decided to give her a name. Her advanced age and her fortitude reminded me of Katharine Hepburn, so I called her "Kate". After all, although her body was blue, she was a redhead!

At first, the authorities at Lamar-Dixon didn't release dogs individually to rescue organizations. Groups of dogs were released to shelters. Then another volunteer told me they had started letting individuals foster dogs under the umbrella of a rescue organization. That opened the door for me to do something for Kate.

My cell phone was my lifeline as I looked for a way to get Kate to a safe haven. To make a call, I had to leave the barn. With all the barn fans going and the dogs barking, I couldn't hear a thing there. Usually, I sat on a bench under a huge old oak tree in the field out behind the barn.

I first called friends Guy and Julie back in Minnesota. By some miracle, I remembered their phone number from calling them the week before; it wasn't programmed into my phone.

Guy told me about Australian Cattle Dog Rescue, Inc. (ACDRI, a national Australian Cattle Dog rescue group,) and gave me a phone number. I called and left a message. Later, Deb returned my call. I had not heard of ACDRI before, but Deb was very supportive. She told me that ACDRI had tried to contact the authorities in Louisiana to offer to help Australian Cattle Dogs (ACDs), but had not been able to reach anyone or get a response.

Being at Lamar-Dixon, I understood why. A rescue group had to have someone on the ground there to navigate the system. The HSUS wasn't working with breed rescue groups at Lamar-Dixon at that time. They seemed to be focused on what to do with all the pit bulls. Worse, the system was changing all the time and it was hard to figure out.

During breaks from working in the barn, I made many calls on Kate's behalf while sitting under that old oak tree. Deb and I had many strategic phone conversations. We discussed the Lamar-Dixon situation and contemplated our options. Lying on the bench under the tree in the heat of the day, I noticed that its branches splayed out so precariously that the tree was held together by steel cables. It may not have been safe to sit there, but all of life seemed precarious that week.

Connie and I added a card to Kate's log sheet saying that rescue would pick her up. We hoped this would give us time to work something out before she was pulled to take her chances on an airplane. Rumors about the possibility of fostering the animals, either individually or via a shelter sponsorship, continued to cycle around Lamar-Dixon. For a person to foster a dog, the dog had to be under the umbrella of a 501(c)(3) – a registered charitable organization. On top of that, the HSUS would only work with national breed rescues if they had a main shelter location, and few did. Many breed rescues operate through networks of foster homes.

I filled out the paperwork to foster Kate as an individual dog, but then the system changed again. Every group sponsoring rescued dogs now had to take a minimum of six pit bulls. Some of those dogs had been fighting dogs and many groups were not prepared to handle them, transport them, or adopt them out. Although the rule was a way for the HSUS to deal with the large number of pit bulls they had to manage, it put up a roadblock for many rescue groups. It felt like another case of passing the buck – poor problem-solving and a lack of leadership.

When I found out that ACDRI wasn't eligible to sponsor Kate, I called Nancy. Even though she lived nearby and had offered to foster Kate, she wasn't allowed to. She would have had to foster under the umbrella of her local Louisiana shelter, which was already over its space limit. As crazy as this may sound, this made Nancy ineligible to foster Kate in her home.

Nancy said that if I could pull Kate, her mother would care for her in an air conditioned home while I worked at Lamar-Dixon. But I still needed a shelter to sponsor Kate. Eventually I was able to reach the Minnesota shelter that had sent volunteers to Mississippi. They agreed to sponsor Kate and said maybe she could take their transport from Mississippi to Minnesota later that week. If I could get Kate out of Lamar-Dixon, I would take her to them in Mississippi, then catch my flight home.

That day, I made many visits to the air conditioned HSUS trailer to complete Kate's paperwork. The crisis counselors sat out front in the heat and the decision-makers met inside. I waited there in the mid-day heat while we took a break from walking dogs, trying to work out a way to get Kate to Cliff's air-conditioned home, or to Nancy's mother's house. The crisis counselors helped me race to fill out paperwork before the rules were changed again.

Lois, one of the counselors, gave me water when I was about to pass out from the heat. She became a bridge between the decision-makers and the people on the front lines, who put blood, sweat, and tears into caring for the animals.

As I filled out the paperwork from Lois, a man emerged from the trailer and told her that he had decided not to take applications for individual dogs. I spoke up to say that this dog was older, would not be chosen by the shelters as adoptable, had been passed by for export, would not do well on an airplane, needed to get out of the heat as soon as possible, and had been through enough! I could get her to an air-conditioned local home that very day if he would just tell me what I needed to do to legitimately take her!

He told me that he would be right back and ducked back into the trailer. I waited for a while, but he didn't return. Eventually I went across the street to the food tent for shade and some lunch. Lois promised that she would find out what she could.

A few minutes later, I ran into the same man in the food tent. Naively, I thought that he had come over to find me. But when I spoke to him, he had a "deer in the headlights" look, as if I had caught him unaware. He apparently had forgotten about me waiting out there in the heat, or thought he had ditched me, and there I was again. I'm sure he was under a lot of stress, but it left me with a bad taste in my mouth. I later found out that he was in charge of a national humane organization.

Off and on all day Monday, between caring for the dogs in Barn 5, I tried to get Kate released. The authorities probably didn't want to adopt out dogs one at a time due to record-keeping issues. Plus they didn't know what to do with all the pit bulls and urged breed rescues to take them in order to rescue their own breed of choice. They told me a few times to come back later. I went back to work in the barn, then returned at the specified time, but they weren't there. When one official finally took my application into the trailer for consideration, she said that she knew the director of the Minnesota shelter. That sounded promising, but she still could not make a decision. After repeated trips to see her, following her instructions to return at a specified time, she put me off again.

I went back at 9:30 that night, per the woman's instructions. Nobody answered the trailer door. I went back again at about 10:00 p.m. and found her. She seemed to have forgotten that she had told me to come back. Perhaps she hoped that I would give up. She was very flippant. In a "valley girl" voice, she dramatically announced that it had been a very long day, she was just *too tired* to make another decision that night and I should return in the morning.

Her announcement made me feel that the authorities didn't realize that lives were on the line. I thought, yeah, it's been a long day in that air conditioned trailer while I've been slaving away in the barn and standing out here in the mid-day sun waiting for someone to make a decision to save a life, hopefully before it's too late. I couldn't tell her what I really thought because I still needed to get Kate out of there. True, these people were under a lot of stress. But perhaps they weren't the right people for the job.

In the evenings, the line of rescue vehicles returning from the city with rescued animals snaked out in front of the complex, waiting to be processed at intake. On Monday evening I first met Monica and Veronica, sisters from Texas returning from a day of feeding and rescuing animals in New Orleans. They were in their vehicle, in line for the intake area, when I stopped to find out what they were seeing in New Orleans. They provided food and water for the many stranded homeless animals that wandered the streets, trying to buy them more time. If they could get close enough, they picked up the animals that seemed to be in the worst condition. But they could only fit so many animals in their vehicle and there were still many more out there needing help.

Monica and Veronica invited me to join them the next day. But I was concerned about what might happen to Kate if I was gone that long. If she wasn't there when I returned, I might never find out what had happened to her. Feeling a responsibility to Kate and having already given away my rubber boots, I decided to stay at Lamar-Dixon. Rubber boots were needed to wade through the muck and I had given mine to an animal control officer who had gone into New Orleans the previous day.

Monica and Veronica from Dallas-Fort Worth

Tuesday, September 20th

In the morning, my frustration boiled over. I dealt the official a well-deserved rant. I told her that the time I was spending standing in line to wait for her again could be better spent caring for the animals in Barn 5, where we were already very shorthanded. If she would just make a decision and let me take care of this dog, I could get Kate out of this heat to an air-conditioned local home and get back to work.

Apparently, it worked. The decision and the paperwork to let me foster Kate finally came around lunchtime. I rushed to get her to a cool, safe place before they changed their minds.

It was mid-day, time for a break at the barn. I found a donated collar and leash for Kate and wrote my cell phone number on the collar. Animals leaving Lamar-Dixon went with donated supplies needed for the journey. I picked up some canned food and then drove the Excursion around behind the barn. There I found a 3-door wire crate, a crate pan, and a soft pad. I struggled to load the crate into the Excursion in the mid-day heat.

It's funny how a few minutes one way or the other can change one's life. With the Excursion ready for Kate and papers in hand, I walked her across the street from Barn 5 to be processed for export. We waited in line in the heat to get a microchip, vaccinations, and the remaining paperwork Kate needed to leave Lamar-Dixon. There I first met Cindy, who was waiting with Gonzo the rat terrier to get him vetted for departure.

Cindy had traveled with Sarah from Virginia and they were taking some animals back to Sarah's rescue organization, Lost Fantasy Stables and Animal Rescue. At Lamar-Dixon, Sarah walked the "aggressive" dogs while their cages were being cleaned. She was known as the pitbull lady who wasn't afraid of anything. Sarah and Cindy became my treasured friends and are now a valuable part of my rescue network. Sarah remembers saving dinner for me, but having a hard time getting me to sit and eat. I remember feeling that stopping to eat was a poor use of time when so many dogs still needed care. But I was glad that meals were saved for me, and even more fortunate that I stopped to eat and got to know Sarah and Cindy.

Once I got Kate through export, I took her to the Excursion and turned on the air conditioning. While I was loading her into the vehicle, another volunteer stopped to talk. She wanted to know how I had obtained Kate's paperwork. She was very concerned about a dog that she had been caring for and begged me to take him then and there. That would have amounted to smuggling the dog out. I had to tell her no, but I was happy to help her find her way through the paperwork process.

Her main problem was that her shelter back home could take a group of animals, but she had no way to get them there. During my time spent waiting in line at the HSUS trailer, I had learned about flights donated to move dogs to other locations. She could request a plane to take animals to her shelter and include 'her' dog in the group.

When I ran into this woman later, she was very excited that she had secured a flight to transport animals to her rescue group. I was glad that I stuck with my instincts and was relieved that she not only was moving the dog she was most concerned about out of the heat, but had arranged transport and care for many other animals as well.

After all of my efforts to secure the documents for Kate, the Lamar-Dixon guards didn't even come out to check. It was too hot. I probably could have driven her out without the paperwork. I planned to take Kate to stay with Nancy's mother until I could work out her transport to Minnesota, but we stopped at Cliff's house first. Cliff's daughter Addison and I gave Kate a bath and the family invited me to stay for dinner. It was nice to experience some normal family life, get out of the heat, and rest. I enjoyed a delicious dinner with this delightful family. I didn't want to impose Kate on them but they were happy to watch over her, so she stayed.

Wednesday, September 21st

Early Wednesday morning, I fed Kate and took her out in the yard. Cliff's family took care of her that day while I worked at Lamar-Dixon. I called them mid-day and they said she was doing fine. They had taken her outside and she was resting in her crate. They told me not to worry about her—they would walk and feed her. What great people.

I spent time with her early in the morning and again when I returned late at night, hoping she recognized that I would return for her. Knowing that Kate was safe, I was able give myself completely to another long day of caring for other rescued dogs.

At Lamar-Dixon, I met many people with good hearts and plenty of stamina who cared for rescued animals from sun-up to sundown. But some of those who volunteered were not good matches for the work that was needed. One woman tried to walk, or drag, a starving dog that didn't want to move. We could see all of the bones on this young, black dog. He probably wasn't at a healthy weight even before the storm. With all that he had been through, he looked very ill and likely didn't even have the energy to walk. Sarah lost it with this woman and told her to carefully pick the dog up and be gentle with him. Sarah spoke the words we were all thinking.

Some people who came to volunteer were clearly not dressed for working in the barn and usually didn't last long, although they meant well. People in flip flops and white shorts usually didn't last more than an hour or two. But they deserve credit for having good hearts and showing up to help.

Most people who appeared to be too clean were usually only looking for a photo opportunity. Some administrative staff from the rescue organizations came in the barn only to take pictures of the animals. Sometimes taking photos of the animals in our care felt wrong to me. It seemed to be a violation of their privacy to flash them in the face when they were lost, overheated, and not feeling well. It was hard for me to see people enter the barn, snap a few photos and then leave, while we struggled on short-handed, trying to give the animals better care. Frankly, I was later surprised to see some of these people shown on their websites holding a rescued animal because I never saw them even touch an animal at Lamar-Dixon.

Some of the volunteers wanted to pick and choose the animals they cared for, instead of working their way down the aisles in a systematic way so that no animals were missed. They weren't careful about recording information in the dogs' logs, which created chaos. The logs were important for recording when each dog had been given food and water and had a potty break. It was also important to note any signs of health problems and submit a vet request form if needed.

On Wednesday, a group of vet tech students arrived and introduced complete chaos into aisle D-E. They didn't follow instructions for walking, feeding, or watering the dogs. They didn't make notes in the logs, or even bring the dogs back to the crates they had come from, where their paperwork was located. We tried to train the students to work within the system and speculated that they must have been first semester students.

That afternoon, we ran out of bottled water at Barn 5. The person who had stocked it was gone and we couldn't work without water. So I drove over to the food tent, loaded bottled water and ice into the Excursion, and drove back to Barn 5. When I returned, Sarah and Cindy were taking a break in front of the barn. I think they were amused by my new job. They knew

I didn't have the patience to wait for someone else to solve the problem. But how could I? We were drinking gallons of water, and would have quickly become dehydrated without it.

A photo from that day shows Cindy holding Gonzo the rat terrier. Gonzo was taken into Sarah's rescue organization and Cindy fostered him at her home. This is one of the few photos we have of Gonzo.

Cindy (with Gonzo) and Sarah (Lost Fantasy Stables and Animal Rescue), Virginia

Besides Kate and Gonzo, several other dogs stand out in my mind. That young black dog being dragged was so very thin that for the first time I truly understood the expression "skin and bones". An old Golden Retriever "Bruce" appeared to be disoriented and we discovered that he was nearly blind. Sarah took him into her rescue and later learned his life story (told in Chapter 7). One dog's records had a note from his rescuers stating that he had eaten the other dog in the house to survive.

Bonnie, a vet tech from the Humane Society of Missouri, had to isolate a dog one afternoon. He appeared to be very sick and began having seizures. We were concerned about a parvovirus outbreak and he was taken across the street to be vetted. I didn't see him after that and don't know what happened to him. Canine parvovirus is a highly contagious, flu-like virus that can be fatal to dogs.

Bonnie was an excellent crisis manager and worked very well without much sleep. I was sorry when she began working on exports in the middle of the night and we didn't see her as much during the day.

On Wednesday I finally discovered the air-conditioned restroom across the street from Barn 5. I had to walk through the veterinary area to get there, which was not encouraged. It was so hot and I must have looked really worn out, so someone urged me to take a break there to cool off. In the restroom there were cages with overheated rabbits that appeared to be in tough shape. I was glad that a kind soul had brought them there to cool down. Later that day when I returned to the restroom, the rabbits had been evicted. They'd been replaced by signs stating that animals were not allowed in the restroom—by order of the health department! It was another frustrating clash between those of us who would do just about anything to care for the animals and those who seemed to think that the "rules" were more important than the lives of the animals.

We had all heard that Hurricane Rita was on the way. Knowing that another hurricane was coming was terrifying, especially since not much had been resolved since Katrina. I hadn't been able to reach the people from the Minnesota shelter who were volunteering in Mississippi. If I had to take Kate with me, I would have to drive home in the Excursion instead of flying.

When I realized that I might be driving home with Kate, I called Deb of ACDRI. She asked me what route I would take, but I didn't even have a map, other than the Louisiana map that came with the rental car. I didn't have internet access either. So Deb consulted an online map and laid out a route for me over the phone. Then an amazing bit of serendipity happened. As I was walking back to the barn, I passed the volunteer tent and saw a stack of folded U.S. maps, free to volunteers. I had not seen them there before, even though I had been at the tent many times. They seem to have appeared from nowhere just when I needed one. I took a map and I still have it, even though it is now well worn. I used that map to find my way home.

Deb got on ACD-L, an online cattle dog group, and asked for places for Kate and me to take a break or stay overnight on our way home. Through ACD-L, Rosemary offered a place for us to stay in Jackson, Mississippi. I had not heard of ACD-L before, but subscribed to it after I got home.

Late on Wednesday night, the dogs had been cared for and the barn was quieting down for the night. I took a rare social break with some people, including Lori from Wisconsin, in front of Barn 5. We were sitting there chatting when, out of the corner of my eye, I saw a loose dog wander into the aisle. He was a large brown pit bull without a collar, and he seemed to come from nowhere. Just then, a woman came around the corner at the back of the barn with another pit bull straining at his leash. She noticed the loose dog and our eyes met briefly in an "Uh Oh!" moment.

The loose dog was still looking toward me. I jumped out of my chair and ran toward him to distract him and block him from seeing the other dog. At the same time, the woman wheeled around and took the other dog back around the corner, out of sight. The loose dog's eyes were locked on me and I froze. The dog could easily have felt threatened by my quick movement. I didn't look him directly in the eye, and I stayed still. One could cut the tension with a knife. I heard Lori behind me and asked her to bring a leash. It seemed like it took forever for her to creep over, speaking soothingly to the dog, and eventually place a leash around his neck. Once she had the leash on him, we all relaxed.

Later Lori told me that she had taken so long to get there because, in her haste, she had tied her shoelaces together. I missed that comedy while I was standing like a statue with my back to her. Since then, I've thought about what might have happened if I'd ended up between the two dogs and a fight had broken out. I'm relieved that I wasn't turned into mincemeat!

Nobody had come looking for the dog, so we searched for an empty crate and finally found one with his photo and paperwork. Apparently, someone had put him back in the crate after walking him and had locked the front door without noticing that the crate's side door was unlatched. When the dog discovered the open door, he decided to take a walk. I learned later from people who know pit bulls that even fighting dogs are usually gentle with people. But I didn't know this dog. He was big and he would naturally feel very threatened by the way I moved quickly toward him. So I was glad that Lori had been able to gently restrain him.

Back in front of Barn 5 later that night, we found people gathered to wish Steve a happy 50th birthday. It was his last night there before returning home to Alaska. Steve was an amazingly efficient, very hard worker, and he had given up a tropical vacation to volunteer in Louisiana. When he gave me his contact information, I was interested to learn that he was from Alaska and worked for Alaska Airlines.

When I got back to the house very late that night, Kate and I spent time out in the yard. I wanted her to know that I was there for her. Then, barely able to stand after being on my feet all day, I leaned against the wall under the shower for a very long time. I was trying to wash away the dirt, the smells, and the sad images of all the dogs waiting... waiting... waiting to be cared for and to find their way home.

Thursday, September 22nd

Wednesday unexpectedly turned out to be my last full day at Lamar-Dixon. On Thursday morning we were told that we had to evacuate; Hurricane Rita's approach was sending us home early. Many of the animals had already been exported in anticipation of Rita's arrival, and things were slowing down. I didn't get a chance to say goodbye to many people, but already had contact information for some of them. Others had left notes on the board in front of Barn 5.

Making arrangements to leave was difficult. I still couldn't reach the people from the Minnesota shelter who were working in Mississippi, and I couldn't get through the phone system to speak with anyone at Hertz or

Northwest Airlines. My departing flight was scheduled for Saturday and Rita was due to arrive on Friday. I didn't want to put Kate on a plane, especially with bad weather and high winds on the way. A plane ride would be very traumatic for her and might even kill her. So I decided to take Kate home with me in the Excursion.

Early Thursday afternoon, back at Cliff's house, I took a shower, finished packing my things, and loaded the Excursion. It was very tough to say goodbye. Everyone had been so generous and I didn't know when I would see them again. What a wonderful family! We took photos with the family, friends and neighbors.

I wanted to take Kate inland before she sensed another storm coming, and I was anxious to stay ahead of Hurricane Rita. I was concerned about Cliff's family staying there with Rita approaching, but that is part of life for them. As I drove down their long driveway, my heart swelled with gratitude for their generosity, and hope for their safety. I turned and waved one last time.

Kate and Jenny with Louisiana friends in Baton Rouge

> *"What lies behind us and what lies before us*
> *are tiny matters compared to what lies within us."*
> Ralph Waldo Emerson

Chapter 4
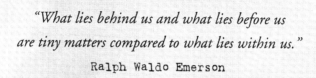
The Long
Road Home

Thursday, September 22nd

Kate and I left Baton Rouge in the afternoon, heading for Jackson, Mississippi, where we would spend the night at Rosemary's house. Kate's crate sat on a towel on the back seat of the Excursion, on the right side where I could see her when I glanced over my shoulder. Right away we were caught in stop-and-go traffic and I wondered if we would even make it the 180 miles to Jackson that night. The slow pace made us intimate with our fellow travelers. The traffic included all kinds of odd vehicles, many packed solid with belongings, perhaps all that the occupants owned. It looked like a mass exodus—people weren't taking any chances after Katrina. I wondered if the traffic would be this slow all the way through

Mississippi. Eventually, though, we passed an accident site and the traffic began to move.

As we drove, Katrina's devastating effects on the crops and livestock in Mississippi were discussed on Public Radio. I started to realize how widespread the effects of Hurricane Katrina will be for many years, beyond the flood waters of New Orleans.

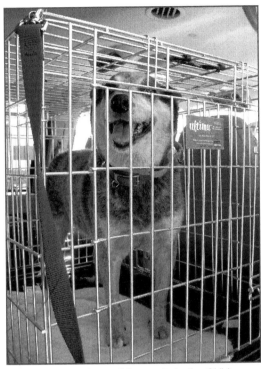

Kate heading to Minnesota in the SUV

I took Kate out for a break at a rest stop. She was wary of another dog nearby and seemed jumpy. I was concerned that she only had a buckle collar. Her only identification was my phone number on her collar and the new unregistered microchip. Although I didn't think she would leave me, I worried that she could get spooked by something and back out of the collar. So, I kept our break short.

We arrived in Jackson during the evening rush hour and found Rosemary's house before she arrived home from work. I took Kate out for a short walk and then we waited in the driveway. I gaped at a huge tree that had fallen across the backyard, another victim of the hurricane.

Rosemary fed me delicious barbecue, and we relaxed. For the first time since we had met, Kate had the run of a quiet house with no other dogs. Rosemary's husband Jim had moved to Salt Lake City ahead of her while she finished her job in Jackson. She had driven their dogs up to stay with him in Utah before the hurricane. It was a perfect set-up for Kate.

Kate explored the house and tried to get into the garbage, something she apparently knew how to do! I don't think she was used to being inside a house though. She followed her nose everywhere, smelling the dogs that had lived there. Later she found a protected spot in the closet, curled up and went to sleep. She was exhausted, and relieved to find some peace and quiet at last. We set up her crate in the spare bedroom, where I would sleep, and she found comfort there. Late that night, I called people back home to tell them I had moved inland ahead of Hurricane Rita. I still couldn't reach Hertz or Northwest Airlines. They weren't expecting me until Saturday, so I had one more day to get through.

Rosemary gave me canned dog food and a martingale collar for Kate to get us through the rest of the trip. She knew that I was concerned about Kate's security in the buckle collar. A martingale collar, also known as a limited-slip collar, tightens when the dog pulls. The dog can't slip out of it, and yet it doesn't choke like a choke chain collar. Having the martingale put my mind at ease.

Friday, September 23rd

In the morning, I thanked Rosemary for her hospitality and we headed north on I-55. Kate and I had a long drive ahead of us through Mississippi, Tennessee, Arkansas, Missouri, and Illinois. I listened to borrowed music CDs and occasionally tuned in to Public Radio for updates.

At rest stops, Kate continued to be wary of other dogs. She hadn't reacted to other dogs in the sweltering heat and humidity of Louisiana, but that was common. She and many of the animals there had shut down in order to cope. Whatever she had been through had traumatized her and she was still shell-shocked. In the quiet of the SUV, she felt protected and was glad to escape the heat. I kept glancing over my shoulder to check on her. She was exhausted and slept most of the time. When she got up and started

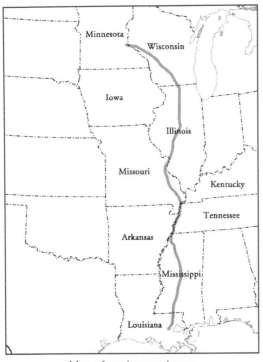

Map of our journey home

looking restless, it was time to take her out for a break. She must have wondered where in the world we were going, but she seemed to trust me.

The traffic heading north was not nearly as heavy as it had been before Jackson, but we still found ourselves in the company of power company trucks and other heavily-laden vehicles. Half the country must have dispatched utility workers to help, and now they were headed home. Many vehicles looked as though they were carrying everything a family owned as they made their escape from hurricane alley.

We approached St. Louis just before the afternoon rush hour. A kind family that had learned about us on the ACD-L had offered us a place to stop, rest and take a walk. But Kate was acting sensitive around other dogs and I decided to push on so we could get past St. Louis before rush hour. The family sounded pretty disappointed when I called to thank them and let them know we wouldn't be stopping there.

I tried to make good time driving, hoping to reach my parents' summer home in southern Wisconsin that night. But traveling through Illinois, I was suddenly exhausted and had to find a place to stop. I didn't know what to do, since I didn't have the energy to look for a place that would accept Kate, and it was too hot to leave her in the Excursion for long. At a rest stop along I-55, a very helpful clerk found us a "dogs allowed" room at the

Holiday Inn in Lincoln, Illinois—requiring another hour of driving. I was very grateful for her help.

When we arrived at the Holiday Inn, they gave us a first floor room with a whirlpool bath, near an outside entrance. The clerk thanked me for volunteering in Louisiana and gave me the room at half price. She told me they had accommodated other volunteers already and half price was their policy. I thanked her for their generosity.

I didn't want to leave Kate alone and I was wiped out, so I picked up my supper at a drive-through. It was Friday night and this small town was fired up for a high school football game. It felt strange to see people going about life as usual. I felt shell-shocked. Hurricane Rita was on my mind and I wondered how the people and animals that we had left in Louisiana were faring. The stress of seeing some of Katrina's aftermath and working with the lost animals stayed with me. Even though we were a few states away, imagining the one-two punch that Rita would bring weighed me down.

I took Kate for a short walk in a field behind the hotel. We both needed to stretch our legs, and Kate needed a potty break. She seemed a little spooked by the traffic and other sounds, but was happy to get out of the SUV. While we ate our supper in the hotel room, I turned on CNN. I drew myself a hot bath and tried to relax. Kate paced the room and then settled down on her crate pad. Then I watched, horrified, as Hurricane Rita struck the very place we had left the day before. As exhausted as I was, it took a long time to get to sleep that night.

In one of those odd occurrences that permeated this whole experience, just before leaving Lamar-Dixon I had met Beryl, a woman who lives within ten miles of my house in Minnesota. Beryl worked for the Minnesota Department of Transportation and had the proper credentials to stay at Lamar-Dixon for Hurricane Rita. Here's her account of what happened:

Huge exports were scheduled for Thursday and Friday before Rita hit, hundreds of animals were exported to other, safer facilities. Some by plane, some by refrigerated semi trailer and some to any accredited rescue group able to transport (one local shelter took ALL the exotics to protect!). I would guess well over 350 animals were exported right before Rita hit. Also rescue efforts in New Orleans were halted through Sunday (though some die-hards still went in to the city to gather what animals they could). We stowed, tied down and shrink wrapped EVERYTHING in the entire compound, took down ALL the tents (including FEMA) and tarps, and tied all the hundreds of crates together. All campers and such, including rented budget rent-a-trucks and several semi trucks with trailers were parked along the open exposed ends of the barns to protect the animals as best we could from the winds, which were sustained at about 60-70 MPH for several hours. All of the volunteers were evacuated by bus to Baton Rouge except those few of us deemed "essential, emergency" personnel. I was fortunate/unfortunate enough to be deemed critical and was allowed to stay. Most of us slept in the barns in stalls with the animals or in the rented trucks (what sleep we could get). Lamar-Dixon fared well; we had 3 tornadoes near enough we had to all evacuate to the brick bathroom areas; it rained about 11" (my guess), but nothing flooded very badly except the surrounding streets and neighborhoods. The animals of course were freaked out, at one point right before the worst of the storm hit, ALL the dogs simply stopped barking. It was deathly, eerily quiet. They knew, and were understandably VERY frightened. It was business as usual for us, as well as we could, cleaning, feeding, watering, walking (until it became too dangerous to do so) and just talking to and trying to calm the animals in our care. I think the horses had it the worst... they were very nervous and frightened.

Saturday, September 24th

In the morning, I turned on CNN again to get an update on Hurricane Rita. The newscasters seemed to think the Gulf Coast had dodged a bullet this time. Although Rita's effects were much less dramatic than Katrina's, this one-two punch must have deeply affected those who were still reeling from Katrina.

After breakfast, Kate and I headed for Wisconsin in a light rain – the first rain I had seen since arriving at Lamar-Dixon a week before. Kate and I stopped at my parents' place for lunch. They live out in the country, back from the road. Mom fed me while Dad walked Kate around the property on her leash. Although they must have worried about me traveling to Louisiana, they hadn't tried to stop me. They were undoubtedly relieved to see me back in one piece and I appreciated their support.

After lunch, Kate and I continued northwest to Minnesota. After her eight state journey, I dubbed her "8 State Hurricane Kate". We arrived home in Minnesota on Saturday evening. I left messages to let the Minnesota shelter and the shelter director know that Kate and I were home.

When I picked up my two dogs, Bandit and Rainbow, from my friends, we tried briefly to introduce Kate to them on neutral territory, but she wasn't going for it. She lunged and snapped when the other dogs came close. She had been through a lot and needed time to settle in. Bandit likes to be in charge and can be a bully with other dogs, so I continued to give Kate her own space.

That evening, I sent an e-mail message thanking Cliff's family for their hospitality. I was anxious to hear how they had fared through Hurricane Rita, yet I was too exhausted for a phone conversation. I needed to take care of my dogs and cat, and get some sleep.

The Excursion had to be returned the next day. I hadn't exactly been given permission to take it all the way to Minnesota, and it took considerable persistence to finally get through to Hertz on the way home to let them know where their vehicle was. The one-way rental fee was well over $1,000. Once I explained the situation, they eventually agreed not to charge the one-way fee.

Sunday, September 25th

I dropped off the Excursion, unpacked, did laundry, bought groceries, and spent time with my cat and the three dogs. I was exhausted and had to return to work the next day.

Events in Louisiana and Mississippi weighed heavily on me. Throughout that week, and in the weeks and months to follow, I went online frequently to check on the Gulf Coast area. The worst part was not being able to stay down there to help while the need was so great.

Post-Traumatic Stress Disorder (PTSD) was common among those who went down to help. Even people who had not been through the hurricane or flood, but had only seen the resulting devastation, were profoundly affected. We felt guilty for leaving when help was still so badly needed. Day-to-day life back home didn't have as much meaning, and staying in touch with those we had met in Louisiana and Mississippi helped. We knew that in the aftermath from the hurricanes, the need for help was far from over. It was hard to see some of the people at home go about their business as though we hadn't experienced a major tragedy in another part of our country.

Monday, September 26th

I returned to work and began learning my new job. At home, my new job was to figure out how to handle the dogs. I kept Kate separate from the others. Officially, she would be quarantined until October 1st to protect local dogs from whatever diseases and parasites she might still carry.

In the mornings, I took Kate for a walk outside the fence, while the other two dogs ran and played inside the fence. During the day while I was at work, we began a rotation with Kate crated upstairs and the other two dogs in their 4' x 4' chain link kennels in the basement. In the evening, I took Kate for a walk off-leash in my fenced field, then put her back in the house and took the other two out for their time to run. Although Kate had supposedly been de-wormed in Louisiana, I always picked up all of her poop.

Kate seemed to be housebroken, except she thought it was okay to go potty on the cement floors in the basement. She quickly learned not to though. She was an expert at digging in the garbage, and seemed to think she should be fed from the table. She thought it would be all right to get on the bed. Although she didn't seem used to it, Kate walked well on a leash. She liked her crate,

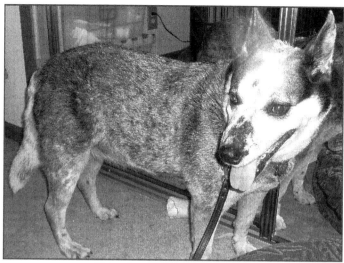

Kate after arriving in Minnesota

where she felt safe. One of our challenges was that Kate seriously thought the cat was food. She thought it was just *wrong* to have a cat in the house.

Kate needed veterinary attention, so I contacted a vet who had worked on my older dogs. She was happy to help out. She had wanted to volunteer after Katrina but was unable to travel because of family responsibilities. She donated some care and an initial exam for Kate.

Kate was afraid at the vets. She might not have seen a vet before and wasn't used to being handled that way. She was diagnosed with parasites: hookworms, whipworms, and giardia. Her ears were bug ravaged and she had fly strike bites on her muzzle. Her face was sunburned and was missing patches of hair. She also tested positive for heartworm. Her teeth were broken and worn down. X-rays showed advanced arthritis in her spine. We wondered if she was pregnant, but fortunately she wasn't. She had a burly build and was probably bloated from the parasites. She was missing a toenail, had tendon damage in her foot and walked with a limp. The vets thought that she was at least ten years old. But she had a very strong will and a big heart.

Fortunately, due to Kate's and my emotional states after arriving from Louisiana, and the recommendation to quarantine her until October first,

I had kept her separate from my other dogs. She pooped in a separate area and I always picked up her poop right away. I was thankful I had taken those precautions when I learned of the parasites she still had in her system. Nothing was passed on to the other dogs.

Kate came out of her shell a little more every day. She learned how to sit, ate voraciously, followed her nose everywhere, and loved to roll on her back in the grass. She didn't get along with the other dogs, but I hoped that would change. I knew it would take time for her to settle in, but I thought that I might have to find her a more relaxing foster home.

Kate had many good reasons to be on edge. Between August 29th, when the neighborhood flooded, and Sept 7th when Kate was rescued from a roof, helicopters were flying over continually to patch the breach in the 17th Street Canal. When the breach occurred, photos showed whitecaps roaring through the streets as they quickly filled with water up to the rooftops. I could hardly imagine Kate clinging to a roof for a week in the heat and humidity, with helicopters buzzing over and almost blowing her off. Did her family survive? Were they away and was she home alone? She seemed to be missing somebody. She froze when a plane flew over and jumped into my lap when a motorcycle went by. She was one brave girl, with a few things haunting her mind, and stories to tell if only she could speak.

I was still waiting for the Minnesota shelter that sponsored Kate to return my calls. Their sponsorship helped get Kate out of Lamar-Dixon; otherwise she might not have survived. But I didn't hear back from the shelter for over a week after we arrived in Minnesota. The woman who finally called insisted that I take Kate to the shelter so they could photograph her, enter her information into the system, 'process' her, and decide if I would be able to foster her. The caller was inflexible about this. By then Kate was getting comfortable at my house, she trusted me, and I felt responsible for her. It was one more of those times when bucking the system seemed like the right thing to do. I hadn't planned ahead for Kate's future; I had just planned one step at a time to keep her safe.

I wanted to protect Kate from any more hassle. I had made a commitment to her and I needed to keep it. When I realized that going to the shelter meant that she would likely go back to being a 'number', I couldn't let that happen. I asked to speak with the director, who had made the agreement with me to get Kate out of Lamar-Dixon. Although I left messages on his cell phone, he never called me back. I told the woman that I would send a photo, they could come to my house to take a photo, or we could make other arrangements, but at that point it would be very traumatic for Kate to go to the shelter. I had not intended to fight the system, but it became apparent that they were not able to look out for the best interests of this one dog. They had taken in a lot of animals and were about to bring another truckload up from Mississippi.

My dilemma was that I wanted to give Kate peace and a chance to recover. I also wanted to follow my vet's recommendations for her care. The shelter wanted my vet to follow their protocol for treating heartworm, and to donate the care, or for me to pay for it myself. But the shelter's protocol didn't agree with my vet's recommendation, and worse, the shelter's recommended protocol changed several times through the course of our conversations. I found myself in a difficult situation.

Everyone was trying to do their best under the circumstances. But I had fought to get Kate out of Lamar-Dixon, and she had become my personal responsibility. Others were trying to do what they thought was best for a *group* of animals. I was looking out for Kate as an *individual.* After all that she had been through, I wouldn't give up on her or put her in a situation where she could again become just another face in a crowd.

On October 3rd, I subscribed to ACD-L, the Australian Cattle Dog e-mail list. Deb of ACDRI had told everyone about the Katrina cattle dog and I sent them an update, including the following:

...Kate is a survivor with a very strong will to live. She follows her nose everywhere and can be very hardheaded. I can hardly imagine what she went through up on a roof to escape the flood... She does not like helicopters, or anything

that sounds like one… She is very tough to have survived up there, especially with the arthritis in her back. I don't know how much wear and tear she had on her old body before, or whether she had worms or heartworms before. But in spite of it all she has a beautiful coat, a very sweet temperament and a lot of heart.

I listed Kate on Petfinder, with a clear photo and my phone number. Petfinder (www.petfinder.com) is a database of pets needing homes. Over 10,000 animal welfare organizations in the U.S., Canada, and elsewhere use it. The site assisted in ten million adoptions in its first ten years and I had found my rescued dog Rainbow through Petfinder. After Hurricane Katrina, Petfinder.com created the Animal Emergency Rescue Network (see Appendix), which was a central means of reuniting people with the pets they had left behind. Through this network, an estimated 3,000+ pets were reunited with their people.

I wanted to get the information out, so that if someone was looking for Kate, they would be able to find her quickly by contacting me. If the Minnesota shelter couldn't return my call for over a week, anyone looking for her would have a tough time getting through to them too. The official (HSUS) listing for Kate, with her

Pet Detail

TYPE: FOUND   STATUS: open   PETFINDER SYSTEM

I.D.: PF3941   SHELTER/RESCUE-ASSIGNED ID: 0001-1442

DATE POSTED: 2005-09-13

DISASTER: KATRINA

ABOUT ...

Dog Australian Cattle Dog/Blue Heeler

AGE (YRS): 0   COLOR(S):

SIZE: M   MARKINGS:

found poster

WEIGHT: 0   ALTERED:

DESCRIPTION: Check Louisiana SPCA

Rescued from roof at 17th street canal, black brown and white

same ID number, LA-SPCA 0001-1442, didn't show up on Petfinder until almost a month later—they were that far behind in entering the data. Ironically, the authorities didn't want to send individual dogs out to be fostered because they were concerned about keeping track of them, but handling that volume of animals made it hard for the system to keep track of them too. The official photo of Kate just after she was rescued was not very good—she looked very anxious—but I could tell it was her by the markings.

These two Petfinder listings showed up even later:

Pet Detail:

TYPE: FOUND STATUS: open PETFINDER SYSTEM I.D.: PF4775 SHELTER/RESCUE-ASSIGNED ID: 0001_1442 DATE POSTED: 2005-09-13 DISASTER: KATRINA

Pet Detail:

TYPE: FOUND STATUS: open PETFINDER SYSTEM I.D.: PF32449 SHELTER/RESCUE-ASSIGNED ID: 0001-1442 DATE POSTED: 2005-09-20 DISASTER: KATRINA

As much as I wanted to re-unite Kate with her family, thinking about someone claiming her left me with mixed feelings. I didn't want to send her back to go through a storm like that again. And it was difficult not to think that someone had done her wrong, abandoning her in the disaster. But I didn't know what had happened, so it wasn't fair to judge. If I had lost my dog in the storm, I would want to find her.

Meanwhile, Kate's veterinary needs had to be taken care of, especially the heartworms and her teeth. She may have come from a home where there was no money to fix the people's teeth, let alone the dog's!

On Friday, October 7th, two weeks after we arrived in Minnesota, Kate and I returned to the vet to have images taken of her heart. Dog heartworm is common through most of the U.S. It is caused by a roundworm, and spread by mosquitoes. The adult worm lives primarily in the heart, interfering with heart function and eventually choking off the blood flow, killing the dog. Fortunately, the images showed no heart enlargement.

Kate was mostly asymptomatic, with no coughing or other symptoms, but one of her blood readings indicated that she might have Stage 2 instead of Stage 1 heartworm. Treating her with Immiticide injections (a recommended treatment for Stage 2) could be very hard on her so I also looked into treating her with Ivermectin tablets (a less invasive treatment, sufficient for Stage 1), to keep the disease from progressing. We gave Kate an Ivermectin tablet, in compliance with the shelter's protocol. She had been given one of these monthly tablets before leaving Lamar-Dixon and was due for the second tablet while we figured out what further treatment was best for her.

Living with Kate, I was struck by the cultural differences in the lives of dogs. Some dogs sleep on the bed with their people, go to the dog bakery, get shuttled to different classes and activities like middle class children, are taken to the vet for minor injuries, and are otherwise pampered. Some dogs live outside, have never been to the vet, and yet are still people's companions, loved just the same. As I grew to know and love Kate, I could tell that she had loved and been loved by someone. But she didn't appear to have had an easy life by my standards. I suppose her people didn't have an easy life either.

Some days I was afraid that someone would claim Kate and she would have to go back to hurricane alley and a place where she would live part of her life on a chain. Other days I sensed that she missed her people and her familiar life, and hoped that she would be reunited with her family. I came to believe that much of what I put her through was unfamiliar and stressful. She had not been well socialized before the storm.

We lived on a country road that wasn't busy most of the time. When Kate first came to Minnesota, she stopped what she was doing and paid close attention every time a car went by. Traffic unnerved her. She didn't seem to be a city dog and may have come from a remote area. When a helicopter flew over the yard, she stiffened in fear.

It really bothered Kate that there was a cat in the house. Kate saw my 16-year old kitty as prey and I ensured that the cat had her own safe space. Perhaps Kate's job before had been to chase away critters, including cats.

Kate didn't seem to know what to do during the infrequent times when she had free run of the house—when the cat was protected in her own room and the other dogs were downstairs or outside. I doubt that Kate had ever spent much time inside. She seemed confused, even startled, by sounds from the radio and TV. When a rooster crowed on a TV commercial, she stopped what she was doing, cocked her head, and looked around. She seemed to be most comfortable with having boundaries in the house—a leash, a crate, some guidance. Yet outside in the fenced yard, she was happy. Eventually, she ran and played and mostly stuck by me. She noticed everything in her environment. To a girl who had probably lived her whole life in Louisiana, the air, the trees, the birds, the sounds, and the smells in Minnesota were new and different.

I became hyper vigilant around Kate as she took in her new environment, and as I came to learn the things that concerned her. She was unnerved by loud noises, sudden movements, and anything out of its usual place. I used Rescue Remedy regularly on Kate as she got used to being at my home and began to relax and recover from her traumatic experience. During October, she learned to let me brush her and touch her ears and feet. Grooming must not have been part of her previous life either!

Overall Kate was a pretty tough dog. In some ways, she was very tough because after all she had been through, she was still able to love. She trusted me at first because she didn't have a choice—I was her only way out. After a while, I earned her trust and we bonded.

Kate's paperwork said that she had been rescued from the 17th Street Canal area in New Orleans. I looked online at all the photos and stories that I could find about the breach in the 17th Street Canal. I even scanned through photos from that first week post-hurricane, looking for a dog on a roof! I wanted to find out where Kate came from and what had become of her family.

And then I came to know grief firsthand when I lost a member of my own family.

"If anything is worth doing,
do it with all your heart."
Buddha

"Lots of people talk to animals.
Not many listen though."
Winnie the Pooh

Chapter 5

Rainbow

On Saturday, October 8th, I was dealt a terrible blow. My friends Eric and Jenny brought their dogs over to play. We were out in the field with the dogs when Rainbow escaped through the fence. We called her and followed her, but she galloped through the woods and bolted toward the road. We think she was chasing a rabbit. My heart was pounding. I was running as fast as I could go. My stomach sank as I heard a loud thump. By the time I reached the road Rainbow was lying on her side, motionless. Blood trickled from her nose and she appeared to be dead. A gigantic Buick with a very shocked-looking elderly man had stopped. He said that she had just appeared in front of his car and there was no time to stop. I couldn't do CPR because her airway was filled with blood. We rushed her to the emergency vet, but I think she died instantly. My only consolation is that running as fast as she could and chasing a rabbit is how she would want to go.

Rainbow was obedience trained and normally would not run into the road. It's a mystery how she even got out. I saw her go through the fence, not over it, and we couldn't find anything wrong with the fence where she had escaped. I wondered how I had failed her, and I just didn't know.

Rainbow had always been full of life and energy and was faster than the wind. She had more energy and was harder to wear out than any other dog I've known. She was bold, she was bright, and she was full of personality. She stole my things and paraded them around to get my attention and start chase games.

She weighed about 60 pounds and we think she was a cattle dog-hound mix. She was reddish brown with black ticking, a short, coarse coat, a long tail, and red and white speckled forelegs and belly. Her ears looked like undersized pointed cattle dog ears that had flopped over. They were as soft as velvet.

Rainbow had been picked up by animal control as a teenage stray, an unspayed female in heat. She was rescued from the city pound on the day she was scheduled to die, and she joined my family in April 2002. She was very smart and never did anything halfway. She had a spotted belly and when I said "Show me your spots!" she threw herself onto her back. I swear she laughed every time she did that—I know I did! She had learned to navigate agility weave poles by herself. I sat in a lawn chair, pointed across the yard at the weave poles, and said "go weave". She dashed over by herself and blasted through the weave poles, never missing a turn.

Rainbow was only about 4 ½ years old when she died. It was agonizing to go all the way to Louisiana to help rescue animals, bring Kate all the way home, then have Rainbow die right there in front of my house, almost in front of my eyes. Life can take cruel twists that happen so quickly and take a while to sink in. I felt badly that the week I'd spent at Lamar-Dixon was one of Rainbow's last weeks.

Lisa, our dog walker, framed "The Rainbow Bridge" poem beautifully for me in memory of Rainbow. That helped keep me going for a while. It begins: "Just this side of heaven is a place called Rainbow Bridge". It tells of the place where animals who have passed on are restored to health and happiness and wait for their special people, to be reunited again one day.

Not long after Rainbow passed on, when I was out walking Kate one day, I found a feather that had Rainbow's markings—red with black highlights on one end, and white spots on a red background on the other. The feather looked so much like Rainbow's colors and markings that I took it as a sign from her that she was okay. I had never seen a feather like that before. Later I learned that it came from a wild turkey.

My friend Sharon offered to make a beaded amulet bag for the "Rainbow" feather. I wanted a cobalt blue bag, with rust, black and white beads. When Rainbow's ashes arrived, much to my amazement, they were in a cobalt blue velveteen bag—another sign, perhaps.

Rainbow had a tremendous presence. After her passing, she continued to visit me. I felt her presence very powerfully and sometimes I wondered if I was losing my mind. I had worked with local animal communicators, but had not experienced communication from an animal like this before. One of the communicators who Rainbow had met was also "visited" by her after her passing, even though this woman had not seen her for a long time and had not yet been told of her death. Rainbow's presence was very strong and hard to ignore, and opened new intuitive doors for me. Had I not kept an open mind, I might have missed these messages.

Rainbow, *on right*, with puppy Bandit

> *"The world is full of suffering;*
> *it is also full of overcoming it."*
> Helen Keller

> *"No act of kindness, no matter how small,*
> *is ever wasted."*
> AESOP

Chapter 6

Back at Home...
Coping and
Reconnecting

Reuniting Katrina's evacuees with their pets was much more difficult than anyone had expected. The people and the pets were scattered far and wide. As this realization sank in, the fostering periods for these pets were extended beyond the original date in October. Those who were fostering or sponsoring pets were asked to keep them in their care longer before concluding they wouldn't be claimed. This meant that the fostered pets could not be adopted into a new family for months instead of weeks.

Many people were still missing after Hurricane Katrina and others were spread out across the country. They were going to need time to get their lives back together, and it would take them a while to find their lost pets. Some were in situations where they couldn't keep pets, but still wanted to get their pets back, eventually. At the same time, the foster families were becoming attached to the animals, and it became harder to think about returning them. Even though that was part of the original deal, the longer the fostering continued, the harder it would be to give the animals back. The situation was unprecedented.

I felt driven to learn more about the loss and sadness caused by Katrina – maybe so I could come to terms with it. I spent most of my lunch hour each day looking on Petfinder and searching the internet for Hurricane Katrina news. It was hard to accept the degree of heartbreaking devastation. I didn't want to forget, and yet found it difficult to explain to those who hadn't been there. I felt out of sync with most of what was going on around me, and Rainbow's death hadn't helped.

I stayed in contact with and received updates from Sarah and Cindy in Virginia. On October 26th, Sarah sent the following message she had received about the rescued pit bull "Missy" that she took home to foster. After becoming very attached, she was relieved that she wouldn't have to send Missy back.

Subject: Katrina dog- Missy

I was the person who initially took in Missy. She IS an owner surrender. She was found on top of a kennel tied to a post- she belonged to a guy who left the dog and his girlfriend. The girlfriend went to get her things from the house and she was scared of the dog, so she left her there without food or water!! Then she (and the boyfriend) expected the dog to be dead... she returned in a week to get more stuff... dog was alive and someone called us to come and get the dog. Find her a good home- she was a sweet skin and bones lady :)

Meanwhile, Gonzo's owner found him through Petfinder. Gonzo the rat terrier was with Cindy when I first met her in the export line at Lamar-Dixon. Sarah's rescue organization had sponsored him and Cindy had fostered him at her home in Virginia. Cindy had taken care of Gonzo for weeks and had become attached to him.

On October 31ˢᵗ, Cindy wrote:

Gonzo went back last Monday. I finally received an e-mail from the owner AFTER I sent one to him letting him know that I had waited all night for my phone to ring saying that Gonzo made it home okay. He had promised me he would call me the minute he got Gonzo off the plane. He said that Gonzo did well but was tired, that they took him and their cat that they found also to the vet to have their microchips updated and that they both were in good health thanks to the rescuers and the people who took care of them... It was terrible. You should have seen the look on Gonzo's face when I drove him down to Sarah. He looked so pitiful, like he knew I was sending him somewhere without me. I will never forget that.....but I had to let him go.

I believe that they are "asking" people to hold the animals until the end of the year but the paperwork that is legal says Oct. 15th. I know that is why I HAD to send Gonzo back. That guy called with just hours left on the 14ᵗʰ...It is hard, believe me. I had Gonzo longer than the owner had had him before the storm. It still hurts like hell...but I have to believe that God knows better than I do and that there is a reason for all of this.

I looked at the pictures you sent that your other friends took down in NO [New Orleans]. Some made me cry all over again. A friend told me that I needed to stop looking and reading about it and I told them NO WAY. It is too easy to cover your eyes and turn your head and act like it never happened. People who did not go down there have NO idea what happened and I refuse to forget or pretend that it didn't happen. It makes me cry but in crying I remember all those who never had a chance or a voice—the animals—and if the only thing I can do is let people know that this happened in our own backyard and animals suffered because of it—then so be it. That is my mission. To never let this be forgotten.

I wondered if someone was still looking for Kate. I looked on Petfinder every day and had not seen a lost dog posted that fit Kate's description. But

I knew that many hurricane survivors didn't have computer access. The whole situation was very complicated. The HSUS was now recommending that the October 15th fostering deadline be extended until the end of the year, and possibly until March 1st. The need for the extended deadline was obvious, but it was a lot to ask from the foster families—to care for the pets until January or March when the original agreement was until October. That is a long time to care for a dog and then have to give her back.

At the end of October, Kate was re-tested for heartworm because she had been feeling much better and her energy level was up. The results came back negative, so the vet decided to forgo the more severe treatment. Kate's personality was coming out more and more. She was probably feeling better because she had been treated for the other parasites.

Kate and Bandit were starting to cooperate through the fence, but still were not allowed to be loose together. With a barrier between them, Kate felt safe and was relaxed and Bandit didn't try to charge at the fence any more. But Bandit was especially lonely since we lost Rainbow. Getting Kate and Bandit together would allow both of them more time to be outside and play, if only they could get along.

In November I re-connected with Connie, the Pasado's Safe Haven volunteer from Washington State who I'd met at Lamar-Dixon. She was also caring for Katrina dogs in her home. I reminded Connie that I wouldn't have met Kate if she hadn't dragged me to the other side of the barn to look for dog rustlers. We discussed my mixed feelings about whether Kate would have to go back to Louisiana.

I had spent many hours trying to figure out where Kate had come from. She had an old mark where the hair had been worn off one side of her neck. It looked like a wear mark from a chain collar, indicating that she had been tied out and had traveled a circular path, with the collar rubbing on just one side. She had shown some signs of abuse, although it also could have been post-traumatic stress from the storm and its aftermath. The longer Kate stayed with me, the deeper my attachment—and my concern for her welfare—grew. If someone claimed her now, I'd have a hard time sending her back. I didn't think she'd had a very good life by my standards, although there were signs that someone had cared about her—she bonded to people. It might not be fair to impose my values, but I cared so much about her. Without me, and her other rescuers, she might not have survived.

On November 10th, Connie wrote:

So sorry to hear about your lost dog [Rainbow]. At least you have the comfort that its last days were not spent in those horrid conditions. That is the feeling I had about the dog (Mama Katrina) I brought home. The vet in Louisiana said she should be "put down" and that she wouldn't live at all, much less to be transported somewhere else... After several days of begging Hertz to let me take a car out of LA, I got one and we drove home to Seattle. She improved daily on the drive and has continued to do so since our arrival here four weeks ago. She is now undergoing the heartworm killing process—has had her first treatment... and is scheduled to go in for #2 next Tuesday...Her hair is growing back, she has regained the sweetest little personality and is the terror of our house. The other little dog I brought back... respects Mama. My original dogs (an enormous black lab and an afghan) both walk the line when she is around. Yes, lots of sadness, but we also did a lot of good and when we're down, we have to keep reminding each other of the good and how hard we worked and tried. And we're not about to quit yet, are we?????!!!!!

Several of us here in the Seattle area are starting a letter writing project to try to get in touch with people from NO who don't have access to the internet to find their pets. My feeling is that by this time, many of the evacuees have forwarded their mail and perhaps we'll find a few owners. Cross our fingers.

It was great to hear from Connie. She knew Kate and it was nice to be in touch with another person who understood what we went through.

By November, Kate had begun to settle in at our house. We were getting to know each other better as she continued to come out of her shell. She trusted me more and learned new things. She tested negative for hookworm, whipworm, and giardia. Her hair and broken toenail had grown back and her feet looked better. She started to act years younger, and it was rewarding to see her personality emerge. She had learned "sit" and "down" and really played for the first time since I'd known her.

Kate in September and November

Kate had walked by the toy box in the basement every day since September without showing interest. But on the morning of November 9th, she dug furiously in the toy box, discarded about half of the toys and came up with an old rubber ball. She started bouncing it and chasing it around the basement. It was an odd shape, so she was chasing it all over and bouncing around like a puppy, so silly! This was the first time I'd seen her cut loose and play. Suddenly, she was ready and was ball crazy! Could this have been the first time in her life that she had a ball to play with? She was feeling better, rewarding me for my trouble. Kate had a very sweet temperament and a lot of heart. She was amazing.

In November, Kate also experienced her first snow, which was clearly new to this southern girl. Even though she wasn't used to the cold, she loved the snow and was happy to be out playing in it. She rolled on her back and wiggled around as though making her own snow angels. I loved to see her let loose and have fun!

Kate and Jenny, November 2005

Kate was fully present in the moment. She thoroughly enjoyed tossing a ball up in the air and chasing it. She threw herself completely into every one of her snow angels, pushing her back into the snow and waving her legs in the air.

When we walked outside, she had an unmatched intensity. She was keenly aware of everything around her and of anything that might upset her. In a sense, she was drinking in new sights, smells, and sounds. But in another sense, she was wary of what might be around the next corner. It was all so different from Louisiana.

She panicked whenever I headed for the truck—she wanted to get in first. She loved riding in the truck and felt safe there. She didn't bark wildly at anything, just rode along and observed the world from the safety of our truck 'den'. She must have been used to going for a ride with someone. Perhaps she remembered that last time someone had driven away without her and had decided not to let that happen again.

I learned that Kate's reactions were those of a dog who was not well socialized to other animals, was probably isolated, likely lived part of her life tied outside and didn't spend much time in the house. She was still wary of other dogs and of strange noises. She froze and panted profusely when startled, and lunged out barking if another dog came too close. She sometimes behaved like a dog that was used to being tied up and couldn't move away or easily defend herself. Anyone who has lived with a sensitive (or 'reactive') dog has likely learned a lot. When with Kate, I became very tuned in to our surroundings, to anticipate anything that might disturb her.

I was still working on integrating Kate and Bandit. I saw some progress every day and appreciated the advice that I'd received from people on the ACD-L. With the help of structure, treats and coaching, the dogs had gradually learned to approach one another calmly from across a fence. They both slept in my bedroom at night, with Kate in her crate and Bandit loose, lying on his bed nearby. They rode in the truck in side-by-side kennels and stayed in adjacent 4 x 4 foot chain link kennels during the day. They had learned to peacefully co-exist, as long as there was a barrier between them.

Kate and Bandit, peacefully co-existing

Bandit missed Rainbow terribly. She had been his best pal ever since he was a small puppy. They played, ran, and wrestled together every day for probably as long as he could remember. So losing Rainbow left a huge hole in Bandit's life. I didn't know if he associated Kate's arrival with Rainbow's leaving, but I knew that he missed his best pal.

ജ ♥ beginning

My friend Mary took a class from animal communicator Mary Getten. She offered to look at Kate's photo and practice her new skills. She said:

I started to feel quite a connection with Kate just looking at her picture and a few thoughts came through. She seems very happy with you and doesn't want to be sent back! I sensed she was living with an older man named Bill who may have kicked her once in awhile. Don't know if any of this is correct. It just came to me as I looked at her.

I found that interesting and didn't know what to think. I later was told by Mary Getten that Kate had likely lived with an older person or couple.

On November 20th, I called Nancy in Louisiana to tell her that a PBS TV special about the Katrina animal rescue efforts would be broadcast that evening. We talked about what was happening with Kate. Nancy said that the people who brought Kate in to Lamar-Dixon told her that they had rescued her from a rooftop in Plaquemines Parish. This was news to me. Kate's paperwork said "17th St Canal" in New Orleans. But rescuers were bringing so many dogs in at a time that Nancy suspects the paperwork got mixed up. I had never heard of Plaquemines Parish. Nancy had to spell it for me.

Plaquemines Parish is a largely rural parish (county) southeast of New Orleans, along the coast at the mouth of the Mississippi River. It was ground zero for Katrina, experiencing damage from the fierce eyewall winds, the storm surge and the flooding from failed levees. Nancy wasn't sure what group brought Kate in, but she told me that Plaquemines Parish had a lot of cattle. Many of the people who lived there were elderly and ran range cattle. Some of her friends used to live there and lost almost all of their cattle and horses in the storm.

Nancy, who lives near Baton Rouge, checked with one of her co-workers whose father lived in Plaquemines Parish. They asked around and had not found anyone who was missing a cattle dog. Kate didn't seem to be a city dog, so it made sense to me that she could have come from Plaquemines

Parish. I still wondered whether anyone was still looking for her, or if they had died in the storm.

Where had Kate been from the time Katrina hit on August 29th, until she arrived at Lamar-Dixon on September 17th? Her Petfinder 'Found' poster showed LA-SPCA number 0001-1442. Someone must know where the number was issued and the photo was taken, but I hadn't been able to find out.

Online I found photos of the devastation in Plaquemines Parish and animals rescued from that area. I began corresponding with Laura at PAWS (Plaquemines Animal Welfare Society), the animal shelter in Belle Chasse, which is along the only road that was open into and out of Plaquemines Parish after Katrina. The officials and vets in charge of rescuing and caring for stranded animals took them to Belle Chasse from the southern parts of the parish. For a while, they didn't allow rescuers to take animals out of the parish. They were trying to keep the animals together in Belle Chasse so that their families would be able to find them.

I also tracked down Lori at the Rescue Ranch, a non-profit horse rehabilitation center that was mentioned in one of the rescue stories on the parish website. Neither Laura nor Lori knew about anyone who was looking for a blue cattle dog, but they offered to ask around.

I even looked at the reports of missing and dead persons from Plaquemines Parish. I was following up on my friend Mary's animal communication experience, curious to find out if an elderly man named Bill had died in the storm. But the records were incomplete. There was no way to track what had happened to the residents who were no longer in the area. A person could have been washed out to sea or could have evacuated with nobody knowing whether they were alive or dead. It must have been horrific for those looking for missing family and friends after Katrina. No wonder the date when the rescued/fostered animals could be adopted out had been moved out to March 1st.

☙ ❤ ☘

> *"Our lives begin to end the day we become*
> *silent about things that matter."*
> Rev. Dr. Martin Luther King Jr.

Chapter 7

Finding Kate, Losing Pip, and Bruce's Story

Friends recommended animal communicator Mary Getten to help me find the answers I longed for. A skilled animal communicator can facilitate a two-way conversation with an animal. You may direct the conversation by asking questions or by providing information to the animal. A gifted animal communicator can hear and understand your pet and help you both gain a deeper understanding that generally results in more harmony.

Although I didn't understand how animal communication could work over the phone, I gave it a try. The first time Mary (in Washington State) communicated with Bandit in Minnesota, he wandered around the house looking behind furniture, clearly trying to find something. I have not seen him do that before or since. Although I couldn't explain it, I was convinced that something was happening between them. Without being told by me, Mary also verified things about my animals that I knew to be true. So I came to believe that her abilities and talents are real, and now consult with her regularly.

On December 2nd, I saw a male cattle dog called Bo on Petfinder. He was rescued from New Orleans, and was in a Kentucky shelter. He looked so much like Kate, with the same unusual coloring and markings, that they could have been littermates, or mother and son. He had gone through Lamar-Dixon, where I found Kate. His file named the street where he was rescued and stated 'Reunion pending', meaning that his original owner had located him at the shelter in Kentucky. Even though he came from a different neighborhood than either of the two Kate was said to be from, I thought his owners might know of Kate. It was a long shot, but I tried to follow up and wasn't able to get through to anyone. This turned out to be another loose thread. Bo's picture and description are on the next page.

&❤︎

Every day I told Kate how I was trying to find her people. I also told her that I loved her and wanted to keep her, but I felt that she was missing someone.

On December 2nd I received a long e-mail about the thousands of animals that still desperately needed rescue following Katrina. The crisis was far from over.

My heart was drawn to the rescue groups in Plaquemines Parish. When I learned of the ongoing needs at PAWS in Belle Chasse, I put out the word. People at work were eager to help, and donated needed items. They even helped pay to ship the items to Louisiana. It was a small contribution to a huge need, but it all helped.

reference id number:
PF46023

Description: ABOUT ...   Bo

Dog Husky, Australian Cattle Dog/Blue Heeler Mix

Age (YRS): 0 Color(s): black gray

BIRTH DATE: 2005-01-01 size: M

Markings: brown   Weight: 0 altered:

Sex: M   DESCRIPTION: *Reunion pending*

Found at 2622 Castiglione. Dog was transferred from Lamar-Dixon shelter to UAN/EARS Shelter in Monroe, LA. EARS Intake #:E1516. This dog is now at the Shelby County Humane Society in Kentucky.

While collecting donations, I learned that Gina, a woman from work, had served in Louisiana in the Minnesota National Guard. Just after Katrina, she had unloaded cargo planes at the air base in Belle Chasse. Gina and I bonded quickly over stories of our time in Louisiana. She told me about the devastation in Plaquemines Parish. Her unit had helped load rescued animals onto outgoing cargo planes in the middle of the night, to be flown to shelters around the country. Guys from her unit had rescued a dog from the river and cared for it until the original owners were found.

The need in Louisiana was calling me to go back to help. Lori (Wisconsin) of Lamar-Dixon and I discussed going back down together over the Christmas holiday break. But Kate's needs took precedence both financially and time-wise. Much of December was spent working on improving her health.

Kate's mouth looked like she had chewed on rocks her whole life. On December 5th, I took her to see the veterinary dental surgeon. A few years earlier, I had spent about $3,000 to have the vet dentist fix my rescued dog Rusty's infected teeth. I was relieved that the vet was willing to donate Kate's initial exam.

It was tough to examine Kate's mouth. She wasn't used to being handled and was especially sensitive about her mouth. We got the best look when we rubbed her belly and looked at her teeth upside down while she laid on her back. The vet dentist told me that she would need to examine and clean Kate's teeth under anesthesia. Kate also had a growth in her mouth that should be biopsied to determine whether it was cancerous. The starting estimate for the surgery was $550-$600. I planned to attend the procedure, which we scheduled for the holiday break. We would first re-test for heartworm just to be sure, since Kate had tested positive once, then tested negative later. While Kate was in surgery, the vet dentist would determine whether any additional dental surgery was needed, which could increase the total cost greatly from $600. I asked the vet dentist if she could donate the procedure for this Katrina foster dog. Her students offered to take up a collection to help cover the surgery. Donations would make a huge difference. The surgery could amount to $1,500-3,000, or more, and I wasn't in a position to spend that kind of money.

I'm not very good at asking for help for myself, but there was something about Kate and her needs that made me ask people to help her. People were often very generous and appreciated the opportunity to help a Katrina dog. The Minnesota vets who helped care for Kate enjoyed being able to help a hurricane rescue dog without leaving home.

I was especially grateful to my new ACD-L friends who gave both moral and financial support to Kate and me. Although Kate seemed healthy enough for anesthesia, I was concerned because she was probably over ten years old. One ACD-L friend offered encouragement when Kate was about to undergo surgery: *Fingers are crossed for a good outcome for Kate! She has come a very long way in a short time. Please don't be too concerned about her age with anesthesia. Tremendous advances have been made in the past years and it is no longer the terrible risk it used to be.*

The plan was to take Kate to my regular vet for heartworm and fecal re-checks on December 23rd, to clear her for the dental surgery on December 27th. But Kate came into heat on December 22nd. That answered the question of whether she was spayed or not! We hadn't found an abdominal scar, so I had planned to have her spayed as soon as some of her other health issues were resolved. Fortunately, Bandit was neutered and I was able to keep Kate mostly isolated at home.

During her heat, Kate became restless and irritable. She nested and hoarded toys in her crate. She had never refused food before, but she overturned her full food bowl. She was bleeding fairly heavily so I bought her denim "Pet Panties". I didn't know if she would tolerate them. She had been shredding her bedding and soft toys, so I thought she might rip off the panties and shred them too! Her behavior was apparently normal for a bitch in heat. (She was certainly acting like a "bitch".)

Before Christmas, in the middle of the commotion with Kate, my 16-year old kitty was going downhill fast. Pip (a.k.a. "Pippi Longstocking") had been stressed since Kate joined the household. Kate viewed Pip as prey and was never left loose with her in the house. My friend Mark had cut a hole in the wall so Pip could get directly from my computer room to her litter box downstairs without having to dodge dogs. She also had a cat tree by the hallway, so she could make a quick escape if needed.

One evening before Christmas, while I was working at my computer, Pip had a seizure. Before I could react, she fell off the desk onto the floor. She was drooling and losing control and I thought she might be dying. I had never seen her have a seizure, although she might have had one before when I wasn't home. I cleared the space around her and watched over her until she recovered. When I took Pip to the vet he thought she was okay. After we came home, I stayed tuned in to her because I had the feeling she was preparing to die.

I consulted Mary Getten and she told me that Pip was not ready to go yet, but that she was feeling increased pressure in her head. Mary had to repeat questions and Pip was not quick to answer. The pressure in her head felt like a ticking time bomb. She appreciated time alone with me, while I worked at my computer and at bedtime. Mary asked Pip why she sometimes howled loudly in the middle of the night. Pip indicated that when she woke up she felt disoriented. Mary suggested that I leave some lights on for Pip and that I put Rescue Remedy in her water and on her ears and feet at bedtime to relax her.

Pip wasn't keen on the dogs. Mary reassured her that she could come in the bedroom at night because Kate was in a crate. She also suggested that I crate Kate in another room at night so Pip would feel safe to come in the bedroom. Bandit had grown up around cats and had been taught not to chase them.

Next Mary spoke with Bandit. He understood that Rainbow had been hit by a car and he said she kept him company by 'visiting' him. Bandit thought there was something wrong with Kate and he didn't trust her. She was fearful and he thought there was something wrong with her emotionally. Bandit associated Kate's arrival with Rainbow's leaving. He dearly missed Rainbow and took it out on Kate. That's attributing human-like emotions to a dog, but that was the message that came through to Mary. Kate didn't have the energy that Bandit was used to and he wasn't getting enough exercise since Rainbow left.

Mary suggested that I continue to talk to Bandit and Kate about becoming friends, send them positive mental images, and give them opportunities for positive interaction. She reminded me to talk to them about what I *want* and to give them the mental picture of what I *want*, not what I *don't want*, because dogs will focus on the picture. Mary also sent me a mix of flower essences to put in their water that I called "friendly juice".

Next Mary communicated with Kate, who gave the picture that she was from a rural area outside the city, but not a farm. She was the only dog, but there were chickens and ducks (that might explain why she recognized the sound of the rooster crowing on TV). She had not worked cattle. She was used to being out and about more, running around outside. She was looking forward to having more freedom and not being crated as much. She thought that Minnesota was *very* cold.

Kate didn't want to fight with Bandit, but would defend herself. She was willing to let him be the top dog. But any move that Bandit made toward her, including play moves, threatened her. Mary told Kate that the cat was part of the family and must be treated with respect. Kate indicated that her former job was to chase off critters and it was hard for her to agree that it was okay to have a cat in the house. Mary told her that part of her job was to take care of Pippi and show me that I could trust her around the cat. That was tough for Kate, but she wanted to try.

Kate indicated that her old life and people were gone. She thought her people were dead. During the storm, there was a lot of wind and rain and the house was smashed up. She was outside hiding under something in the yard and was terrified. She'd had puppies in the past, but didn't have any when the storm came. She didn't know Bo, although Mary said that if he had been a littermate or her puppy, she might not know him after a period of time. Kate wanted to stay with me. She wanted to put Louisiana behind her and to get along with Bandit, but didn't know how.

After I consulted with Mary, I was very mindful of my time alone with Pip. I didn't think we had much time left together. Pip did fine for a few days, but then seemed to be losing it again. She began climbing up on my tall file cabinet to look out the window. When I was with her, I put her up there on a quilt to rest, but the risk of another fall was troubling. It was a long way down. Over the next few days, Pip became more and more disoriented and agitated. She cried a lot and became frailer, and I believed that she was ready to go. I didn't want to leave her alone while we were away to visit family at Christmas, and it would have been too stressful for her to go somewhere. She seemed more and more uncomfortable and unhappy and so I took her to the vet before Christmas to say goodbye.

Pip had been with me for all of my adult life. She was a beautiful gray, orange, and white calico cat with tiger stripes, white feet, and one long white stocking (hence her name, "Pippi Longstocking"). She outlived Nike, my first kitty, and had been the only cat in the house for a while. She was a feisty kitten, a real character, knocking all the spare change off the dresser and taking crazy runs across the bed in the middle of the night. In recent years, she slowed down and became my constant companion while I worked at the computer. She also slept on the bed at night and kept me company with her purring. She had been losing her way more and more since the seizure. Still, it was tough to say goodbye and I missed her.

Losing Rainbow and Pip made the months following my Katrina trip even more difficult. I was lucky to see Kate heal and enjoy life. Bandit, my "recreation director," raised my spirits by insisting that I play ball with him every day.

Pippi Longstocking, December 2005

On December 23rd, my regular vet did Kate's heartworm and fecal re-checks. The fecal came back negative, but the heartworm results wouldn't be available until after Christmas. Over the holiday, Kate went along to visit my family in Wisconsin, while Bandit stayed with my friend Becky in Minnesota. Kate did well with the pet panties, plenty of walks outside, and some crate time.

Due to the holiday, I was unable to get the heartworm test results before December 27th, the day of Kate's dental surgery. That day, I got up at 5:15 a.m. to take Kate to the clinic. It was too early to reach my regular vet before leaving for the dental clinic, which was forty miles away. After we arrived, I called the other clinic and was told that the heartworm test results were a "slight" positive. My regular vet told me that he was not overly concerned since she had also previously tested negative and had been on HeartGard® Plus since the end of September. But the vet dentist's tech insisted that the heartworm antigen and antibody tests be performed again, at the same time by the same lab. The tech (we didn't see the vet that day) said that surgery was too much of a risk under the circumstances.

Knowing how stressful it was to draw Kate's blood, I wasn't looking forward to doing it again. But the blood samples were taken and the results were expected back in less than two days. That still left time to do the surgery before I had to go back to work. If the results came back negative, we would do the dental surgery and hip, knee and tail x-rays two days later on Thursday. If they came back positive, I would have to come up with another plan. After all the ups and downs, I would be heartbroken if Kate was heartworm positive. She didn't seem like a sick dog at all—she was happy and energetic for an older girl—but heartworm disease can be deceptive.

Besides the uncertain heartworm test results, the other bomb dropped on me that morning was an uncertainty about how much would be donated towards the dental surgery. The woman who had volunteered to collect donations for Kate's surgery was out of town and had not left any information. It was going to be difficult to make decisions in surgery without knowing how much would be donated. Kate deserved the best care in the world, but I didn't have thousands of dollars to put into the care of my foster dog.

My anxiety level shot up. It would be so much easier to take care of Kate's recovery while I was on holiday, as originally planned. I was praying that the heartworm tests came out negative because the treatment is very hard on an older dog. After waiting three months to get her teeth taken care of, I was ready to get it over with, along with her spay and a biopsy of the growth in her mouth.

The vets had done a lot for us already, but the uncertainty about whether the dental surgery would be donated was troubling. It would be just the beginning of a string of vet bills to get Kate taken care of. I was anxious to get Kate's more serious health problems resolved as soon as possible. Since they had made the offer earlier, I thought the vets would donate most of her care.

Animal rescuers often have to ask supporters for donations toward the rescued animals' veterinary bills. Knowing that so many dogs had urgent needs, I wasn't prepared to ask the rescue community to donate money toward Kate's bills.

On Wednesday I called to get the heartworm test results and confirm that Kate was scheduled for surgery on Thursday. The heartworm antigen test came out negative but there was one more delay. In a mix-up, the lab had not done the antibody test. Those results wouldn't be available until Friday. So, the surgery couldn't be done that week. That fourth heartworm test had used up another $100 and my whole week off.

I was in tears that day. I had waited three months to get Kate's mouth taken care of. It was hard to enjoy my holiday, and I couldn't afford to use much more vacation time for her. Now that we had discovered the growth in her mouth, the situation felt more urgent. I decided to ask the other two vets if they could take care of Kate's teeth. I wanted to have a back-up plan for Monday (my last day off) if the vet dentist wasn't able to donate part of Kate's care.

On December 30th, Kate's heartworm antibody test came back negative. This didn't surprise me, but I was relieved. The vet dentist had left me a message, telling me to quit "chasing" the heartworm issue. Ouch! She must have forgotten that her clinic had refused to do the surgery without the fourth heartworm test. The dental vet's office wanted to put the surgery on my credit card and determine how much would be donated later. As much as I was devoted to this foster dog, I couldn't afford to do that.

ଓ 💜 ଔ

In December, my friend Sarah from Virginia sent me the rest of Bruce's story. At Lamar-Dixon, Sarah had noticed an older, blind Golden Retriever. She was very concerned about how he would cope with being exported to a shelter. So, she sponsored him and took him home to Virginia to care for him until his family was found. He had a tag with his address and the name "Bruce", but the phone number didn't work. This information was listed on Petfinder and eventually Sarah was contacted by the daughter of the dog's owner, Al.

Sadly, Al, at age 87, had not survived Katrina. Sarah was troubled about sending Bruce back, but eventually Al's family decided that Bruce belonged with Sarah. He stayed with her in Virginia and she takes him to visit the elderly in a local nursing home, where he gives love and comfort to others.

(photos courtesy of S. Dutton)

Bruce at Lamar-Dixon in 2005   Bruce the therapy dog at work in 2007

Sarah sent me the rest of Bruce's story, as told by Al's daughter Carolyn:

My Dad met Bruce one day while he was taking his daily walk to the mailbox. Bruce was probably about four or five years old. My Dad called me up excited telling me he found this beautiful loving Golden Retriever, with no tags. My Dad tried to find the owner to no avail. He knew the way Bruce acted and the way his coat was all shiny that he had to have an owner; he was very well kept. Well after thirty days, my Dad decided that Bruce was his.

Because Bruce was so loving and playful it was easy to fall in love with him very quickly. He adapted to his new home with no problems. My Dad and Bruce would take their daily walks together every day. In Bruce's younger years, he would play with his water bowl by jumping into it with his two front paws. He would also stand on top of his dog house. My Dad built Bruce's dog house, also equipped with a heater and plenty of room. The dog house issue did not last long. Bruce then came into the house and began sleeping with my Dad. Mom was not so happy with a dog in their bed, although she loved him too. So Bruce had to sleep on the floor next to them. Lots of times my Dad would go out and sleep on the living room couch so he could be closer to Bruce. Bruce never left his side.

Then one day my Dad decided to get a new brother for Bruce. He picked out a Dalmatian and named him Duke. Duke was raised by my Dad from eight weeks old. He was hoping that Duke would grow up and be a playmate for Bruce. Unfortunately, Duke seemed to be very independent and jealous of Bruce. My Dad could not let them play in the yard together. Duke was stronger than Bruce and he did not like the idea that he was second in line. My Dad still loved both of his dogs. He would let Duke out of his cage on a daily basis to romp and play with him alone. Duke was fine when Bruce was not around, but it was still very hard for my Dad to handle because of his strength.

Bruce became an inside dog and unfortunately Duke had to stay outside. But he had a very well-built dog house equipped with everything. My Dad would check on Duke regularly trying to give him equal attention. Yet, it was Bruce that had been his favorite from the start. Bruce followed my Dad everywhere. When my Mom died on July 24th, 1999 my Dad was devastated. They had been married for 49 1/2 years. Bruce became more of an anchor with love and affection to get my Dad through a very tough time in his life.

Anyone who came to the house always fell in love with Bruce. My Dad was already very involved with his church and always was the instructor every year for vacation Bible school, teaching the kids how to make things with their hands. When my Dad decided to take up dancing lessons, that was the turn around for him. He was happy again, and having fun. Had to put this in about my Dad because one of my Dad's requirements for anyone of his dancing buddies was to meet Bruce first… His motto "like me, love my Bruce". If you did not accept Bruce, well you knew where the door was.

Bruce and Duke were always taken care of on their annual exams, with their shots and heartworm medicines. When my Dad figured out that Bruce was not seeing too well he took him to the doctor. The doctor explained to him that he had degenerative eye problems and was slowly going blind. He tried to see if there was an operation to help Bruce but was told no. So the vet maintained a watchful eye on Bruce while giving him medicine to slow down his blindness. My Dad did not want to just shove the pill down his throat, so he would make meatballs for the month, put them in the freezer, and give Bruce one a day with his pill placed in the middle of the meatball.

When Hurricane Katrina came knocking at Dad's door, he refused to leave his dogs. I explained to him that we were evacuating to a pet friendly hotel and we were taking our dogs too. Dad was stubborn. He did not want to leave. He had to stay home and protect his dogs and his home. He also had four other people who asked him to leave. I did not know till later that I found out my Dad was maybe contemplating leaving but would not because of Duke. What a simple solution... put them in separate cars or a dog carrier for Duke. I found out from his neighbor later that he had told her he would handle it differently next time.

Still my Dad used to work for the Sewerage and Water Board for over 25 years. He would pump the water out of the city. He was there during [Hurricane] Betsy, 1965, pumping out water and doing it again during Camille in 1969. Dad believed the city would never flood.

The last time any of his neighbors saw him was after the storm. He was outside checking out the wind damage and his car stating "Well, we dodged another one". That was before the levees broke. I cannot begin to imagine how frightened and alone my Dad must have felt when the water started pouring in. I know his first priority was to save his dogs. He decided to put Duke in the garage thinking he would be safe there.

Unfortunately, we buried Duke in the back yard where he belonged. That was his home. All I know is that Bruce was at my father's side all during Katrina and never left my Dad's side. My Dad had left enough food and water for him for about three weeks. I know that Bruce was comforting to my Dad in his last hours on this earth. I know my Dad is looking down and smiling that his Bruce made it and is being so well taken care of.

Everyone including his neighbors thought that my Dad had been rescued. I kept calling the search and rescue department and they assured me that they were on the way, but could not call me when he was picked up. All I know is when my sister drove down from Georgia, she found everything boarded up, plywood still on the windows. On the front of the house was a big red X/0 meaning that house was checked and no bodies were found. Search and Rescue never went into the house. My sister pulled off the plywood, broke a window, and climbed through. There she found my Dad, (dead) and Bruce so much alive. She did not have room in her camper to bring Bruce home with her. So the animal rescue was called in to retrieve Bruce. I do not know how long poor Bruce stayed in the house or when he was rescued. All I know is there was three feet of water in the house, furniture, smashed, broken, smelly and hot. How Bruce survived was simply a miracle. We tried from California to locate Bruce. We were on the phone sometimes three or four times a day with Animal Rescue trying to find him. We actually did find him finally in Gonzales and he was in barn #5. I explained to the girl, please hold him! I'm coming for him, but I cannot get a flight into New Orleans for five more days. She explained they could not hold the animals and they were being shipped daily to all parts of the country. We finally arrived in New Orleans, late at night. The next day bright and early my daughter Andrea and I immediately drove to Gonzales to find him, only to find he had been shipped out to anywhere. I kept searching the internet, making calls, till I found him in Virginia. But you know what, he was already safe in loving arms, and is only alive today, because of our angel Sarah, who refused to see an old blind dog die in the heat. There is a place in heaven for you, Sarah, and my Dad will be the first one to greet you!

My Dad had a love for his animals and loved to work with his hands. He loved fixing things. He was the neighborhood handyman. At his burial, we placed in his coffin pictures of Bruce and Duke, a hammer, screwdriver and measuring tape.

His love for the animals is never ending and I know he is taking care of all the animals up in Heaven and patiently waiting for his Bruce (when it is his time).

Once again thank you for taking care of "Bruce"...

Al on his 87th birthday in July 2005   Remembering Al and Duke

(photos courtesy of C. James)

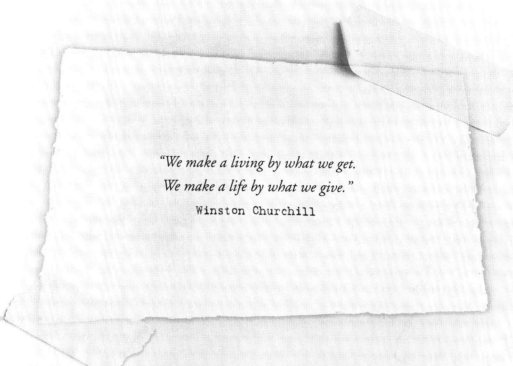

> *"We make a living by what we get.*
> *We make a life by what we give."*
> Winston Churchill

Chapter 8

Seeking Harmony

On January 5th, I took Kate to my regular vet for basic dental work, hip, knee, and tail x-rays and removal of the growth from her mouth. I dropped her off before work in the morning and picked her up that evening. This vet wasn't able to do extensive dental x-rays, but he was able to take care of Kate's basic needs, work within a budget, and help me decide whether she would need more extensive dentistry. I still planned to have her spayed once she was safely out of season.

The vet cleaned Kate's teeth, extracted two, removed the growth from her mouth for biopsy, and removed a black skin tag from her chin. The appearance of the growth didn't concern him and the biopsy results came back negative—good news! He reported that her hips had shallow sockets, but no arthritis. The x-ray showed severe arthritis in her lower spine and a congenital kink in her tail. Her knees were normal, with no arthritis visible on x-ray and no laxity on physical exam. He estimated that she was at least ten years old, due to her spinal arthritis and the condition of her teeth. The vet techs took care of her ears, toenails and anal glands, which was a blessing since Kate didn't put up with those things well while awake. Amazingly, all this work cost less than $500.

These results, along with the heartworm results, were great news! We would probably still need to x-ray Kate's mouth to make sure no problems were brewing below the surface. The spinal arthritis was a known progressive problem, and she was fairly pain tolerant.

Kate bounced back from the dental surgery quickly. Mouth pain was probably an everyday thing for her and it's hard to keep cattle dogs quiet, even the old ones! Shortly after returning home, she played ball and didn't seem to favor her mouth at all. She appeared very happy, playing with all the toys. Her coat was soft and silky, not coarse and hard like before. Most of her obnoxious "in heat" behavior had disappeared, but I knew that she could still get pregnant at this stage. I had to limit her outings for a while, but soon I'd be able to get her out more.

Eileen from the ACD-L group wrote:

All of this is WONDERFUL NEWS!!! I am so glad it went well. Consider putting her on glucosamine/chondroitin/MSM as a supplement, and ask your vet about Metacam—it has helped my 15-year-old dog's arthritic pain TREMENDOUSLY—even after the very first dose. And—thank goodness for the "low" vet bill! Give tough ol' Kate an extra hug from me and mine tonite!

I had not known Eileen before going down to Louisiana, but she quickly became a supporter and a friend. I had started Kate on Cosequin and MSM in December and decided to also look into Metacam, a prescription anti-inflammatory pain reliever.

I also heard from Cindy, who reported on the progress of Little Man, a beagle from Lamar-Dixon that she was fostering in Virginia:

Hey, you're getting closer and closer now… Little Man is doing well. He is wide, slam open!!! Not the quiet little dog we saw at LD!…He gets neutered on the 24th! I think it will help him a little bit. He is definitely food and toy aggressive…I don't think that he had much handling by people before the hurricane. He has his little quirks that tell me he isn't used to being handled. But he is getting much better about it. He is such a little sweetie—such a suck up! I am so glad I got to bring him out of that hell hole down there. I still miss Gonzo…Oh well…At least I had him for a month—and I have pictures of him.

Now that some of her health issues were getting resolved, I envisioned Kate prancing in the Parade of Rescue Titleholders at the Australian Cattle Dog National Specialty, which was to be held in Minnesota in October of 2006. To participate, a rescued dog needs a title. Kate had a great nose and I thought she would do well at tracking. I didn't have any formal training or experience with tracking yet, but we could learn together. Perhaps we would have enough time to earn a Tracking Dog (TD) title in the coming months.

I expected to pay for Kate's routine veterinary care once the major issues were resolved. But I was concerned that her further dental needs could cost thousands of dollars. Although Kate was with me as a foster, I would continue to take care of her if nobody claimed her. Since I had not taken her to the Minnesota shelter, they weren't covering any of her expenses. Kate and I were in a kind of limbo where I was responsible for her care, yet she didn't really belong to me. Her original owners could still claim her. One thing that pushed me to get her medical issues taken care of was that if she did go back, she would likely return to people who couldn't afford vet bills. Eileen and Nickie encouraged me to let people on the ACD-L know that Kate needed financial help – not to ask for money, but to let people know that there was a need, in case they wanted to contribute. They knew that some people on ACD-L would appreciate the opportunity to help Kate and me on our journey. I decided to wait because I didn't want to take money that would otherwise go to dogs in more urgent situations.

I had been reporting Kate's progress on ACD-L. In addition to asking for advice, I became a contributor. I had some experience with rescued dogs and posted this segment at the beginning of January:

...My experience with Kate... is that she calmed down... after we got home from Louisiana and she realized that she could depend on me. That was after driving about 1,200 miles from her original home to a completely new environment... where there are different dogs and a cat. Kate had to be isolated... because she tested heartworm positive and was also being treated for other parasites. After a few weeks here... we got rid of the parasites and she started feeling better. She was with me for over a month when one day she decided to play ball! Gradually, her personality came out more and more and she is feeling more comfortable mentally as well as physically. She made up a new chase game with me just yesterday. She now seems like a much younger dog than we originally thought. I can hardly imagine all the things that she has been through, and watching her heal has been one of the most gratifying things that I've done. I can guarantee that if I had pinched between her toes (a common shelter temperament test) at Lamar-Dixon in Louisiana in September, she would have gone through the roof. I would have too!

Years ago I adopted a shelter dog who turned out to be an ACD mix... He had kennel cough and was very sick when I brought him home. He was a cage chewer... and tore his way out of a crate, so we built him a 4' x 4' chain link kennel in the basement. When left in the kennel, he defecated on himself and danced in it almost every day for over six months. I didn't have to leave him for but a few minutes for this to happen. He lifted his leg on things in the house, but learned quickly not to. When I moved to throw a ball for him, he ducked. God only knows what this poor guy had been through. I knew that I was his last chance and that if I took him back to the shelter, that would be the end for him. Once he bonded to me, he sat on my feet and followed my every move. We got through this period and people who met him years later thought he was the sweetest, greatest, most beautiful dog. Everyone wanted to take him home. When

I told them his story, they couldn't believe how he had started out. And I was so very proud of him and how far he had come. My point is that this wonderful dog who everyone wanted was inside that sick, anxious, scared and dirty dog who everyone passed by at the shelter... he just needed a home where he would be loved and feel secure to learn how to behave in a home environment.

... I encourage everyone to consider fostering an ACD and also adopting a rescued dog. I think that ACDs are especially misunderstood and do not do well when confined in a shelter. They need all the help they can get from ACD lovers who understand them. I also think we need to get at the root of the problems more, via legislation, education, and other means.

During January, I was anxious to get Kate and Bandit living together. Bandit, my two-year old ACD, was the product of a carefully planned breeding. He had been to puppy kindergarten, obedience, rally, and agility classes, and herding lessons. He went to the dog park until he was about six months old (when my other dog was jumped by a larger dog that stood on her neck, cutting off her air and threatening her life). Bandit had dog friends that came over to play. He had always been bossy with other dogs, and he had learned a very bad tail-grabbing habit from another dog at the dog park. He also wanted to protect me or "own" me and keep other dogs away from me.

As Kate's health improved, I exposed her to Bandit more and more. Kate and Bandit seemed to miss each other when they were separated. They were okay riding together in the car with a wire barrier between, and crated next to each other in the same room, or with Kate crated and Bandit loose. They weighed about the same, and Kate showed many signs of submission. They started acting more like a pack, with each one checking for the other when they had been separated. But Bandit bit Kate's ear through the fence one day and sometimes tried to grab her tail. This wasn't okay with her or me! They had been okay loose in the same room for short sessions, but I wasn't comfortable with them loose in the house yet.

Normally, I'd expect an older bitch to take over, but Kate seemed content to let Bandit be the top dog. She would show her belly to him and look away. But she wasn't used to being around other dogs and wouldn't put up with any rude behavior from him either. He didn't seem to know how to be top dog, at least not like a benevolent leader, so he naturally stirred things up.

I expected to have Kate as a foster for a while longer and thought that Bandit would initially have a problem with *any* new dog in our household. They had come a long way and I asked myself some tough questions. Would more patience and continuing to gradually get them together work, or was I making things worse by keeping them apart? Did I need to let them work this out? Would they just make a lot of noise and resolve things? I was concerned that Bandit could really pound Kate if given the chance. If they got into a serious fight, I'd have a hard time pulling them apart.

Sometimes it seemed like Bandit was trying to play with Kate. He used to play rough with Rainbow, hanging on her collar, grabbing ears and tail, running full speed, and wrestling. He needed to be taught an alternate way to interact with Kate. His playful attempts to get her attention were obviously threatening to her.

I wanted Bandit to be able to play and didn't want him to associate punishment with every interaction with Kate, yet he needed to know her limits. Kate was very sensitive to a verbal correction. She cringed and hid if my voice was raised, even though it wasn't directed at her. When the blinds got tangled up one day, I let out a $%^&#@* in frustration. The next thing I knew, Kate was hiding behind the bed in another room.

Kate thought I was her mom and I should protect her. Bandit thought I was his mom and *he* should protect *me*. That didn't make for good pack dynamics. I thought that I might have to ask two other dog-savvy people to get them together and leave me out of it. Then maybe the two dogs could work out their stuff without the complication of "my stuff" and we could be one big happy family. I'd be less anxious with them around the house once they'd had a chance to be together and settle some things without me in the middle. But, when we got back to the house, I would still be in the middle, wouldn't I?

It would be difficult for me to monitor Kate and Bandit closely and let them have contact because Bandit is at least a thousand times quicker than I am. He and Kate would have to learn to respect my rules about behavior without having any major fights. I looked for a good trainer who knew and liked cattle dogs to work with us on this. I knew that I had to take charge of the situation.

On January 26th, I returned from a business trip. Bandit and Kate did very well kenneled side-by-side while I was gone. After pondering the advice I'd received on ACD-L, I decided to let them be together. Ever since Kate had been out of heat, they had shown signs of bonding and acting like a pack. After greeting both of them individually, bringing them home, and letting them unwind, I let them out in the fenced yard together. First I told them each what I was going to do and how I expected them to behave. Bandit was playing with his Jolly Ball and Kate carried a rubber ball. They did well together in the yard, not really interacting, but each playing on their own. Kate tried to chase Bandit a few times, but couldn't keep up. So I took them up to the 'playpen', which is about an acre of fenced land.

We walked and played ball for about 45 minutes and all went well. It was almost 50 degrees, which is warm for Minnesota in January. There was one tense moment when a fat rabbit inside the fence made a break for it and struggled to squeeze out the 4"x4" opening in the fence wire. Both dogs dropped their balls and ran together for the rabbit. I had visions of them playing tug of war with it, but the rabbit got through the fence just in time and the dogs went back to their balls without incident. When we returned to the backyard, I took pictures of Bandit and Kate sitting side by side—a milestone. But Kate is looking away from Bandit in the photo, and I should have paid more attention to that.

Kate and Bandit together, January 2006

When we went in the house, I made a big mistake. I was so comfortable with how well Bandit and Kate had behaved in the yard that I was too relaxed in the house. They seemed fine for a few minutes, and then I went into another room. Suddenly, they were seriously latched onto each other and I couldn't get them apart. Bandit had his jaws around Kate's face and her teeth were sunk into his shoulder. I yelled (of course that never works, but it's instinct) and tried to pull them apart without getting bitten. I eventually grabbed Bandit's collar and got him to let go, but Kate wasn't going to back off. I had Bandit in a tight hold with my hand twisted in his collar. Kate was still trying to latch onto his shoulder. I grabbed her collar and tried to pull them apart and get the baby gate between them. The fight moved from the living room to the dining room to the kitchen, a more confined space. I resorted to beating on them with the baby gate to get them apart, and put the gate between them.

This all probably happened in minutes, but seemed to take much longer. Once I got the gate up, I put Kate in her crate and then put Bandit in his crate next to hers. All was calm. Both were worn out. I let them settle down and caught my breath. Kate had a puncture wound over her left eye. At first I thought the eye was bleeding, but it was okay. Apparently the other tooth mark was inside her cheek. No wonder she was upset! Her face swelled up around her eye. Bandit was covered with saliva and his skin was black and blue, but otherwise he seemed fine. Later I discovered that his throat was swollen, so Kate must have grabbed him by the throat first.

I took Kate to the vet to have her eye examined. He put her on antibiotics and injected her with an anti-inflammatory and a sedative to calm her down. The left side of her face looked like she was part St. Bernard (droopy eye) and part hamster (swollen cheek). We were all bruised, but luckily I had been able to break them up without getting bitten. Kate looked pretty beat up, and Bandit had sore spots too.

I don't know what started the fight. They may have gone for the same toy. Bandit may have tried to play with Kate, which she saw as a threat. It may have just been that I left the room and wasn't there to enforce the rules. I don't know if they settled anything, or started something, but that fight was exactly what I was trying to avoid.

After the fight, they were calm when crated together in the house and in the truck. Neither had tried to start a fight once they had a barrier between them. They both knew that I expected them to get along and figure out a way to live together without fighting. Putting them together started out successfully and in hindsight I should have quit with the outside session and built on that. When a dog is afraid, like Kate, she will fight for keeps in order to survive.

I signed Kate up for a beginner obedience class starting at the end of January. Now that her health issues were being addressed, I wanted to give her more opportunities for socialization. I contacted the instructor (who had helped sponsor my trip to Louisiana) to let her know about the fight between Kate and Bandit. I told her that I thought Kate would be fine by the start of class, but that she was probably going to need a lot more socialization work than I had originally thought. She had bounced back physically, but still seemed weirded-out mentally. I had to be very careful with Kate around other dogs. Knowing that many of the handlers in beginner obedience classes are inexperienced, I warned the instructor that Kate was an older dog who would not like other dogs approaching her or jumping on her. Kate was very smart and learned quickly, but the school environment would be a challenge. The instructor suggested that we arrive late, after the class started. She agreed to give Kate extra space to let her get used to the environment.

I had taken Kate to the obedience school for short sessions before, to see how she would do in the building with other dogs at a distance. She seemed to be overwhelmed. Plus, beginner handlers often don't know how to read or handle their dogs. Kate didn't feel comfortable if another dog lunged toward her, even if it was six feet away. I didn't blame her since some handlers don't have control of their dogs and have no idea what signals their dogs are sending.

Ours was a fairly large beginner class. The instructor had told the others about Kate and they were very supportive. Kate was anxious in the room with all the other dogs, but we gave her plenty of space. She panted constantly but amazingly enough, listened to me and paid attention most of the time. I realized, though, just how difficult it was for her to be in this environment. When something scared or upset Kate, she panicked and seemed like a wild animal. Donna, an assistant, was like an angel by our side. She helped shield Kate from other dogs when needed and did some hands-on T-Touch (Tellington Touch) work to help Kate relax. Donna also told me about anxiety wraps to provide a calming effect, and other things that I could do to better prepare Kate for the next week of class.

Kate and I left near the end of class before the moving exercises began. I wanted to end on a good note and didn't think the movement would be calming for a herding dog! Overall, Kate's first class was a positive experience and I was very proud of her. It was one more step in the right direction... I taught her the exercises at home, but at class mostly focused on getting her comfortable around the other dogs.

Our experience at class made me see more clearly just how fearful Kate was around other dogs and helped me understand her reactions to Bandit. Her distress around other dogs had not been noticeable at Lamar-Dixon. She must have been very shut down at that time.

I received the following input from ACD-L.

Having gone through a huge learning curve with one of our dogs years ago, I learned that a lot of dogs that appear dog-aggressive are actually just terrified. Our dog put on a very impressive threat display but according to his shrink (and our experiences with him) he just wanted the other dogs to go away... I suspect Kate is frightened also.

Kate had reason to be afraid. She was an older dog with a sore back, being exposed to new things. Her teeth were in bad shape and couldn't protect her very well. She trusted me for the most part, but became overwhelmed easily. Bandit was a big goof who mostly wanted to play, but he was used to playing rough and he wanted to be in charge. When upset with him, Kate didn't appear to give a warning; she just went straight for the throat. Neither dog would back down from a fight easily.

But they played and teased each other when there was a barrier between them. Kate cried to go along when Bandit went outside. I thought they might still be able to work out a peaceful co-existence.

When Kate was outside, she enjoyed running, playing ball, and rolling in the snow. She even chased a rabbit when she got a chance.

Once Kate was no longer in season, I started taking her along in the truck when Bandit and I went to herding lessons and obedience school. She loved to go along and hated to be left behind. She was gradually getting to see more things. When out of the truck, she still tried to lunge at other dogs if they were too close. I think she wanted to eat the small ones and was afraid of the big ones, or just plain didn't know how to interact properly with other dogs. She had *seemed* to be okay around other dogs in Louisiana, so it took me a while to realize how serious her issues were.

I once had a Bernese Mountain Dog who became reactive to other dogs when she was about ten years old. I then found out that she had severe spinal arthritis and back pain, and was trying to prevent other dogs from approaching her and jumping on her. Kate's behavior seemed similar, although more serious.

I received more helpful input from ACD-L:

We tried gradual exposure from a distance with our dog as you are doing with Kate. One thing his shrink suggested was to teach him a special trick (his was shaking hands) and have him do it for really good treats when you knew he was about to be in a stressful situation. I guess it served as both a distraction and something positive to become associated with having other dogs around. He had two opportunities to do serious harm to other dogs that got too close and never did more than roar and slobber. He really did just want them to go away.

We did find a trainer who helped us with him. He and I stood on one side of her semi-advanced class and she explained to her students that he was just afraid and asked that they say hello to him and toss a treat as they and their dogs walked by. We did that for a while and then were able to stand in the middle of the class with them walking around us. He never did become completely normal though.

Kate probably feels safe behind the baby gate or crate and her wanting to play with Bandit can be expressed then. This is a tough problem, but think about how far she's come in a really short time.

While trying to resolve the issues at home, I received another message on January 21st reminding me that the situation on the Gulf Coast was still very desperate. There were still many starving animals in need of rescue. Since many of them were not neutered or spayed, they were reproducing.

Knowing how much work it took to take care of just one rescued dog, this felt overwhelming.

At that time, I couldn't go back to the Gulf Coast to help, but I was able to help with rescue closer to home. I volunteered to drive for a transport of nine dogs that were being brought to rescue in Minnesota from a kill shelter in Kentucky. Another volunteer drove the same route, transporting five of them while I transported the other four.

The other driver, Louise, was the president of RAGOM (Rescue a Golden of Minnesota). She lived a few minutes from me, across the state line in Wisconsin. She was a good friend of Beryl, who I had met at Lamar-Dixon. Louise and I drove the dogs from Eau Claire, Wisconsin to Homeward Bound Rescue in Albertville, Minnesota. There I met Katie of Homeward Bound, and started a very effective rescue relationship.

*"All kids need is a little help, a little hope,
and somebody who believes in them"*

Magic Johnson

Chapter 9

Back to the Vet

On February 6th, Kate went to her second week of obedience class. She showed improvement from the first week, panting less and relaxing more. Unfortunately, others in the class were more comfortable too, and didn't always give her enough space. That sparked her impulse to lunge at the other dogs. I had to be vigilant to ensure she had a safe space. Would gradual training and getting rid of her tooth pain and arthritis pain help with this response, or was it too ingrained? I looked for new experiences that would build her confidence.

While working through these issues, Kate was my teacher. I learned more from her than from any other dog.

Once I realized how worried Kate was around other dogs, I thought back to the big January fight. Bandit had probably tried a "play" move on her which terrified her; she had gone for his throat, which surprised him, and then he went for her face, making her think that was his intention all along. In February, I worked on getting them friendly again. One day, Bandit went up to Kate (in her crate) and touched noses very nicely with her. They often looked after one another from the other side of the gate. I talked to them and hoped that when Kate felt better and became more comfortable around other dogs, with stronger leadership from me, we could give it a go again.

On February 7th, Kate was spayed by the vet who had first seen her when we returned from Louisiana. I learned that her clinic could do the more extensive dental x-rays that Kate needed. When we had first worked with that vet, she had offered to donate $1,500 worth of care for Kate. Our initial visits used up half that amount, so I thought we still had about $750 of donated care available. But since we last saw that vet, she had helped other hurricane victims. The amount she had set aside to donate was used up, so I would have to come up with more funds for future vet work. The vet gave me a very detailed written estimate for the dental work so that I would understand the costs.

The morning of Kate's spay surgery started at 2:30 a.m. for us, with the sounds of Kate retching, preparing to vomit. I leapt out of bed. By the time I got Bandit into his crate and opened Kate's crate, she had already re-ingested most of the vomit. Yuck! Too bad, because she was not supposed to eat anything after 9:00 the night before. I lay awake in bed wondering if we would have to postpone the spay *again*.

I actually cried over this because I had been warned that Kate could get pyometra, a hormonal abnormality following a heat cycle without fertilization. It's a painful and acute condition of the uterus that has been compared to appendicitis. It can be fatal if not treated right away and is one of many compelling reasons to have female pets spayed at an early age.

I wanted to get Kate past all this vet stuff and on to some sort of normal life. I continued with the original plan, got up at 5:00 a.m. and drove the 45 miles to the vet clinic. At that time of day, I couldn't reach anyone to ask if the surgery would have to be delayed due to Kate's vomiting. We had to be at the clinic when the doors opened and couldn't call ahead.

They weren't concerned about the vomiting incident. Kate's blood work went well and the spay surgery went ahead as planned. Along with the surgery, they trimmed her toenails, she expressed her own anal glands (atta girl, save me a few bucks!), they determined that the bump behind her ear was just fluid, and did the dental x-rays. But they couldn't do the dental work at the same time as the spay surgery, so this wasn't our last health milestone as I had hoped.

Kate would need to have more teeth pulled, requiring another $1,000 of surgery into her jaw. The vet recommended doing this surgery later in February to avoid further problems, but first I had to figure out where the money would come from. The bills for this foster dog were adding up.

I believe that Kate was put in my path for a reason. She had come a long way since September and we had become very attached. She was a wonderful dog, in spite of her fears. She was a survivor and was very tough, but I don't think she would have survived the aftermath of the hurricane—the system set up by humans—if I (or someone) had not seen her as an individual and taken her home to foster. As an older ACD who was afraid of other dogs, she would have been terrified if shipped with a load of other dogs and put in a shelter.

When I brought Kate home, I took her out of a life or death situation. I didn't think of what would come next, but I knew she deserved another chance. Being able to care for her and see her blossom was therapeutic—a way to keep helping one lone survivor after Katrina.

The local vets had donated some care in 2005. But, by mid-February Kate's vet bills for 2006 were over $2,200, and my financial resources were stretched. The company I worked for was being sold, which put my job at risk. My truck had needed new brakes. I would put my tax refund toward Kate's vet bills, but that wouldn't be enough.

Many people who want to help rescue dogs cannot foster a dog themselves. They sometimes contribute by donating money to help others who are doing the fostering and paying the bills. But Kate was safe and had a good foster home with me, so I didn't want to take any funds from dogs that were in more desperate situations. I was torn, and started wondering if I should let more people know that Kate's vet bills were piling up.

Eileen was very supportive and encouraged me to let the people on ACD-L know I needed help. She also shared the starfish story with me (told in Chapter 20), which helped me a great deal. The moral support I had received had been fantastic, and any additional support that people could offer would make my role in caring for Kate easier. Some fantastic people from ACD-L sent donations toward Kate's bills. Sometimes it really does take a village!

Jim of Kansas City sent a donation and told me about his five cattle dogs, all from a rescue organization or the euthanasia list at the shelter.

Alex of California sent a donation and told me about her ACDs, "Fox" and "Bandit." Bandit was 11 ½ years old, blind and was losing his hearing, but was otherwise healthy and happy.

Bazza and ACD Winkipop of Florida sent a donation and posted the following message to ACD-L: *I'm sending $20.00 to "8 State Kate" to help with her dental bills. Anyone care to match me???*

Luis of Pennsylvania wrote: *Having read your many postings, and having family who have suffered through multiple hurricanes in the panhandle... I would like to offer a small donation towards Kate's vet bills... God bless, and the Bentleys here are glowing.* [which means that we're thinking about you, praying for you, pulling for you...]

Christine from Georgia sent a generous donation and told me about her rescue dog Shelby, who, she reported, *was an ole gal of age 10 when dumped at a shelter in bad, bad shape. Her furry little butt is now 13 and while still battling some health issues is a happy camper!* Christine and I have since worked together on rescues.

My newfound friends from ACD-L were a Godsend, and I began to realize how many people from across the country had been following Kate's story.

I also heard from Lori (Wisconsin) who I had met at Lamar-Dixon. She offered to send some funds if needed, told me of other possible funding sources, and gave me encouragement. She said: *I truly believe the tough cases… are given to people for a reason…I am not sure I fully understand them, but it seems to work out that way.*

I responded, in part: *I think that Kate was put in my path for a reason. I don't know if she would have survived otherwise and she really is a great dog, baggage and all. I hate to think what would have happened to her if we had not met. I'm learning a lot from her and realizing just how much I learned from my first rescue dog Rusty. Helping her to heal is good for me since I feel like I was able to do so little in comparison to the vast need.*

The evening that I brought Kate home after she was spayed, she was so out of it that she wouldn't take her antibiotic or painkiller. I hoped it wouldn't matter and let her rest in her crate. She was very uncomfortable and practically panicked in the cone-like Elizabethan collar that was meant to prevent her from licking her stitches. A friend lent me a "BiteNot®" collar—a smaller stiff collar that's made to keep the dog from turning back around to lick or bite herself. But it wasn't the right length for Kate and needed to fit precisely to keep her from turning around. So I made her a custom-fit bite-not-like collar out of a plastic vinegar bottle, sheepskin fleece, duct tape, and a shoelace.

After Kate was spayed, my friend Sharon wrote:

Great news that Kate came through fine with the surgery, I know how worried you were. I think you're right, dogs like Kate and my Beau do come into our lives for special reasons—they help to make us more human and compassionate for starters. I learned this week that while I'm traveling, Beau just sits on the landing by the garage door waiting for me to come home—it's kind of sad, but very sweet.

Kate did well for most of the week after the spay surgery. Then we had a rough weekend. Her skin was very sore where the hair had been shaved. It looked like razor burn. I applied cortisone cream with aloe and later tried a lidocaine spray from the vet clinic. Apparently the spray irritated her skin more. Her belly became red hot, she panted profusely, and I called the vet at 11:00 p.m. I was worried that Kate had an infection, but the vet warned me against taking her temperature with a glass thermometer since it could break inside of her. My neighbor Becky had an unbreakable thermometer, but I couldn't reach her and had to leave a message. I almost took Kate to the emergency clinic, but decided to wait until morning. Becky came over the next morning with her thermometer. Kate's temperature was normal at 101.2 degrees. One thing I learned from that long night was to buy an unbreakable digital rectal thermometer.

When we tried to clean the shaved area on Kate's belly with a damp cloth, as the vet had instructed, Kate almost hit the ceiling. I put more cortisone cream on her belly, which seemed to provide some relief. Then I discovered that she could reach the edge of the shaved area with her back feet. She had been scratching it with her foot, making the irritation worse. I looked for a sock to cover her toenails. She didn't like to have her feet handled, so I wasn't sure how we would manage, but the sock helped for a while.

At this point, I couldn't remember the last time that I had enjoyed eight hours of sleep. Bandit was playing ball by himself since Kate was getting so much attention, and Kate was tired from fighting the treatment.

The week following the spay surgery, we missed obedience class due to Kate's rash and upset stomach. People on ACD-L recommended that I put a T-shirt on Kate to protect her belly, so she sported a hot pink T-shirt from the Angry Trout Café in Grand Marais, Minnesota. The shirt served double duty as protection for her belly and as an anxiety wrap to help calm her.

The rash seemed to be improving. Her belly was still warm, but not as hot as before. She had been on Rimadyl and an antibiotic since the spay surgery, and I was still applying cortisone cream to her belly. She had learned to roll over to let me inspect her belly when I said "belly up"!

Unfortunately, Kate vomited again on February 13th, almost a week after the surgery. The vet decided to take her off of all oral medications until she was able to keep food down. I gave her a small amount of a prescription canned food for sensitive stomachs, hoping she would keep it down. I was concerned about having her off the antibiotic too long since she didn't seem to keep any of the food down that day. If she had an infection brewing on her belly, I didn't want it to get out of control.

Kate's blood work had been normal prior to the surgery and she had done well for the most part. But on February 13th, she curled up in her crate into the smallest ball she could form, and became clingy. I wondered if she had eaten something that was causing her to throw up, but I couldn't think of anything she might have gotten into, especially since she had been wearing an Elizabethan collar when unsupervised. She still had an appetite; when she vomited, she tried to eat it right back up.

Kate had been nesting a lot and hoarding toys in her crate. This wasn't unusual for her, except that she was doing it more and seemed more obsessive about it. Lisa, the dog walker, said that Kate had acted strange outside that day. She dug a hole in the dirt by the house, peed in it, and then buried it, like a cat. I'd never seen her do that. Some of these unusual behaviors may have been hormone-related.

I wasn't sure what was going on and asked people on ACD-L for their thoughts on Kate's strange behavior. I decided that if Kate didn't keep her food down that evening, I'd take her straight to the vet in the morning. Alex (from ACD-L) wrote:

I just read your update on Kate on ACD-L. My girl Fox does the same thing—if she has something in her stomach that doesn't belong there, she'll gag and vomit until she gets it up and out. Fox also tends to eat strange stuff when she has an upset tummy. I can't keep tennis shoes out because she always goes for the shoelaces if she's not feeling well. She's given me a few scares with this, but once she vomits up whatever it is, she's fine. Hopefully Kate will be the same.

Alex was a prophet. That evening, Kate threw up a nasty, compacted wad of cloth and a piece of a rubber ball. That explained the swollen, sore belly. Apparently her shredding activities had led to her swallowing the cloth. Later that evening, she had another normal stool, indicating that food was getting through her system. I hoped everything had come out and she didn't have a blockage. A while after she threw up, I fed her about 1/4 can of her prescription food and waited to see what would happen. She was more alert when she went outside at 10:00 p.m., then just wanted to curl up in her crate. I needed to get some sleep myself!

Kate ate 1/4 can of food again at 3:00 a.m. The next morning, she had kept all the food down and was more alert. She peed, pooped a small amount of normal-looking stool, and drank water. She felt better and had more energy. She also shrieked for her breakfast and ate 1/2 can of food. I started her on the antibiotic again. Her incision looked nice and her rash was improving. The T-shirt was protecting her belly.

Looking back on that week, here's what I think happened:

Kate's skin had a reaction to the shaving and/or stuff they scrubbed her with. Something that I put on her skin to help made it worse, and her skin was flaming hot. A stomach upset from the Rimadyl and/or hormonal changes from the spay surgery made her shred her blankets and eat them. She ate some stuff that caused a blockage and later threw it up, along with a piece of a rubber ball that had probably been in her gut for a while. While she had this blockage, it may have also put pressure on her abdominal area and caused a local (hot) reaction, although she didn't have a fever.

But had Kate expelled all the junk that was in her gut? She was eating food and appeared to be processing it normally. Could she be having a reaction to the sutures underneath her skin, which was closed by medical adhesive? With all the other stuff going on, it was hard to tell. But she was on an antibiotic and seemed to be feeling much better.

I was ready for Kate to be out of the woods and on the way to recovery. After being up again for half the night, taking 90 minutes to drive to work in a sleet storm, then finding out that I had to give an impromptu presentation, I'd had enough excitement for one week.

By the next morning, Kate seemed to be back to her old self, except for the belly rash that was still healing. She was cranky and decided that the T-shirt had to go. I, on the other hand, had developed my own weird, unexplained rash, which was very unusual. Hmmmm... My rash hurt like crazy and looked like I had severe burns on my neck and arm. I had read stories about an animal taking a disease from a person and vice versa. I wondered if it was possible that I took Kate's rash because I was so worried about her—and so stressed and short of sleep. But my rash seemed to be much worse! My body was wiped out. My immune system had taken a beating after being up these nights with Kate, on top of everything else we had been through.

Kate did a happy dance when I got home that night. She was feeling much better and had more energy. I kept an eye on her belly in case she was having a reaction to the internal sutures. I also watched to make sure she didn't eat weird and dangerous stuff.

The next day I worked at home. Kate didn't mess with her incision or lick her belly much. After her post-surgery complications and some very late nights, she was feeling better, but I was exhausted! Soon, she was back to playing ball, but she wasn't used to the zero-degree weather we were having.

The following Sunday, I took Bandit and Kate to visit local animal communicators. I took the dogs in one at a time. The overwhelming message from Bandit was that Kate was like a wild animal. He thought she wasn't normal and wasn't like other dogs. He thought she was strange and didn't like her. Kate gave the message that she wasn't comfortable around other dogs. She had a wild, undomesticated feel. She trusted me, but there was a lot of tension in the household.

The animal communicators strongly suggested that I consider finding Kate a home without other dogs. The idea upset me a lot. I realized that they were simply responding to what they had learned from the two dogs, and I tried to have an open mind. If I were going to re-home Kate, I didn't know where to start. I didn't know of anyone who had the expertise to handle her, yet didn't have any other dogs. She had come to love and trust me, and I didn't want to throw her another curve. Yet, Kate and Bandit might never be completely comfortable together. March 1ˢᵗ was fast approaching. Soon someone would be allowed to adopt Kate if she wasn't claimed by her former owners.

I told my online Lamar-Dixon friends on the DARR (Disaster Animal Rescue Responders) list that the animal communicators thought Kate would be better off in a home where she was the only pet, and that it wasn't fair to either dog (or me) to keep them in the same house if they couldn't get along. I wrote about how we thought Kate came from a rural area and wasn't used to being around other dogs, about my efforts to get her healthy, her progress over the past few months, and how she and Bandit were doing together. I let them know how smart Kate was, how she learned quickly and loved people, and how strong our bond was. Her reaction to other dogs was almost like that of an undomesticated animal—she acted wild sometimes when afraid. If Kate never became well socialized and Bandit didn't understand her, they might never be completely comfortable together. I loved Kate and felt very responsible for her. I loved Bandit and felt very responsible for him. Kate and I had been through so much that it would be very hard for me to find her a home and let her go.

I wrote: *I'd appreciate your advice and comments, especially if you have experience with a similar situation. Do you think that dogs in this situation from such different backgrounds can be taught to get along, and that I should work with them longer? If so, do you have any advice on how to do this? Do you think I should look for a home for Kate where she will be the only dog and have more freedom to have the run of the house and yard?*

In response, Dee Green (Canine Behavior Therapist, BalancedDogs. com) wrote:

I'm a dog behavior specialist, with almost 15 years of experience, primarily with the so-called "aggressive breeds."

I've followed your posts about Kate with great interest. Rehabilitating an older dog is always a special challenge, but for me, the ultimate reward. I once rescued an 8 year old Pit from a crack-house. She'd never been to a vet... and lived her days mostly chained to an electrical meter. At first, she had no benevolent interest in people or other animals. In fact, when I met her, the new land owner was pushing a bowl of food to her with a rake. He couldn't get any closer or she'd attack him. When he didn't get the metal rake out of the way in time, she grabbed it and tried to "kill it," violently shaking it until her mouth bled.

Against the advice of my vet, other trainers, and everyone I knew, I let her live in my dog run, while I worked with her. Along the way, I came to really love the old gal, and respect all that she'd lived through. I eventually decided to integrate her into my pack of three (a Rottie, a Chow/Golden X, and a Lab X). She lived another four years, and I had only one significant fight in all that time. Thankfully, I knew how to handle it, and it never happened again.

I feel I have a reasonable idea of what you're dealing with, and in my experience, it's not a matter of any two dogs choosing to "get along." Dogs are instinct-driven animals, above all. They operate according to their biological impulses, which are predicated upon their being either dominant, or submissive, in any relationship. Be it with other dogs, humans, or other animals. There are no equal relationships where dogs are concerned.

Consequently, they expend a good deal of time and energy communicating where they perceive themselves to be in that hierarchy. This posturing can be quite loud, and appear aggressive and dangerous to the average human, but 99.9% of the time if the people don't respond (by not touching or speaking to either animal), there will be nothing more than some wet fur from the mutual saliva exchange.

On the other hand, if the dog has poor "social skills," they might over-react to the other dog's posturing, or behave inappropriately towards the other dog, and provoke an aggressive response. Fearful and insecure dogs will frequently "strike" pre-emptively. [Note: I think this is what Kate did, out of fear.]

In my experience, dog-dog aggression within the same pack is usually a matter of leadership. Again, there are no equal dog relationships, even with humans. If a human isn't behaving how a leader is supposed to behave (according to their biological blueprint), they're genetically programmed to take control. In your dog's mind, if they're in charge, you're subordinate. That means you don't eat, sleep, or leave unless the leader tells you to. Pack leaders maintain order through strict control. So when you don't behave in a way that's consistent with either blueprint (leader or subordinate), an unbalanced dog will quickly become frustrated and anxious. That pent-up energy has to go somewhere, and it's usually directed at another dog they perceive as submissive. In your pack, if both dogs are feeling this pressure to lead, then they're going to compete (fight) to see who's stronger. That's how dogs resolve leadership issues.

Attempting to address issues by avoiding the trigger (in Kate's case other dogs), is a great disservice to the animal, from my perspective. No matter where Kate lives she's going to encounter other dogs, if not at home, on the street, or at the vet. When the inevitable happens, and she connects with another dog, if her humans haven't established clear rules, boundaries, and limitations, she's still going to "suffer" and behave accordingly. If that energy is unleashed on the wrong animal (or human) at the wrong time, the end result could legally label Kate "dangerous" and her fate could rest in the hands of animal control.

As for your question "Do you think that dogs in this situation from such different backgrounds can be taught to get along, and that I should work with them longer?"

I think if they regard you as their leader (determined by their behavior), they'll get along with whomever you tell them to accept in the pack. The "work" required to achieve this is pretty much yours...

Based on all I've read, I urge you to ignore the naysayers, and act from the heart in concert with dog behavior experts who support you. Kate's been through a lot, and you're likely the only human that's shown any real interest in her. Losing you could set her back.

Best of luck with Kate. Thanks for being there for her, and all of the other Katrina dogs you touched.

Connie wrote:

Dear, dear, Jenny, my heart is heavy for you today... my first reaction would be for you to keep her and keep working on it. As with my little old Mama Katrina, the worst health problems are probably behind you and as she starts to feel better, my...expertise... tells me that you must keep her. You've done so well so far and I'm sure after all you've put into her, she'll continue to improve and you'd never forgive yourself (nor would she) if you gave up now. I don't envy you having to make such a decision.

I have a funny about my little "cattle" dog. Today, she was out in the back yard and I thought the neighbors had gotten a new dog—I heard barking from a strange voice...for the first time since I've had her she has found her voice (bark) and is very proud of herself... I have to laugh at her... She has brought me such pleasure—as has your little Kate to you...

As for advice, you've made it this far—hang in there! You have to be so proud of what you have accomplished with her.

Monica (of Homeward Bound Animal Rescue in Texas) wrote:

I too feel that changing Kate's environment may make her issues worse. You are most likely the only "for sure", secure thing that has come into her life. No one will ever have the history and bond to her like you do. No one will be as committed to her as you. If you were to find her a home she will most likely come back to you because the average person will not deal with such issues. This bouncing around would not be in her best interest. This will not be an easy road at all. It will take a lot of time and is a huge commitment to take on. Her health issues may be compounding her behavior as well.

With my dogs I have found that they all eventually get along. They may not like each other much but they know they have to at least tolerate each other. I have nine dogs here right now and they do not all like each other but they can be in the same room. Every new foster dog I get always goes through the same process… We get lots of growling and teeth showing at first… but it is not tolerated.

I know Kate means the world to you and I know you two will be able to work this out…

Do whatever you know is right for you, your dog and Kate. You have done so much for her already so no matter what you decide you have changed her life already in a great way.

I appreciated having this amazing support from people who went to the Gulf area after Hurricane Katrina. I understood that the animal communicators were probably getting some disturbing messages from Bandit and Kate, and were trying to give me a way out. But I also felt that the people who had been down south, and had rehabilitated traumatized dogs, understood better what Kate and I were going through. I honestly didn't know where she could go if I didn't keep her and felt that I would be letting her down if I gave her up. If the "perfect" home had presented itself at that time, I would have considered it.

I wrote back to the DARR group:

Thanks for your support and suggestions. I want you all to know that I have not given up on Kate and I haven't given up on Kate and Bandit getting along. I was just passing along a strong suggestion from a trainer friend to find out what you think. Kate has come a long way since she's been here, and has dealt with a number of health issues. This environment is very different than the one she came from. I do think that if Bandit and Kate were to never get along, it would be tough to keep them in the same household. But for now I'm working with each of them individually and they have a lot of contact through baby gates and kennels throughout the day. I'm working with Kate on resource guarding, "give" and other obedience commands. Kate did very well in class last night. I was surprised how far she has come in less than a month. I'm continuing to work with Bandit in agility, herding and obedience, and reinforcing that I am the pack leader...

Sharon wrote:

Here's what I think—you have to follow your heart, no matter if conventional wisdom says otherwise. You have given Kate a home where she knows she will be cared for and loved. Rehoming her could be more traumatizing than keeping her with you. I would think that time will work its magic and Bandit and Kate will come to terms... I would suggest taking all the feedback you've asked for, taking some quiet time and ask yourself what you think is best and feels right. I know it's hard with 'special needs' dogs, and I know you've worked yourself into exhaustion with Kate's health problems. I doubt that anyone else on the planet would dedicate themselves to her the way you have. So, you know what side I'm on. Your friends are really watching out for you—keep that in mind when they counsel you on this subject. However at the end of the day, I still believe you should listen to your spirit and let it guide you...

I do believe you are a special angel for cattle dogs and that Kate is where she is supposed to be. When I rescued Beau and was asking friends for advice, my closest friend said those same words to me, "Beau is where he is supposed to be." Part of me didn't want to accept that because it is more work, more stress, more expense. However, the rewards and amazing love that he gives me everyday more than offset those feelings. Rescued dogs will 'read' wrong to a lot of people, they are still in a state of flux and not their natural self. I hope you are able to come to peace on this soon.

The responses indicated a unanimous "thumbs up" for keeping Kate and continuing to work with her and Bandit. Their advice matched my own instincts. I continued to work with Kate and Bandit, and tried to keep an open mind in case a new, better opportunity for Kate presented itself. I wrote an article on Kate as a Katrina survivor and submitted it to the Australian Cattle Dog Club of America (ACDCA) Quarterly publication. To open the door to other possibilities for Kate, I mentioned that we might be looking for a home where she would be the only dog.

Meanwhile, I was working hard to keep Bandit busy. He lost his best friend when Rainbow died, and did not have another companion like her. His favorite game was carrying one Jolly Ball while herding another one around the yard. He was so good at so many dog sports that I began to think about entering him in the versatility competition at the ACDCA National Specialty in October. After all, the Specialty was being held near our home in Minnesota!

I also applied for an AKC indefinite listing privilege (ILP) number for Kate. She needed an ILP number to be eligible to work toward a title. Perhaps she could be ready to participate in the Parade of Rescue Titleholders at the Specialty.

By the end of February, Kate was feeling much better. She was playing ball and was back to her usual daily exercise. At obedience class, she was becoming more comfortable around the other dogs. She even calmed down enough to perform some of the exercises in class. Kate was like a sponge, learning all kinds of things. She was amazingly smart when she was feeling well and wasn't overstressed. But she still seriously thought the small dogs were food!

Kate and Bandit had agreed that Bandit was the top dog. I'd been working with both dogs on NILIF ("nothing in life is free") principles, and was teaching Kate not to guard resources so intensely. NILIF principles are a non-confrontational way of handling dominance aggression in dogs. When used properly, these behavior modification techniques kindly, yet firmly, reinforce the person's role as pack leader.

Once she got a ball or a bone or some food, Kate acted like it was a survival situation (which it probably was in her old environment) and very seriously protected her prize. I taught her to give up the ball—without growling—when asked. When she gave me the ball nicely, I gave it back, or gave her a treat, or threw it for her. Occasionally I just took it, but most often she was rewarded for giving it up. I also got her used to having me around her food bowl. I held the bowl and fed her one handful at a time, or just held the bowl and let her eat out of it. I was trying to change her attitude, so she wouldn't think the world was going to end if someone came near her stuff. As she became more relaxed about these things with me, I hoped she'd eventually be more relaxed about them with Bandit too. She had a lot of potential if she could just relax some of her ingrained survival instincts.

Bandit and Kate were starting to play through the baby gate again, but Kate was still afraid he would make contact. One day when I was in the shower, Kate was in her crate and Bandit was loose. I heard some barking and rushed out to find out what was happening. Bandit stood in front of Kate's crate, waving his rubber chicken, trying to initiate play. The chicken had always been one of his favorite toys. He left it for Kate, in front of her crate. Sweet. There was hope, although we might end up needing two chickens!

Kate didn't know how to play with another dog. Bandit wasn't the gentlest playmate, and her physical issues probably made her sensitive to rough play. Kate sometimes slipped going up the stairs. This might have been due to her spinal arthritis since her hips and knees seemed to be fine. I made sure I stood behind her to break a fall if needed.

My friend Janna gave me referrals for a behaviorist and a

Kate with her ball

TTouch practitioner who did energy work. So far, I had been busy enough just taking care of Kate's veterinary needs and working with her at obedience school. I looked forward to the day when her major vet needs were behind us and I could afford the time and money to see the behaviorist and TTouch practitioner. But first we had to take care of those troublesome teeth.

At the end of February, our obedience school offered to help raise money toward Kate's vet bills. Our friend and agility instructor Amy donated specially-made dog bandannas, and classmate Donell made special dog cookies to sell.

I was asked to make a poster telling Kate's story. I bought some poster board and set to work telling the story of how we met in Louisiana, how Kate got the name "8 State Kate", and how she had progressed since arriving in Minnesota. To show what she had escaped, I added photos of the Katrina destruction in Plaquemines Parish.

Through Kate's poster, I wanted to show how Katrina had shattered lives and left everything changed. I wanted to give people another way of seeing what happened in Louisiana, particularly in Plaquemines Parish. I put a lot of time and emotional energy into the project. The process helped me better understand why going to Louisiana had been a life-changing experience for so many of us. I wanted people to *notice* what had happened, and to understand what Kate had been through. When I delivered the poster to obedience school for the fundraiser, I felt like it was sacred and had high hopes for raising awareness as well as money.

Kate was scheduled to have dental surgery on March 7th to remove the diseased teeth from her jaw. I hoped it would be her last surgery for a long time, but knew that her teeth would need ongoing attention.

℘ ♥ ℘

*"To be followed home by a stray dog
is a sign of impending wealth."*

Chinese proverb

Chapter 10

Getting by With the Help of Our Friends

March 7th was coming, and I still had bills to pay from Kate's second surgery. The fund drive from Kate's poster at the obedience school brought in over $100, which I was very grateful for. With outstanding vet bills though, I still felt anxious about the money. I finally agreed that Eileen and Nickie could let the people on ACD-L know that Kate's medical bills were piling up again. The generosity of people on that list was heartwarming. Donations came in from all over. More important than the money, it was great to know that people all over the country and even the world were rooting for us.

Susan, from North Carolina, sent a donation and mentioned her rescued ACD Zephyr. Dana, from Virginia, sent a donation. She mentioned her rescued ACD named Zee and said that she enjoyed reading about Kate and the work I had done to help her. Trish, from Colorado, donated and told me how others had helped bail her out when her rescue dog had health issues. She liked reading about Kate's progress on ACD-L and was glad that I was able to help her.

Nicole donated and said that she had two 12 year-old seniors in her pack of six. If anything ever happened to her, she prayed that someone like me would care for them! Barry (Bazza) of Florida sent a larger donation than promised and said, *I hope it helps with your truly wonderful work with Kate. I'm glad you two found each other! Keep up the super job!*

Christine from Georgia sent a donation even though she'd had unexpected vet bills for her own old rescue girl. She wrote, *Just got paid today and can't think of a better way to spend some money then helping another senior kid. Thanks for all you have done to help her.*

And on it went...I thanked everyone from the bottom of my heart. Their supportive messages meant as much or more to me than the money.

At the beginning of March, Kate was doing well and her last (I hoped!) dental surgery was coming up. Even though she had missed some of the obedience classes due to her health issues, she now pranced like a show dog when she heeled, even at school. I was proud of her and how far she had come.

At the vet clinic they told me that Kate was like a different dog. She wagged her tail on her way in the door, was happy to see them, rolled on her back and let them scratch her belly, and was much more relaxed and friendly. She now had a waist and had gained some muscle from our daily walks up and down hills. They told me to keep up whatever I was doing with her. Wow, that felt great! If I'd had a Bentley it would have been aglow with pride that day.

It was exactly one month since Kate had been spayed and I thought that spaying her had contributed to the change in her attitude. I also noticed that the more positive and confidence-building interactions she had, the more comfortable she became. It was nice to know that the clinic staff had noticed her improvement in just one month. She did better in obedience class each Monday too, although she still wasn't completely comfortable around the other dogs. I thought it would be a while before she achieved that, but she showed progress.

Kate came out of her dental surgery well. I drove her home through rain and rush hour traffic. Since she'd previously had trouble stomaching Rimadyl, the vet put her on Metacam this time. The vet had handed me a medicine bottle containing her pulled tooth, like the mechanic giving back the old car part that had been replaced! The extracted upper tooth was very worn down; a short section of the tooth had been exposed with the rest embedded in the jawbone. The vet told me that normal canine teeth are about 1/3 exposed and 2/3 within the jawbone. Most of Kate's teeth were worn down like that, with not much left exposed. I wanted to show Kate's supporters what we were dealing with, so I took a photo of the tooth next to a nickel and posted the link to ACD-L, along with other photos of Kate.

The response to the photos was amazing. People I had never met or spoken with wrote to me to tell me how well Kate was looking, and congratulated me on what I had done for her. Messages like that really picked up my spirits. With so many people now interested in what became of Kate, I started planning a website to track her progress.

When Kate's tooth was extracted, the vet inserted bone graft material to fill the hole and stitched a flap of gum tissue over it. It would take a few weeks for the tissue to grow into the graft to make it sturdy enough to chew with. I had to prevent Kate from putting too much pressure on the graft before it was healed. Once she came home, we stuck to a regimen of canned food. Although Kate was very oral, I kept her from chewing on things and picking up balls. She went outside on leash and wasn't allowed to pick things up. I left some toys out around the house and yard because Bandit needed something to play with. I had to be careful to only let him have the toys when Kate wasn't nearby.

Kate still had about $1,600 in vet bills due later in March that weren't covered yet. Posting her story on a website could be a far-reaching and effective way to raise additional funds. I sent my friend Eric a photo of the poster from the obedience school fundraiser and he began setting up a website, www.8StateKate.net.

I woke up on March 13th to find that Kate's mouth was bleeding. Kate had been feeling great and it had been tough to keep her from playing. Even with all the bones and hard toys taken away, somehow she had overdone it. It appeared that she might have ripped out her graft, so I called the vet right away. I tried to find a creative way to look at the graft because Kate didn't want me messing with her mouth. But I couldn't get her to a vet that day. We were having a blizzard and the road was getting snowed over right after the plow went by. Cars were going in the ditch everywhere and my driveway had not been plowed yet.

The next day, we dug out and I took Kate to the vet. She had opened up the original graft, and it was becoming infected. Some healing was apparent, but the sutures had to be redone. The vets took Kate into surgery, flushed out the site, and re-stitched the wound. They stitched her up even more securely, adding another $450 to the bill.

After we got home from the vet, when I took Kate out to go potty, there was a loose dog outside the fence. I didn't notice him until it was too late. I tried to keep her calm, so she wouldn't burst her stitches, but this imposition put her over the edge. She went crazy. This strange dog in our yard was just *wrong*, out of order, not the way it should be. I had to drag her back to the house. Fortunately she was in her harness, on leash, and inside the fence. It took her a long time to calm down after we got in the house. Me too.

It had *not* been a great day. Kate growled at the vet and acted uncivilized. She probably wasn't feeling well at all. Getting her through the next week without damaging the new sutures was going to be a challenge, and might require putting her on a sedative. To make things worse, Bandit wanted to go after her when she acted so strange.

I was discouraged and found myself wondering if Kate would ever be comfortable around other dogs and in different situations. My doubts weren't fair to her at that moment. Kate was hurting and feeling vulnerable, so of course she reacted the way she did.

Kate was put in my path for a reason, but that didn't prevent me from questioning whether I could give her what she needed. Was she a time bomb waiting to go off? If she had been outside the fence when the loose dog came in our yard, the results could have been disastrous. He looked like a wolf at the edge of the woods and was big like a Malamute, but had blue eyes and dog tags. I had never seen him before and didn't know where he came from, but his timing was *very* bad. I still didn't know if the incident had caused Kate to damage her new stitches, and it would be a while before she calmed down enough for me to take a look.

The day was also stressful for Kate and me because two clients at the vet clinic came in with loose dogs. One of the dogs was running around loose in the parking lot when Kate and I arrived. Neither dog was well-trained or under control. The receptionist supplied leashes, and we avoided any major clashes. Often people think that as long as their dogs are friendly, everything will be all right. But Kate was in pain and feeling vulnerable. Her response to being approached by even a friendly dog would have been extreme. That could have been a disaster and the people were oblivious. With Kate, I learned to be hyper-alert, so I could protect her from this kind of thing.

Following the repair surgery, Kate had to wear the basket muzzle or the Elizabethan collar (E-collar) all the time, which she hated. She couldn't have hard or soft treats, but a squirt of easy cheese or Kong liver paste kept her happy for a while. Lisa, our dog walker, came over mid-day to take the dogs out when I was at work. Since there was always the chance that the loose dog would come back, she was extremely careful with Kate, keeping the E-collar on her and keeping her on leash inside the fence.

A couple days after the second dental repair, Kate was doing better. I started giving her Benadryl, which made her drowsy and mellowed her out. When I took the E-collar off, I immediately put a black leather basket muzzle on her so she couldn't pick anything up. I wasn't leaving anything to chance, wanting her mouth to heal completely this time. Showing true cattle dog spirit, even with the basket muzzle on, Kate wanted to grab at the ball. She was very oral and was frustrated that she couldn't pick it up. That was especially hard to watch after seeing her joy when she had first learned to play ball. Keeping her busy and happy pushed my creativity to the limit.

When going outside, Kate wore her harness and stayed on leash inside the fence. The harness was also useful for steadying her while going up and down the stairs.

Between trying to wear out Kate and Bandit, breaking trails with my snowshoes, and shoveling what seemed like tons of snow, that week left me completely exhausted once again. The outpouring of support from ACD-L kept me going and brought tears of gratitude. I thanked everyone for being a net for Kate and me.

Nickie wrote:

I'm so glad to hear that our request for help has been so useful. Yippee!!! And Jenny ... you seem to have everything on your plate all at once. Hang in there. It's bound to get easier eventually. Even winter doesn't last forever.

Eileen wrote:

Jenny, I am SO GLAD this has been a help to you. You and Kate surely deserve it! Hopefully Kate will be fine with her sutures... Keep us posted—again, I'm glad that so many have responded! There really are a lot of folks with awfully big hearts out there. :)

I was thankful for the moral support from Nickie and Eileen. The response to their request for donations was fantastic. In two days, ACD-L members gave over $700, with more to follow. Along with the donations, it was even more encouraging to receive people's notes telling us that they were rooting for us. The moral and financial support, provided by generous people we had never met, was a tremendous boost. The past week had been exhausting, but I surely didn't feel alone in caring about Kate.

Even without a website up and running, support flowed in for Kate and me. I managed to post photos online from my time in Louisiana and our long trip home. The website was in the planning stage, and I was depending on busy friends to volunteer their time, so progress was slow. Meanwhile, I ordered note cards with a picture of Kate and Bandit and used them for thank-you notes.

I was on pins and needles until Kate's new sutures healed. She continued to be very unhappy that she couldn't chew on a bone or pick up a ball. We enjoyed playing in the snow, one fun way to keep her busy. Throwing snowballs that exploded when they hit the ground worked, as long as she wasn't near anything that she could smack her face into!

A few days after Kate's graft was repaired, I let Bandit out in the fenced yard while I was attending to Kate. When I returned to check on him, he was outside the fence, eating at the birdfeeder. This had never happened before. The backyard was enclosed by a secure five-foot chain link fence. The gate was not only latched, but I had to shovel away snow to open it far enough to let him in. The yard was next to the deck, which had a three-foot high railing. It was above the garage roof, with about a one-story drop most of the way around, and a huge pile of snow below. The snow was crusted over, with no tracks. Bandit had to stand on his back tiptoes to put his front feet up on the deck railing and had never gone over the railing. So I couldn't figure out how he got out. I was more than a little panicked, since Rainbow had died on that road. But Bandit came back inside the fence without incident.

Bandit kept pestering me to let him out for squirrel patrol, but his days of going out unsupervised were over until I figured out his escape route. Later in the day, he ran across the deck full speed, headed for a squirrel out in the yard. When he reached the corner of the deck, he launched himself and landed with one rear haunch on either side of the corner railing. He perched there precariously for a moment while I sent a quick prayer to the God of No More Vet Bills. Then he flipped backward and fell back onto the deck. He jumped back up, apparently unharmed, but disappointed that the squirrel had escaped.

During his two years with me, Bandit had never gone over that railing. In his excitement to get the squirrel that morning, he accidentally taught himself to fly. At that end of the garage, which is built into a hill, he didn't have far to fall. He must have landed in the huge pile of snow below, but strangely he hadn't left a dent. Once reinforcements were installed, Bandit could go out unsupervised again. We were both lucky that he hadn't gotten into trouble while he was loose outside the fence.

So there I was with the senior Miss Kate, recovering from dental surgery, and two year-old Bandit, my performance event dog who had taught himself to fly! Life was tiring, but certainly not dull!

As the days and weeks of her healing went on, Kate became surly with Lisa, our dog walker. She had been fine with me, but I'd noticed that sometimes she was crabby with other people. She was tired of the Elizabethan collar and may have been sore from walking in the crusty snow. We tried to give her a break from the E-collar and often used the basket muzzle instead, but we still couldn't leave her unattended without the E-collar.

With all this going on, I hadn't had much time to think about the website. My friend Eric, who had been working on it, became busy with other projects. The website didn't seem as urgent since the financial pressure had been eased by donations, but I still wanted to get Kate's story out there. My friend Janna offered to take over developing the site.

ജ ♥ ര

Of the many things Kate taught me, two of the most important were how to deal with dog-to-dog interactions, and how to work with resource guarding dogs. To help me understand Kate, I read Jean Donaldson's books <u>Mine: A Practical Guide to Resource Guarding in Dogs</u> and <u>Culture Clash</u>. Both books have good information on understanding dog-to-dog interactions. <u>Mine</u> has a very good chapter on desensitization and counter-conditioning that can be used to get a dog comfortable with different people, body handling, and unfamiliar situations. I followed these techniques to get Kate used to having different parts of her body touched.

Earlier in March, Kate had tried to bite one of the vets when he bent over her. He was in a very threatening position—I should have seen it coming. It was important to restrain Kate, distract her with treats, or even ask the vet to muzzle her. I wanted her to know that I was watching out for her and I tried to make the experience as positive as possible. Part of her job, though, was to be vettable. This was much more difficult for an older dog who probably had not been to the vet for most of her life. It is so much easier to start with younger dogs and get them used to as much handling and as many different places and situations as possible.

On March 21ˢᵗ, we went back to the vet to have the stitches in Kate's mouth checked. They had looked good to me, but Kate wouldn't let me get a close look. She was getting more uncomfortable and bitchy about going to the vet. They sedated her to examine her mouth and the stitches were mostly intact! She had torn out a small corner of the gum flap covering the graft, but the vet thought it would still heal fine without further intervention.

Keeping Kate content in an E-collar or muzzle for four weeks was hard work. We had about ten more days of restraint left. In spite of her confinement, Kate's attitude was mostly good when she wasn't at the vet.

She loved to walk outside and play in the snow. I bought a soft ball about 18 inches in diameter that Kate could push around the yard while she had the muzzle on. But she didn't do anything halfway. She got too worked up after a while and started crashing into things. Then I had to put the ball away, but at least she had a few minutes of fun.

Kate continued to make significant progress on body handling and resource guarding. But we had to suspend the socialization work while her mouth healed. I signed us up for a Beginner 2 obedience class starting on April 5th and hoped to begin working with her at school again.

Nearing the end of March, I looked forward to the day when Kate wouldn't have to wear the Elizabethan-collar or muzzle any more. As the snow melted, balls that had been buried in the yard resurfaced. Although she was wearing the muzzle, Kate grabbed for them, and got upset that she couldn't pick them up. To avoid tempting her, I tried to keep the balls out of sight, but once in a while another one surfaced.

By the end of March, friends from ACD-L had contributed a total of about $1,100 for Kate's vet bills. I was amazed and very grateful. By then the vet bills for 2006 had topped $3,200, and my tax refund was going to put the total within reach.

Keeping up with work, vet visits, caring for the two dogs separately, and household chores was tough. Having another down day, I wondered if Kate would ever be comfortable in our world. Having two dogs that couldn't relax together was stressful. Sometimes I didn't think it was fair to Bandit. I wondered if, after all the effort, I would eventually have to find Kate another home or put her down. But I was her rock. Many people had supported us and I didn't want to let them down either, unless that was the only right thing to do for Kate.

On my down day, Eileen wrote:

You've had a long road, with a lot of stumbling blocks along the way. It's natural to feel down when you are so tired! But—you have come SO FAR with Kate! Rejoice in those baby steps! Dinia and Rody have much the same problems—I have to supervise them ALL THE TIME when they are in the same room—most of the time they tolerate each other. However, I don't leave them alone together, EVER. It's a matter of management. And I've been doing it for two years so far, with a few scuffles that could have been a lot worse had I not intervened. You may eventually find the perfect home for Kate. Until then, remember those baby steps. After all she—and you—have been through a lot together, I wouldn't give up on her just yet!

Nickie wrote:

Hi Jenny ... Hugs to you! Give yourself (and Kate) a break. You and Kate are going through pretty hard times while Kate recovers from that surgery. Pat yourself on the back for still being upright after all that you're doing just now!

Sometimes keeping your head above water is as much as you can hope for. You just have to keep putting one foot in front of the other to survive the tough times, and then the good stuff can come later on. Tough times don't last forever ... it just feels like it! (That's all the clichés I can think of at the moment, but they're all true.) lol [laughing out loud]

And if at some point it seems obvious that Kate needs a different home, that's not a failure, and it's not letting us down. That's just learning what is best for Kate, for Bandit, and for you. Maybe you're her final destination, or maybe you're the person to get her to where she's going. That's hard to know until life unfolds a little farther.

Hang in there ... we're pulling for you all.

That day, confirmation of Kate's ILP registration was waiting in the mailbox when I got home. For me, it was another affirmation that we were on the right track. I was also feeling better, knowing that the following week her restraints could come off.

Without Rainbow, it was really hard to give Bandit enough exercise for his body and his mind. He appeared to be making moves to play with Kate. It would be fun to teach her to play, but I didn't think she'd tolerate playing hard the way he liked. Once her mouth healed, I hoped that we could take a few more steps forward. Even a more peaceful co-existence would make it possible to relax a bit.

Kate had come so far already. I enjoyed the challenge of teaching her, rehabilitating her, and seeing her learn. In the long term Bandit and Kate would need to co-exist in the same yard and the same room, even if they didn't play together. Trying to wear them both out separately was exhausting! Even if Kate was never fully comfortable in society, she needed to get more comfortable in our home.

At the end of March, Kate and I took a long weekend to visit my friend Mark in northern Wisconsin. There were no other dogs at Mark's place. Bandit stayed with some friends in Minnesota, where he enjoyed good playtime with other dogs. It was a nice break for all of us.

"When you are kind to others, it not only changes you,
it changes the world."
Harold Kushner

Chapter 11

Coming Into Our Own

On April 3rd, the vet told me that Kate could play with soft toys again. Woohoo!! There *was* a light at the end of this long tunnel! Kate was excited to get her rubber chicken and Cuz ball back. I continued working with her on resource guarding by exchanging a soft treat or another toy for the toy in her mouth, or throwing the ball for her once she gave it up. Since she hadn't had her toys for a while, she wasn't sure she wanted to give anything up, but we made progress anyway. In another week she could have hard cookies, bones, jolly balls, and other toys again.

April 3rd was also the fourth anniversary of the day that Rainbow came to live with me in 2002. I missed her and I knew Bandit missed her too. I thought about getting Bandit another playmate. This April 3rd (in 2006) was a nice sunny afternoon, so one-by-one I took Kate and Bandit out to the field to play ball and enjoy the day.

On April 5th, Kate and I started Beginner 2 obedience class. She had already learned the exercises very well at home. In class we mostly worked on getting her used to the other dogs again. Given the opportunity, she still reacted to strange dogs, appearing to show a proactive display of self-defense.

Spring was arriving in Minnesota and Kate was feeling much better. She looked healthy, with a shiny coat and toned muscles. We enjoyed our early morning walks as the sun came up and the birds came to life. She loved to go for walks in the field and play with her Cuz ball. She tossed the ball in the air and chased it across the field—all on her own! She rolled on her back and wiggled back and forth with her feet in the air. She was coming into her own, an amazing dog who looked genuinely happy.

Kate loved to ride in the truck (and *hated* getting left behind, which was probably true of most hurricane dogs) so she rode along to a lot of places. I was careful to give her positive experiences that wouldn't make her feel threatened.

Bandit was a busy fellow and continued to do well in obedience, agility, Rally, and herding. In the spring there was a seasonal overlap in classes, and when summer arrived we would focus on herding and agility. Bandit was two years old and *very* active, especially since Rainbow wasn't around to help him spend his energy.

We three were doing very well, thanks to all the help I had received to get us this far. Now I wanted to give back, but money was still tight for me. The company I worked for was being acquired by a larger corporation, which meant the future of my job might still be in question.

I had kept in touch with Sarah of Lost Fantasy Stables and Animal Rescue in Virginia. Money was in short supply for her rescue, so I began working with her on grant applications. In western Virginia, many people live in poverty and the animals often get the worst part of the deal. The need is great and donations can be hard to come by.

While I was looking on Sarah's website (www.lostfantasystables.org) to gather information for the grant application, up popped "Fred", a red heeler mix. He had the same coloring and unusual markings as Rainbow. This felt like more than mere chance. He looked unhappy in the photo, which was taken just after he arrived there.

Fred's Web Page

Name: *Fred*

Breed: *Shetland Sheepdog Sheltie / Red Heeler / Mixed*

Color: *Red/white*

Sex: *Male*

Current Size: *35 Pounds*

General Potential Size: *Medium*

Age: *2 Years (best estimate)*

Activity Level: *Moderately Active*

Indoor or Outdoor: *Indoor and Outdoor*

Good with People: *Friendly*

Good for Inexperienced Caregivers: *Yes*

Good with Dogs: *Yes*

Good with Cats: *Yes*

Good with Kids: *Yes*

Housetrained: *Yes*

(photo courtesy of S. Dutton)

Description: *Fred is a beautiful guy with a ton of love to give to his very special family. Young sheltie mix, great with kids, cats, and other dogs. Walks well on a leash... housebroken/crate trained. Fred is a big tail wagging, face licking bundle of love who really wants a family of his very own! Fred would make an excellent addition to any family.*

Sarah told me that the enraged man who had dumped Fred threatened to shoot him if she didn't take him. He had stuffed Fred into a tiny chicken crate and thrown it into the back of his truck. He was very rough with the dog and said that he had been chasing sheep. (Imagine that—a herding dog left loose that chases sheep!) After the man left, Fred trembled in fear for a long time while Sarah held him in her lap to comfort him. There was no doubt that he knew his life had been in danger. Sarah named him "Fred", and he had been with her for about three months when I found him on the website.

Bandit needed a rough and tumble playmate again. I needed a playmate for him, too. Without Rainbow, it was really hard to wear Bandit out. If Bandit had another dog to play with, he would be happier and I could spend more time working with Kate. Could Fred be the playmate we needed?

Fred's temperament was crucial to this idea working out. He had to be a dog who knew how to play, and yet would be submissive to both Bandit and Kate. I turned to Sarah for this input. I trusted her judgment, knowing that she had plenty of experience with many breeds of dogs. From Sarah's description, Fred sounded like he would be a good pal for Bandit and would let Bandit be in charge.

We had some time to think it over. I couldn't bring another dog home until the end of May because I had two trips coming up. I also needed to make sure the vet bills were under control before even considering another dog.

My friend Janna had three dogs, including rescues. I asked her about the dynamic with three dogs instead of two. Janna wrote:

Three dogs are NOT that much more work than two. Once you hit two and you feel comfortable with two, anything above and beyond that is just another dog. I do think Fred would be a good addition to your home and I think you would be great for Fred! :)

It depended on the dogs too. I wasn't sure that I even felt comfortable having Bandit and Kate together, let alone adding a third dog. When I first got back from Louisiana, having Rainbow, Bandit and Kate was overwhelming. I consulted animal communicator Mary Getten about bringing Fred to our home. She liked his temperament and thought that he would do well with Bandit. He showed her that he liked to run and play chase games, like Rainbow had. She gave him the picture of Bandit and our home and introduced him to the possibility of coming to live with us.

I looked into what it would take to transport Fred to Minnesota over Memorial weekend at the end of May. I put out an inquiry on ACD-L asking if anyone would be able to transport him along the route from Virginia to West Virginia, Kentucky, Ohio, Indiana, Illinois, Wisconsin, and finally to Minnesota (another 8 state dog!).

80 ♥ ○ξ

On April 11th, I noticed that Kate's mouth was bleeding again. Fortunately, it was during the weekend, so I could keep an eye on her. She had been healing well and playing with the Cuz ball and the rubber chicken. Once she got hold of a jolly ball, which the vet had approved, her mouth started bleeding. I looked at the surgery site and it was still closed, but appeared to be red and sore. It was probably healing okay, growing bone from the inside, but it could still get infected. Kate was cranky again, which made me wonder. I consulted with Mary Getten on Sunday and she confirmed that Kate's upper right mouth and back left foot were sore (both of which I had observed, but had not told Mary).

Later that night, I looked in Kate's mouth again. It appeared red, but not torn up. It was probably tender, but I expected it would finish healing well if we were careful. After I looked in her mouth, Kate bonked my nose hard with her nose, as if to get me back for messing with her! Then I asked her if she wanted to stay with me and continue to be separated from Bandit and have her own space, or whether she would rather go to another home where she would be the only dog. Kate rolled on her back and vomited. She had never done that before, so perhaps the question upset her! Great…my own attempt to communicate with Kate had made her vomit!

On Monday I called the vet about Kate's mouth. She wanted me to take Kate in right away. But her clinic was on the other side of town, and I was in a training class for work that week, so my schedule wasn't as flexible.

Since we had just run out of antibiotic, I asked the vet to renew it until I could get Kate to my home vet the following day. I'd known my home vet for over fifteen years and knew he could help me determine whether Kate's mouth was okay. I wanted to make sure she was healthy before I had to travel in May.

We skipped the second week of our obedience class to visit the vet. He sedated her to look closely at her mouth—you can't muzzle a dog and look at her teeth. He found that Kate's surgery site had healed well! While she was sedated, he also gave her a Lyme booster shot and trimmed her toenails. I was optimistic that Kate wouldn't have to visit the vet again for a while.

My vet only charged me $45 for everything—a much-appreciated gift. Kate had become more difficult to handle in those situations and I probably should have paid him $45 just to enter the room with us. With a longer break between vet visits, Kate would probably become easier to handle again. She had been through a lot in the past few months and we needed some smooth sailing to get her back on track.

Kate made progress in spite of the vet visits. The weather was nice and we spent more time outside. The snow melted and most of the mud dried up. Kate learned to be comfortable on the deck, with Bandit in the fenced yard, while I did chores around the yard and wasn't right there with her. She was also getting used to the higher noise level with the spring increase in traffic on our road. When she first came to Minnesota, she took notice every time a car went by. By spring, there were more motorcycles and other noisy traffic, but she didn't seem to pay as much attention.

Now that Kate had her toys back, she collected them and took them in her crate. One night she hoarded three Cuz balls and one clutch ball! She was getting better about resource guarding, but could be very insecure about her "stuff", especially since all the toys had been taken away for a while. I can't say that I blame her. When you've lost everything, you want to hang onto every good thing you can get.

It was one thing after another for Kate. On April 16th, just a few days after we received the all clear on Kate's mouth, she bumped into my leg and yelped. She had never done this before and I noticed a hematoma on her ear. An ear hematoma is a pool of blood between the skin and the cartilage, essentially a big bruise. Hematomas are caused by burst blood vessels, often due to vigorous head shaking or ear scratching. Ironically, Kate's hematoma may have been caused by her exuberant play!

Kate and I both wanted a longer break from the vet. There was a chance the hematoma would resolve itself, but I knew that if it got worse, it could become extremely painful and require treatment. By the following day, the hematoma had grown. I could tell that it was very painful—it felt like it was going to explode. When I called the vet, he agreed that it needed attention. He recommended that I drop Kate off at the clinic the next morning. The previous week I had promised Kate no more vet visits if she stayed healthy—I was devastated that we had to treat her again so soon. Obedience class was put on hold once again, until she felt better. She was under too much stress.

This time, I gave Kate a sedative before leaving home. She was sort of punch drunk when I dropped her off at the vet clinic on my way to work. The procedure was uneventful and went well. When I picked her up after work, poor Kate was still "drunk" from the anesthesia, but she seemed happy to be going home. She was scheduled to go back in three weeks to have the stitches taken out. The vet was as anxious as I was for Kate to get back to a normal life and enjoy being a dog. I hoped and prayed for no more complications. I took a photo of Kate with her newly stitched ear and posted it for ACD-L. She looked so sad in that photo.

I'm sure Kate preferred that the next time I visited the vet, Bandit should take his turn for a change. That evening, she almost got her wish. After playing ball outside, Bandit came in with a bloody foot. Fortunately, it wasn't serious and healed on its own.

The hematoma treatment pushed the financial pressure back up. My friend Janna helped me set up a PayPal account and a "Help Kate" button on the 8 State Kate website, where people could click to donate. But the website wasn't completed yet.

Sarah offered to finish launching the website, even though she was very busy with her rescue organization. I took her up on her offer. I hoped to include a link to the photos showing the devastation in Plaquemines Parish and add a photo diary of Kate's progress since fall, similar to the poster that had been displayed at obedience school. I was passionate about telling the story of what had happened in Louisiana. I wanted to share Kate's story with people to raise awareness, not just to raise funds. Sarah shared those feelings. She had made two trips to the Gulf Coast to pick up and care for rescued Katrina animals.

During April, my article about Kate was published in the spring edition of the ACD Quarterly, the national publication of the Australian Cattle Dog Club of America. It included some of the photos that would eventually be on the website. I was glad to get the story out.

Connie in Washington State left me a phone message, asking me to call her. She wanted my address to send funds for Kate. It was great to talk with her and hear that her Katrina dog was doing well. I was very grateful for her support, knowing how much she had given already.

I also received a generous donation from Bobbi from obedience school, along with this message: *God bless you for all you are doing for her. I am sure you are the basis for her strength.*

Debra (Illinois) from ACD-L sent a nice donation in memory of her ACD Mick, and asked me to give Kate a special cookie in his memory.

Squad (New York) from ACD-L sent us a very generous donation toward Kate's vet bills, along with a recommendation for a joint replenishing complex. I thanked her for the recommendation and planned to look into the new supplement once our supply of Cosequin and MSM ran out.

I also received supportive notes from Cindy and Sarah in Virginia, who were both scraping by to support their own rescued dogs.

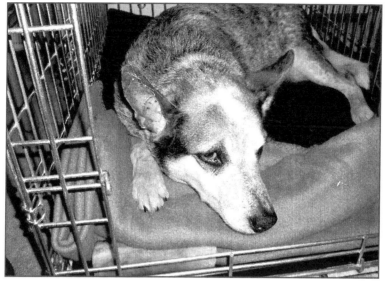

Kate's stitched ear

After the hematoma was repaired, Kate recovered slowly. She was wobbly the following day, and she seemed to have a new limp. I had to keep the sutured ear dry, so we covered it when going out in the rain. The vet told me not to use an Elizabethan collar because it might bump her ear, but I had to somehow prevent her from putting her foot in her ear to scratch it. Getting through the recovery period without any complications was not going to be easy. Eileen warned me that a hematoma could recur, so I kept an eye on it.

The day after the surgery, Kate was already interested in playing ball. She was getting back to her old self slowly but surely. Kate was still kind of dopey and her eyes were droopy, which made her look even sadder. The ear stitches had to stay in for three weeks. She probably thought she'd be better off on her own out on the bayou rather than trying to survive all of my attempts to "help" her. But she was pretty tough and she would feel better soon.

That night we had a thunderstorm. Would it rattle Kate? I still didn't know how she would react to big storms since she'd only been with me since the end of September. Eileen recommended an anxiety wrap, so I wrapped an ace bandage around Kate in a half body wrap. The anxiety wrap is used to calm the dog's mind and body by using a technique called maintained pressure to help reduce stress. Maintained pressure provides even, rhythmic, and repetitive input to the sensory receptors of the brain and central nervous system, providing a calming effect to the mind and body.

As I corresponded with Eileen that night about the storm and anxiety wrap, Bandit waved the rubber chicken at me again, inviting me to play! His only anxiety was to get his play time in.

By April 25th, Kate was doing better. Her stitched ear looked good, with just a small red patch in the middle that I watched like a hawk. Some swelling was normal, as long as it didn't get infected. I continued to give her a break from obedience class. I wanted to just let her play ball and be happy for a while.

Bandit and I had attended a herding clinic the previous weekend. He was my first herding dog and we had a lot to learn. Kate rode along in the truck and I took her out to go potty when there weren't other dogs around. One time when she was getting back into the truck she must have hurt her back. She didn't want me to pick her up, and started to jump for the tailgate when I wasn't looking. But she couldn't quite make the jump on her own, and she missed. I caught her by the harness in mid-air so she wouldn't fall. She went crazy, turned around on the tailgate and started biting at my hands. It was clearly a pain-triggered outburst, and she was blaming the pain on me. Luckily I had gloves on and she scratched my wrists, but didn't hurt me (one advantage to her lack of teeth). I got her into her crate and, once inside, she calmed down. The next day I took along an old ramp, which was much easier for her. From then on, she used the ramp to get into and out of the truck.

On April 27th, Bandit earned his first qualifying score in Novice B Rally, with a respectable score of 92. I was very happy with his performance since it was his first time ever in a competitive Rally or obedience ring. He also did well being crated and getting around in a crowded place. He was even polite when an obnoxious, yappy dog jumped on him, even though I was tempted to let him take a bite out of it. I don't like crowds or poorly behaved dogs any more than he does! Bandit enjoyed the individual attention on our day out, and I was glad to see him do well in spite of the stress in our household.

Kate managed fine being left home alone that day. She still had stitches in her ear, but otherwise her life had been relatively pleasant lately. She was enjoying some gorgeous weather and playing with her ball.

Knowing how much support we had received from the dog community, I wanted to give something back. In mid-March, I received a few e-mails from a woman in Wisconsin who was trying to find a new home her Australian Cattle Dog. She was going through a divorce and was concerned that she could no longer give him the care and attention he needed. I tried to help her find a solution that would allow her to keep him. She was very torn, but made up her mind that it would be best to find him a new home.

I began to share more of the things that I had learned from Kate, hoping that others might benefit. On ACD-L, I replied to a woman who had posted questions on resource guarding:

Sometimes the skills that dogs need to survive make it tough for them to live and be well-socialized in our society. I highly recommend Jean Donaldson's book, Mine: A Practical Guide to Resource Guarding in Dogs. This book gives a lot of specific information with step-by-step instructions for dealing with food bowl guarding, object guarding, location guarding, and more. It's helpful to read the book all the way through, but you don't have to do that to gain insight into the specific problem that you're having with your dog... You can also get Jean Donaldson's book Culture Clash, a longer book that discusses similar issues.

After living with a dog who was not well-socialized or trained, I had this advice to offer a woman who had asked questions about her ACD puppy:

If you can't take him to training class…find other ways for him to learn obedience and get socialized to other dogs and situations. One of the benefits of obedience school, especially for young dogs, is to get them used to being around other dogs, even if they don't get to play. Another benefit is that you become better at working with him. So I'd encourage you to take at least one training class with a reputable instructor. Also, take him places with you (like maybe the local PetSmart, Petco, or feed store) and make sure he gets exposed to different situations.

Kate apparently was not socialized as a pup and is afraid of a lot of things, including other dogs. This is much tougher to manage or change with an older dog…

And while he is still a puppy, get him used to being handled all over (ears, feet, mouth, etc.) and in different positions, including on his back. You can do this as part of a game, while playing. I've been working with Kate on this. She has improved a lot for me, but she is still wary of being handled by strangers.

By the end of April, life was approaching normalcy at my house. We were busy with spring activities and Kate was scheduled to have her ear stitches removed on May 10th. I already had the sedative to give her before we headed to the vet.

৪০ ♥ ଔ

> *"You cannot do a kindness too soon, for you never know how soon it will be too late."*
>
> Ralph Waldo Emerson

Chapter 12
Who Said That Life Would Be Fair? ...and Meeting Fred

At the beginning of May, while walking one of the dogs up in the pen, stabbing abdominal and back pains doubled me over in pain. I could hardly walk. My trip down the hill and back to the house was made one small step at a time. Back at the house, I called my neighbor Becky for help. We put the dogs in their kennels and she drove me to urgent care. A physician gave me pain medication and scheduled diagnostic tests to get to the root of the problem.

The pain subsided and I went home, wondering what was happening. I was planning to drive to Baraboo, Wisconsin that weekend for Noah's Wish disaster response training, and had a solo work trip to Europe scheduled later in the month. A couple of days after my painful incident I was feeling much better.

Meanwhile, Sarah and I were working on a plan to get Fred from Virginia to Minnesota after my trips. In my mind, the decision had been made. Kate would never be the playmate that Bandit needed and Fred could be. When I contacted Sarah to discuss transport plans, she told me that her friend (who had volunteered) was now unable to plan Fred's trip. That's how I ended up coordinating my first transport. We had almost a month to pull it together and I started looking for volunteer drivers.

We planned to transport Fred from Virginia to Indiana on Saturday and from Indiana to Minnesota on Sunday, the day before Memorial Day. Sarah and I assembled and distributed a transport sheet modeled on other transport sheets that we had seen. A transport is usually divided into legs of about 100 miles each. Sarah planned to drive Fred from Ceres, Virginia to Charleston, West Virginia and I planned to pick him up in Wisconsin. That left eleven transport legs to fill. We also needed a place for Fred to stay overnight in Indiana.

Sarah's friend Laura, who lived near Indianapolis, offered to take care of Fred on Saturday night. Sarah had met Laura in Mississippi, caring for rescued animals following Hurricane Katrina. Laura was part of the Indy Pit Crew, a rescue group that takes care of pit bulls and has even rescued an abused woman along with her dog.

Before I left for the weekend of Noah's Wish training, a repair man came to work on the water softener in the basement, which threw Kate into fits. She was very protective of our home and of me, and she still hadn't learned to let it go when I told her someone was okay. I gave her Rescue Remedy and did NILIF work with her to give her something to focus on.

I looked forward to the Noah's Wish training, which would include ways to cope with the stress of disaster situations and a recap of the Katrina experience. I wanted to meet others from my region and train with an organized group that was well prepared to cope with a disaster situation. The experience would also be therapeutic. I was excited to see my friend Lori from Wisconsin, who I had met in Louisiana. Lori and I had considered going back to Louisiana between Christmas and New Year's, but neither one of us had been able to go. We corresponded by e-mail, but I hadn't seen her since we had left Louisiana in September.

Bandit and Kate stayed at Becky's place while I was gone. She had taken care of them before. They had their own space there where they could be near one another, but separate from the other dogs. They also had a large fenced area to run. Bandit could play with Becky's dogs while Kate stayed in her own space.

The three-day Noah's Wish disaster response training was awesome. What a tremendous group of people! I wished I had known about them before I went to Louisiana. Noah's Wish was founded by Terri Crisp specifically to care for animals in disaster situations. They had no conflicting demands or political agenda. They were very experienced at disaster response and had their act together. In Louisiana after Hurricane Katrina, over 70% of the hundreds of animals that they cared for were returned to their owners. This was way above and beyond the percent of animals returned by other groups.

At the training, we received a Volunteer Field Operations Guide and got acquainted with other volunteers from all over the Midwest. We did teamwork exercises. We attended sessions on The Basics; Volunteer Information; Disaster Response; Intake, Reclaim, and Foster Care; the Incident Command System; Shelter and Triage; Facilities and Supplies; Communicating: Internally and Externally; Search and Rescue; Rescue, Handling, and Care of Animals in Disasters; and Disaster Preparedness. We also had our photos taken for Noah's Wish badges. It felt great to be among so many willing volunteers who wanted to be better prepared the "next time". All the same, we hoped there wouldn't be a "next time" like Katrina!

Lori and I bunked in the same room and had time to reminisce. Once we started talking, we realized that we both had many tears left to shed. The enormity of the need that we had seen was still overwhelming. We had done our best and it wasn't nearly enough. Lori apologized for crying; I didn't. I understood our tears and knew they needed to find a way out. The tears still come easily today.

At the training I met many wonderful people, some who had responded to Katrina and some who hadn't but wanted to be trained for future disasters. When I realized that some of them lived along Fred's transport route, a light bulb went on in my head. I passed around my pen and notebook for the contact information of people who would be willing to drive transport legs in Ohio, Indiana, Illinois, Wisconsin, and Minnesota. That's how I started building a transport network that has since served many rescued animals.

Once I got home, I wanted to help create a network of ACD volunteers across the country, trained in disaster response. On ACD-L, I encouraged others to take the Noah's Wish training course. We needed more help keeping an eye out for ACDs (as well as other animals) in disaster situations. Disaster response does not just include field work. It includes walking dogs, cleaning litterboxes and cages, keeping records, procuring goods and services, managing facilities, communications and dispatch, and other jobs. People who don't have the stomach or physical ability for the more hands-on parts of animal rescue can still contribute in other areas.

On May 10th, Kate had the stitches removed from her ear and was doing well. After five surgeries in four months, she was surly with the vets and we had to sedate her to remove the stitches. The vet encouraged me to let her just enjoy being a dog for a while. We hoped for a vet-free existence until she was due for vaccinations in the fall.

Sadly, as I write this, my vet has now become a patient himself. He is losing a battle with cancer. He was always so kind to Kate and me. I think about him often and hope that he, too, gets the best of care in return for the wonderful care he gave to so many animals and their families.

In May I ran into one of the downsides of asking for financial help to care for a rescue dog. I received criticism from someone who had previously been supportive. She questioned why I had put Kate through so much vet care and had asked for money to help cover the expenses. I didn't take this lightly, and did some soul-searching. Re-examining my choices, I felt I had made the right choices for Kate and for me as each situation arose.

This person's concerns were reasonable, but I was the one who had taken on responsibility for Kate. I was riding the roller coaster to recovery with her and following through the best that I could. I hoped this woman's critical feelings weren't shared by others. Kate and I were facing enough obstacles already and it seemed to take a village to support her needs.

Kate was enjoying life and playing with her ball again. I cherished our early morning walks. I wouldn't have taken the initiative to get out of bed so early and enjoy the morning if it hadn't been for her. Bandit and I were training in obedience, herding, and agility. He took his position as recreation director in our household seriously, and kept me busy too.

Before I left for Europe, I received a doctor's approval to travel. The source of my painful attack had not yet been diagnosed, but I had not had another such incident.

While traveling, I had time to work on Sarah's grant applications. I also continued, via e-mail, to organize Fred's transport. As the transport came together, Homeward Bound Rescue in Minnesota (which I had helped in January by driving a transport leg) offered to foster the Wisconsin cattle dog whose family was splitting up. I added him to the transport in Wisconsin and he would ride along with Fred to Minnesota. This was the start of a partnership with Homeward Bound that has helped us rescue and place many dogs.

On the plane, I read the book Cesar's Way by Cesar Milan, the 'Dog Whisperer'. He mentioned that dogs belonging to homeless people often have a more natural existence. They're more likely to be out wandering and foraging all day which is more natural for a dog, like a wolf's life. This made me think of my morning walks with Kate, how tuned in she was to her environment, and how she seemed to be much more comfortable outside. I missed these walks while traveling. I wondered if Kate had been homeless before Katrina or whether she'd had a stable place to live. I had always thought that she belonged to someone, but that might not have been the case. That might explain why nobody had claimed her.

When I returned home from Europe, I was happy to be back with the dogs again. Becky had taken good care of Kate and Bandit. They both did well at her house while I was gone, but it wasn't *home*. Becky told me that she wouldn't be able to board them again for a while because her aging mother needed extra help. I didn't have a back-up place where Kate would be comfortable if I had to travel again.

Fred's transport was scheduled to leave Virginia on Saturday morning, May 27th. Late on Friday afternoon, I found the last driver needed to fill the transport. The woman in Wisconsin was torn up about having to part with her cattle dog, but she brought him to meet the transport as scheduled. She sent all of his favorite things along. It was a very sad day for her, although she felt she was doing the right thing for the dog.

The transport went smoothly. The drivers along the transport route reported that Fred was a sweetheart and behaved well in the car. He enjoyed special attention from everyone along the way. I'm sure he wondered where in the world he was going! On Sunday I met the transport and picked up both dogs in western Wisconsin, then drove them to Minnesota.

When I first met Fred, he hardly noticed me. He was distracted by the sights and sounds in the park. He had traveled a long way and was glad to get out of the car. Although Mary Getten had told him that he would be making a long journey to his new home, I don't think he knew that he would end his journey with me. He had been handed from one driver to the next so many times. He was very cute and sweet, much cuter than the upset dog I had seen in the picture. He lacked some confidence, maybe, but he had plenty of charm. After we crossed the border into Minnesota, I handed the cattle dog off to Melissa, who drove him to his new foster home.

This was the first time I met Melissa in person, although we had e-mailed many times. I had first heard from her online in February. After Katrina, she had gone to Louisiana and cared for rescued animals at the Winn Dixie staging point near New Orleans. Since meeting online, Melissa and I collaborated on many rescues, saving a number of dogs from death row in Georgia and other southern states.

When Fred and I got home, I opened the bag that came along with him. It contained food, toys, special treats, and an ASPCA card entitled "Adopt a Shelter Dog". The card had a beautiful paper maché picture of a dog sitting in front of a house that said "Home Sweet Home". Made by Jamie N. of Fremont, California, it had won the 4th-6th Grade Category in the ASPCA "Make Your House a Home…Adopt a Shelter Dog!" Art Contest.

The card was signed by each of the transporters along Fred's long journey. As I read their notes, I realized how many wonderful people had shown Fred love along the way. Fred was truly a delightful dog looking for a place to call home. And here he was, home at last!

During Fred's first week, I kept all three dogs separate, spending individual time with each one. Then I introduced Bandit and Fred on neutral ground away from home. They did fine together on a short walk, then played well together and got along great. The trainer who helped me introduce them liked Fred and thought he was a good match for Bandit. At home, they played together in the yard while Kate stayed in the house. It was good to see Bandit having fun and Fred settling in. He came out of his shell a bit more every day. He had to learn how to navigate the stairs, and some of the household sounds seemed to surprise him as they had Kate.

Fred loved to play chase games (as Mary Getten had predicted) and I started calling him "Chase" half the time. I liked the name Fred too, but Chase seemed to fit him better. When I told Sarah about his new name, she wrote: *Chase (my youngest son) would be thrilled to have Fred called that...* I hadn't even known that Sarah's son was also named Chase!

I was still wary about the dynamics in the house. Kate was riled that Chase was there. She would get used to him over time, as she had with Bandit. I was careful to make sure she was secure in her own space and got her own walks. Knowing that the two boys were good at wearing each other out helped too.

On the last day of May, Bandit woke me up around 1:30 a.m. and I took him outside. When I came back in I noticed that Kate was lying still in her crate and groaning, over and over. She looked catatonic, staring straight ahead. I couldn't get her to come out of her crate right away, but eventually she got up and came outside with me. She laid on the deck and panted and drooled profusely while I called Becky, and then the emergency vet. Becky lives nearby and has a lot of experience with dogs. She could help me assess Kate and get her into the truck if we needed to go to the vet. At first I thought Kate was in gastric distress and I was concerned that she may be bloating, but her abdomen wasn't bloated. She seemed "checked out", like she was having a seizure but without any movements. After talking to the emergency vet on the phone, I waited for Becky to arrive.

When Becky drove up, Kate jumped up, ran over and barked at her. She seemed to have snapped out of it and was almost back to normal, although still panting more than usual. She seemed to be fine neurologically. We wondered if she had a vestibular (ear) problem because she had a head tilt, but Becky was familiar with that and didn't think that Kate was showing many symptoms. I noticed a pee spot on her crate pad, probably from a temporary lack of control. This was unusual for Kate – she must have had a seizure. I decided to keep her home and watch her; she had become so difficult to handle at the vet. Under the circumstances, I didn't want to have to give her a sedative or take her to a strange vet unless it truly was an emergency.

We went back to bed for a while. At 4:00 a.m. when I got up to check on Kate, her face and neck were swollen. She didn't have the glazed-over look and wasn't panting or drooling, but something was very wrong. When I had put her back in her crate at about 2:00 a.m., she had groomed herself, then scratched at her chin. Now I noticed there was a crusty blood spot under her chin that I hadn't seen earlier, and guessed that she had been stung by an insect. I called poor Becky again and we decided that I would give Kate 50 mg of Benadryl. The only reason I had it in the house was I'd recently stocked a first aid kit for the Noah's Wish training! At 5:00 a.m. Kate was still swollen, but didn't seem distressed. By 6:00 a.m. the swelling had gone down but hadn't disappeared, and she was behaving much more like her normal self.

What a horrible coincidence, if Kate had a seizure earlier, and then was stung by something later. I remembered she was attracted to a flying bug when I took her out to go potty at about 10:30 p.m., but Becky and I both agreed that the swelling wasn't there at 2:00 a.m. In my moments of distress in the middle of the night, I had made up my mind that if Kate was bloating or needed any extensive surgery, it would be time to put her down. The poor girl had been through enough already, but I didn't want things to end that way.

I sent an account of the incident to ACD-L and other dog friends and asked for input. Was it possible that Kate could be stung and not swell up right away, or that being stung could cause a temporary seizure or stroke-like incident? It wasn't clear whether more than one thing was going on.

I called my vet when the clinic opened at 7:30 a.m. He thought that Kate had a petit mal seizure, followed by a reaction to an insect sting—two separate incidents. The next day, June 1st, she was doing much better. She seemed like her usual self even though she was on Benadryl. She still had some loose swelling at her throat, with fluid under the skin. She also had a small bump that I first thought was a tick, but looked like a blood blister. It was troubling not to know what had stung her. There may have been wasps nesting under the deck. I watched her carefully as the vet had recommended. She might have had seizures before, but the one on May 31ˢᵗ was the first one I knew about. Perhaps Bandit's new habit of waking me up in the middle of the night was because he had detected something unusual from Kate.

The stress of having Chase join us might have helped trigger Kate's incident. I hope not. Perhaps it was one stress too many for a dog who had been through a lot. Kate and Chase were always kept separated. She had her own space as usual, but she knew he was in the house. She had the seizure when we were all sleeping and not interacting directly, so perhaps she'd had a bad dream.

The following evening, Kate acted pretty much like her old self again. She seemed so resilient. I wished I could bounce back like that! I had to give an important presentation at work the next morning, which wasn't easy, going on so little sleep.

> *"Courage is being scared to death,*
> *but saddling up anyway."*
>
> John Wayne

Chapter 13
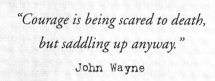
Letting Go

But Kate wasn't the same. She had pulled through the incident and seemed fine physically, yet something was very wrong. I always thought that once we had taken care of her health issues, she would recover completely and live a full, happy life. But the stress of the storm and all that she had been through had taken their toll. Since the seizure, she'd been distressed. Kate had snapped and her brain wasn't the same. She lunged at the baby gate, she lunged at me. She didn't want to be here any more.

Bandit knew. He started acting strangely toward her and tried to pick on her again. Their relationship changed for the worse, and she seemed even less comfortable in our world, ready to snap at the least disturbance. The tension increased in our household.

A trip to the emergency clinic would be extremely traumatic for Kate. She had been through enough. It was time to think carefully about what to do next.

Kate was a survivor. Once the heartworm question was resolved, her veterinary needs were not life threatening. I thought she had years left to live on this earth. She had muscled out, her coat glistened, and she loved playing with her ball. She was beautiful and had such a strong spirit. Maybe I was naïve, being so very close to her. It never dawned on me that she would leave so soon… and that I, the person who rescued her, would be the one to send her on her way.

As I struggled with the choice, Sarah wrote to me:

"I sent you away from this world of pain not because I didn't love you but because I loved you too much to make you stay". Someone sent this to me once when I laid one of our horses to rest and I think that it expresses all that I ever wanted to say but couldn't come up with the right words for.

What matters most is that she has had a good life since Katrina…she has known unconditional love and loyal attention for maybe the first time…she has always had food and good care…a roof over her head…toys to play with…and a safe haven from the storms her life has brought her. I think that you did well by her and she couldn't have asked for anything else. She was very lucky that you found her sweltering in that God awful heat in LD and chose her to bring home. She is very loved and very cherished and will always be with you in your mind and heart. "For God as he giveth he taketh away, in their minds and their hearts a memory shall stay".

You live with her and you know what the choices are… I think if I was in your shoes I would let her go now while she is healthy and relatively happy so she can run free again in a body and mind free from pain. You did save her Jenny…you gave her love…and you can help her leave with the same love you have shown her all this time. She is a very lucky old dog to have had you come into her life and give her a home.

Believe me when I tell you that you are in my heart and my prayers…you are a very good friend to me and I appreciate everything you have done. Many "hugs" and much love…

Sarah's words of wisdom helped me summon the courage to do what was best for Kate. So many people had supported Kate and me. Her life and mine had become public. I had never doubted that we were investing in her future. I agonized that I might be letting everyone down or giving up on Kate too soon. I wanted her to have more time to play and be happy. But my gut told me that the seizure had been a turning point. Kate had snapped and there was no going back. In the end, the decision was between Kate and me.

On Friday, June 2nd, it was time to let Kate go. After all of my efforts to help her get better, what she needed now was to be set free from this earth. I sat in a meeting at work that morning, unable to concentrate. I felt a strong need to get home, so I took the afternoon off.

Stopping at the vet clinic on my way home, I picked up a sedative and asked them about putting Kate down on Saturday morning. They suggested that I bring her in that afternoon—why wait and have to endure another night when something could go wrong? I balked at the suggestion, but then realized that they were right. I just wanted one more day with Kate. I would never be ready to let her go. I made an appointment to return late that afternoon and took home some extra sedative. We planned to meet on the grass outside so Kate wouldn't have to go inside the clinic.

Kate and I spent a nice sunny afternoon walking in the field, playing ball, and sitting together in the yard. Her last day with me was going to be the best day possible. I fed her special treats. I took photos of her and thought about how it felt to sit by her, to feel the breeze and hear the little grunts that she made when she talked to me. I wanted to always remember this.

I tried to be brave. I tried to be positive. I questioned whether I was doing the right thing, and always reached the same conclusion. So I focused on simply enjoying that afternoon with her. I gave her the sedative, five pills, one at a time, during the afternoon. One or two should have been enough to slow her down, but they weren't. She remained vitally aware of what we were doing.

We got in the truck and went to the clinic. I let them know we had arrived, then took Kate out on the grass. Our usual vet was off that day, so a new vet came out to meet us.

Kate was a survivor to the end. With all that sedative in her, she still fought the vet and the technician. Her survival instinct would not leave her. It was amazing, really, and very painful for me. That fighting spirit was what had brought her this far in life, and I had a lot of respect for her. I had to muzzle her and hold her down. The whole process was awful and it took too long.

I held her and looked into her eyes while the fight went out of her, and at last I knew she was gone. The pain of letting her go mingled with the relief of setting her free. I wanted to remember everything about her. It was hard to leave her lifeless body, even though I knew her spirit had gone.

We had been through so much together. I had to wonder if I had done enough.

The drive home was a blur of emotion. I pulled over on the way and called Sarah. We talked and cried until my cell phone battery died. Then I hurried home to take care of Bandit and Chase.

After I got home, I called Lisa, our dog-sitter. Kate's leaving was Lisa's loss too. She had suffered with me through the loss of Rainbow and Pippi in the past few months. She had walked Kate almost every day and was one of the people who Kate knew and loved the most. If anyone knew Kate as well as I did, it was Lisa. She had walked Kate and Bandit separately for months without charging me extra. She gave Kate special care when she needed to wear the Elizabethan collar and when she was the biggest grouch. Lisa and Kate had grown to love one another too, and I was grateful.

That night, I wrote to Sarah:

Sarah, I know you are right, but I miss her oh so very, very much. It hurts physically. She needed so much of my love and attention that there is a huge hole now that she is gone. After Katrina, I needed her as much as she needed me. Thanks for listening and supporting my decision.

The next day, I wrote to ACD-L and other friends:

It is with a very heavy heart that I'm letting you know that we sent Kate to the Rainbow Bridge yesterday... Thanks so much for helping me get her to a safe place and take care of her needs.

It's so hard to put in writing what Kate's spirit was like. She was an amazing dog who could bond well with people, but she had a very wild, almost untamed side too. She was not well socialized to other animals and never would have survived in a shelter. I learned so much from Kate and understood her in way that most people didn't. Kate also had a handful of other human friends who she loved... The bond that I had with Kate... was so different than the bond I've had with other animals. I miss her terribly, terribly much.

Early Wednesday morning, Kate had a seizure and an allergic reaction to an insect sting. After that, she first seemed to be back to her usual self. But then I realized that she could snap without much warning and redirect her reaction at me or the baby gate, or anything else that was nearby. After the seizure... her wiring was just not the same and I was worried that something terrible would happen... I think she had a troubled mind. She was happy when I had her out for a walk with her ball, but did not seem happy much of the time any more.

Kate was most content when we were out for a walk and playing with her Cuz balls up in the field on the hill. She loved her Cuz balls, took them with her everywhere, and kept them in her crate at night. Yesterday was a beautiful day here. I took Kate and her Cuz ball up on the hill in the afternoon. We went for a walk. She played ball and took a dip in the dog pool. I gave her a sedative and we sat together for a long time. Then I drove her to the vet and I sat with her out on the grass. We gave her extra sedation, and yet still she fought the euthanasia. I am so very grateful for the time I had with her and am so very sorry that I had to let her go. She was a survivor to the very end and I hope she forgives me for taking that away from her.

I don't regret any of my time with Kate. She taught me so much and I learned that I can communicate with a dog in ways that I wasn't aware of before. She really was a character and a beautiful dog and I will always miss her. Sometimes the ones who are the most difficult also give the most back.

I couldn't regret anything I had done for Kate. She was an amazing dog and I learned so much from her. She changed my life. Questioning whether she was ready to go tore me apart. We didn't have much time to prepare to say goodbye. I wondered if she could have healed emotionally if she had stayed healthy longer. I wanted her to be at peace and hoped I would get a sign that she was okay and had forgiven me for letting her go. I missed her so much, and her absence left a huge hole in my life. She was a sweet, yet wild thing, and the bond we had was different from anything I had experienced before.

Exhausted, I got by with the help of my friends. People wrote from all over the country, and even the world.

Eileen (Wisconsin) wrote:

Oooohhh, Jenny, I am so sorry to hear that you needed to do this, but, I know you fought so hard for Kate, and I know how much she added to your life. So I also know what a very difficult decision this must have been for you. In a way, it is maybe a relief for both you and for Kate; she did have a troubled life, but the best of it, I have no doubt, was with you. Now you deserve a rest for awhile, and Bandit and Chase can relax and be buddies. Enjoy your time with them as well. Hugs to you.

Eileen's support over the previous months had meant the world to me. Although letting Kate go was probably the right decision, doubts crept in. I had envisioned her healthy and prancing in the Parade of Rescues that fall. But that was my dream, not hers. Perhaps that was denying who she really was. I hoped to get some sign from Kate that she was okay, wherever she was, and that all her pain was gone.

Jaye (Missouri) wrote:

You and Kate are blessed, and you blessed all of us with your will and your power and your spirit for giving. Thank you for sharing so much of yourselves with all of us.

Sharon (Minnesota) wrote:

I had heard that you were facing this difficult decision and my heart went out to you and Kate. Your tribute to Kate is a beautiful testimony to her spirit of resilience and to the power of the loving bond between the two of you. Kate was very lucky to be able to spend the last months with you, knowing she was loved and would never go through something like Katrina again. You gave her a great gift in bringing her into your heart and home and an even greater gift in letting her move on in her journey. There is nothing for her to forgive with you, there is only the love she will always have for you.

Before letting Kate go, I didn't have enough time to fully realize that I would never again get to scratch her belly or throw the ball for her or take her on an early morning walk. I missed her badly, and hoped that I had given her peace.

One of the gifts that Kate gave me was some very supportive friends. I heard from Amy in Minnesota, Rodrica in Pennsylvania, Laura in Indiana, Ann in Minnesota, Carol in California, Di in Cairns, Australia, Eric in Minnesota, Kristina in Georgia, Leslie in Minnesota, Jinna in Georgia, Luis in Pennsylvania, Dorothy in California, and Kathy in Illinois.

Deb of ACDRI (California) wrote:

I can't think of anyone who gave a dog more of everything that life had to offer in such a short amount of time. You were Kate's angel and she knows that. I'm so sorry.

Alex (California) wrote:

I am so, so sorry to hear about Kate. I feel as though I lost one of my own dogs. I was hoping she'd pull through once again, but I guess it was her time to go. She will always be with you in spirit and I am sure that she appreciated all the love and care you gave her during the last year. Sending our beloved animals to the Bridge is the last act of love we can do for them, please do not doubt that you did the best for her. Know that she is happy and healthy again, waiting for you at the Bridge...

Ann and Zoë (Minnesota) wrote:

I am bawling my eyes out right now. I am soo, soo sorry to hear about Kate. I know how much you loved her and how much patience you had with her. She leaned on you for strength and love and I know she had the best life in your care. Nobody would have gone as far as you did to provide her with life...

Lori (Wisconsin) wrote:

I am so incredibly sorry that it was Kate's time. You have done so much for her over the last few months, and your final acts of kindness and love show what an incredible bond you had together. Sometimes those that are with us the shortest times teach us the most and leave a special mark on our hearts. Thanks to you, Kate was able to experience love these last few months, perhaps for the first time in her life. She is now running free and healthy at the bridge, telling all those waiting there about the special person she found.

Milda (Maine) wrote:

I have so much admiration for you and the amazing devotion you have given to Kate. You have given her such dignity and were still able to affirm the dog she was, the issues she struggled with, and the reality of her private demons. I fully understand what you have gone through, on a lesser level, as I have a rescue who has been quite difficult, and I wrestle with trying to know what her future holds... Know that you gave Kate a life that she never would have known otherwise, that she knew you cared for her, loved her and wanted her to be better. The gifts she left with you will always be a reminder of her special soul... Hugs to you and thank you for including us in your story.

Lisa (Texas) wrote:

You are in our thoughts and prayers. I'm so sorry about Kate but know that you will be the one she waits for at the Bridge, yours was the supreme act of kindness, love and compassion...you are now a different person... every act of kindness you do from here on will directly relate to Kate... Kate's last few months with you will help all others that you help and probably more from all the people involved with her. It was not in vain. Thank you for caring so much.

Laura (Minnesota) wrote:

I'm very sorry to hear about Kate; she was a survivor. She was lucky to have survived the hurricane but I think even luckier that she landed with you. Someone else might not have recognized the spirit that she had. She was right where she was supposed to be with the right person, she will be remembered.

Angie (Missouri) wrote:

I'm so sorry for your loss. Thank you for taking her in and giving her the life she probably never had. Dogs live in the moment and I know she had many wonderful "moments" with you. Even though I never met her, I felt I knew her in spirit. She touched many people through your generosity. Thank you so much for all you did for her.

Louanne (Bandit's breeder in Minnesota) wrote:

I am so touched by your reflections on Kate. What you have to say about her and the travel you had together, albeit short, is amazing. And yet what really touches me most deeply is the depth of your compassion and feeling. I admire your ability to put it into words, and the courage it takes to love so deeply and share your intimate feelings so openly. God Bless you in your loss and grief. May all those special memories serve to heal you. Hopefully the survivor in her has strengthened the survivor in you.

After receiving many caring and compassionate messages from people in widespread places, I wrote to ACD-L and others:

Thanks to everyone for your understanding, love and support. Kate changed my life in tremendous ways. If not for Kate, I would not know any of you. She put me in touch with new friends from all around the country and even the world... I was never good at asking for help for myself, but knew I was going to need help in order to care for Kate. And new friends responded whenever we needed help.

If not for Kate, I would not have gotten thrown head first into rescue again and would not have realized the huge need for ACD rescue in this country. Often it is overwhelming. I've found many ways to get involved, although there is always more need.

If not for Kate, I probably would not have taken the Noah's Wish disaster response training to be better prepared if something like this happens again. And thus I would not have met many new friends who share the same level of conviction about such things.

If not for Kate, I would have had a much more difficult time healing from all the things I saw down in Louisiana and all the ones that I was not able to help. Kate did as much for me as I did for her. Whenever I felt overwhelmed by the memories of all that I couldn't do, I thought at least I was able to make life better for this one. And Kate was my teddy bear who comforted me too.

If not for Kate, I would not have had the opportunity to know a creature who was such a teddy bear, yet so wild at the same time. As brave as Kate was, she was afraid of things that I never would have anticipated. And yet she took the greatest amount of enjoyment from discovering snow for the first time, rolling on her back in the grass, tracking a rabbit through the early morning dew, and chasing her ball. Although I knew this intellectually, if not for Kate, I would not have the same level of awareness about how important it is to socialize puppies to all kinds of situations and animals. Kate challenged me to a new level of understanding of dog behavior, and at the same time I was frustrated that many people had no clue how to relate to her.

If not for Kate, I probably would not have become such close friends with Sarah, who I met in Louisiana. And then I would not have met Chase, an ACD-X who was brought to Sarah's shelter cowering in a chicken crate by a man who was going to shoot him… because he was chasing the man's sheep.

Kate was probably backyard bred, but she was beautiful to me. She had an amazing spirit, beautiful markings and the strongest will I have ever known. I thought that I would care for Kate for the rest of her years, not realizing that it would only be months. If I had known that her time here would be this short, we would have spent less time at the vet. I'm satisfied that I was able to make Kate's life better, to love her and be loved by her, and help her to heal. I thought that if I could just get her healthy, we would have the chance to heal her mind and help her to become more comfortable in this world. I'm satisfied that (with your help) I was able to make her life better, I just wish that I had been able to make everything ALL RIGHT. But because of her past or whatever trauma she went through, everything wasn't all right with Kate, and I finally realized that I wasn't able to fix that. We had our moments when all was right, and I will cherish those.

Here's a photo of Kate on her last day here with me. I miss her terribly, terribly much. She was an amazing dog.

Kate on her last day here

I heard from Cindy, of the Baton Rouge family that took Kate and me in, Susan in New Hampshire, Laura from PAWS in Plaquemines Parish, and Stacey in Florida.

Deb (Illinois) wrote:

I'm so very sorry for your loss. I kind of know what you are feeling because I was never able to make everything quite all right with my Mick... All we can do is learn from them and help the next one I guess. You did a wonderful thing by taking her in and she in turn did wonderful things for you.

I replied:

Kate is not my first rescue dog, but she's the first one that I've felt like I haven't been able to make everything "all right" for.

Squad wrote from New York:

I am in tears, both at your pain, and at the fact that Kate had been so damaged by irresponsible and disgraceful human beings. I know you would have done anything to save her and if this is the decision you thought was best for her, then I support you 100% and know it was the right thing to do. At least she is not in pain, and she spent her last months in a loving and caring environment...

I replied:

I think that somebody loved Kate before. I don't know what she went through before or during the storm, but I think somebody did love her or she wouldn't have bonded to me the way she did.

Chris (from Australia) wrote:

Oh Jenny, I am so sad to hear this (Kate's death). I have been following Kate's story with interest and have enjoyed reading your updates. I must admit though, when I read the last one about the seizure, I did have some concerns, as seizures, and their side effects, can be hard to deal with as you have found out.

My first Cattle Dog also fought the euthanasia injection, and that made it even harder, but Kate sounds a lot like he was, tough to the end. You have given her so much in the short time that you had her, and she knew that and wanted to stay. You had not just given her a house to live in, you had given her a home, and probably the first real one she has ever had.... She will always be with you in spirit. Rest in peace Kate... My deepest sympathy to you Jenny.

I replied:

Thank you for your comments on seizures and on the euthanasia injection. I'm not sure that Kate was ready to go yet, and that has been very hard for me. I hope to get some sort of sign that she's in peace, out of pain, and has forgiven me for letting her go...

Chris replied:

Please don't beat yourself up about the injection. I worked for many years in animal welfare and have had to hold so many dogs for that final needle. It is not the needle itself that they fight, but the fact that they are at the vets, (as was in Kate's case, as she didn't like being there). They also pick up on the owner's emotions, and know that you are upset and uptight, but they don't really know why. This also causes them to fight as well. Cattle Dogs especially are so in tune with their owners, being a (mainly) one person dog, more so than some other breeds.

Kate knows that you loved her and cared for her and that you would always do your best for her. She was letting you know in her own way that life was getting a bit much for her and you did the kindest thing. Her struggle was with being at the vets, NOT with you, so there is nothing for her to forgive you for. I'm sure that in true Cattle Dog fashion, if she could have gone with a bit of the vets hide in her teeth, she would have been happy. ;-) I know it's not funny, but you have to look at life through a Cattle Dogs perspective at times.

Please take care and be easy on yourself. I know Kate would also be very approving of your work with other rescues, so that they can also have the same chance at a good life that she had with you too...

I was very grateful for Chris' kind words. It was comforting to know that other people understood what I had been through.

Libbe, our obedience instructor, wrote:

I am so sorry for your loss! I am sure you did what you had to and that in itself took courage. Thank goodness you were able to so greatly improve the rest of her life after the hurricane. You were a blessing to her and it seems like it came back to you in many unexpected ways. That's what giving can do- isn't it wonderful. God bless you-

Connie (Washington) wrote:

I join you in your sadness and... since I received your message my thoughts and prayers have been with you and Kate. I think that anyone involved with animals, and with the Katrina or rescue dogs in particular, can identify with your heartache... all these Katrina dogs/animals opened a part of our being we didn't know existed. I think we are all thankful for that new awareness and for the chance we had to make a difference and will continue making a difference in the lives of animals (and our fellow human beings). As we have said so many times, there has to be some reason for all this.

I, like you, count my blessings to have been able to go to New Orleans and work with the animals and all the many new wonderful and caring people I now count as special friends. Again, like you, I am learning all I can to be able to help again if we are ever so unfortunate as to see a disaster in which animals will be left behind.

Jenny.... Kate has such meaning to you, to us and to the animal world, in general. She personified the determination and fight these poor little creatures had. I hope when the sadness lessens, you will collect all the communications you sent to all of us... and write a book... The world needs to know the paths of these animals and what true pleasure and love they can bring to those who care enough to take them in. Kate's life can have a tremendous impact. As you know, she didn't touch just you and it is all such a beautiful story of love and caring and perhaps she/you have been provided the opportunity to touch the lives of others...

I know you have been blessed by Kate's short time with you, but I think this is just the beginning of what Kate has brought to the world.

I replied to Connie:

The responses that I've received since Kate's death tell me that she has affected a lot of people. I'd like to write a book to remember her (and all of the hurricane survivors and victims) and support rescue.

Nickie (Vancouver Island, BC) wrote:

My heart goes out to you. It's such a tough thing to live through, but it sounds like you have followed the path that was best for Kate. We never know what lies around the next corner for ourselves and for our dogs. Every experience adds something to our lives ... even the losses. And you certainly added a lot to Kate's life.

I replied, in part:

I miss Kate terribly, even though I probably made the right decision. I especially miss our early morning walks and our evening walks with the ball... and just rubbing her belly... I just wish I could have made everything all right for her and she could have lived here longer.

Nickie wrote back:

Some of us humans seem to spend our lives wanting to make everything right for others... But we can't. All we can do is play our part in their lives. They take what they can from it, and we get to learn a lot more about what being alive really means...

You really threw yourself into helping Kate. You both benefited. And she was as 'all right' as she could be, considering the baggage she brought with her. Your wish was for her to be more comfortable in herself. Now she is... no more stresses over things that she worried about, because those things are gone. No more aches and pains. She's at the Bridge... she can relax, and start a new life. And you helped her get there when the time was right. Hugs to you... and Chase probably can't believe his luck!

I replied:

Thanks Nickie. One of the things that Kate taught me is to appreciate living in the moment more...Thanks so much for providing financial and emotional support for us during some very tough times. Although many people were supportive, not everyone was. But I don't regret anything that I did for her—she gave so much back...

Chase is feeling very lucky, except that Sheriff Bandit is compelled to teach him the "ROOLS".

Nickie replied:

... I'm sure you received some pretty negative responses along with the support during those tough times. I'm coming to understand that when we reach out to the world with our lives, we open ourselves to both the negative and the positive. The positive is wonderful ... the negative can be hard to deal with.

I suspect it's better to feel the pain of the negative, rather than to grow a thick enough skin that it doesn't hurt. It's a new world we're living in ... a lot to learn about how to deal with it.

I wrote back:

I still wonder about Kate's life before the storm. My friend Mark, who knew Kate... told me something that surprised me. He always thought that Kate had been a stray, on her own for a long time before the storm, or maybe for most of her life. Having been a "stray" himself when he was a teenager, Mark would perhaps recognize this better than I would. That surprised me... I always thought that Kate had a person who loved her, because of how well she bonded with me. But she was "wild" in many ways, and Mark may be right. That would be so sad and might explain many things about her. I just never thought that a dog could be a stray so long and survive or not get picked up. I hate to think that she never had a family before, or for much of her life. She was such an amazing spirit, probably like many homeless dogs today, that it breaks my heart. She sure knew how to love me, and she saved me as much as I saved her...

I dream that I'll write a book that will help me solve the mystery of Kate's previous life... She seems so amazing to me, even if she appeared to be a plain old dog to other people...

ဆ ♥ �

I returned to work the Monday after letting Kate go. I was completely exhausted, but kept moving. On my way to work, the radio played the song "Feet of a Dancer", sung beautifully by Maura O'Connell. I knew the song, but it had never made me cry before. It begins, "I hope you find the feet of a dancer, I hope you can sing in the rain, I hope you find all the easy answers to your pain..." That is what I had hoped for Kate. The song continues: "I hope you find love and affection, someone who cares..." At least I had been able to give her that.

That week, I also learned of the untimely death of Shannon Hartwick Moore, a Louisiana woman in her 30's. She had passed on at about the same time as Kate's seizure, just as the official 2006 hurricane season began. Shannon was from Louisiana, a Katrina survivor herself, and had worked tirelessly to rescue animals. Although I hadn't known Shannon, her death hit me very hard. Perhaps these creatures, human and animal, could not bear another hurricane season. Katrina, followed by Rita, was enough for one lifetime.

On June 8th, six days after Kate passed on, I wondered if her ashes had come back to the vet clinic so I could pick them up. I had no reason to believe they would be there that particular day, other than a strong feeling. I called the clinic and the ashes were there. Later, when I checked my messages at home, I learned that the clinic had called my home just a few minutes before I had called them. My connection with Kate was still strong.

When I got home that evening, I took the velvet bag with Kate's ashes up to the field where we used to walk and play. I was compelled to do this as I had also done with Rainbow's ashes the previous fall. I wanted to carry Kate with me to a place that she loved and keep her close. I walked with the ashes for a while; I don't know how long.

When I returned to the house, the boys were anxious to go out and play ball. They were full of life, and life went on.

*"I sent you away from this world of pain
not because I didn't love you but because
I loved you too much to make you stay."*

Unknown

*"Those who do not know how to weep with their
whole heart don't know how to laugh either."*

Golda Meir

Chapter 14

Shape Shifting...
Rest in Peace,
Sweet Kate

Following Kate's passing, Chase became my companion on the morning walk. It was a way to stay close to Kate, and feel connected. Chase didn't need a walk separate from Bandit, but I wanted company for this morning ritual. Bandit's company wasn't peaceful; he was so focused on his ball.

For a while after Kate died, I saw the most amazing things each day— different creatures that behaved unusually for wild animals. One morning I saw a woodpecker that I have not seen before or since, along the route that Kate and I used to walk. She had Kate's red head and black/white body. She followed Chase and me along our walk and stayed very close, then watched us from a dead tree. The next morning a lone doe walked very slowly all the way across the south yard, and on across the front yard. That afternoon, when I returned home from work, a lone turkey walked slowly across the front yard. The next morning while we were on our walk, a doe peered at me over the far fence. Even though Chase was with me, she stayed still until we got very close. She watched me for a long time, as I returned her gaze. I made eye contact and she looked right back into my eyes, steady as can be. The next day it was a blue jay. Each time, I saw a lone creature in a place at a time that I hadn't seen that creature before, or since. Each one lingered much longer than a wild animal normally would, and looked me in the eye.

All of these creatures gave me the feeling that Kate was present. It was like she was a shape shifter, taking different forms to follow me, to let me know that she was watching over me and was all right. Rainbow had first made me think about shape shifting, and now Kate appeared to be doing it. You may think that I was sleep-deprived and hallucinating, or you may believe that these creatures were really there. Either way, you are not alone.

During the second week of June, I continued to receive condolences from my online friends.

Cheryl (Connecticut) wrote:

I'm really sorry for your loss. This part of animal ownership never gets any easier, does it? I lost my blue girl January 15, 2004. I got another ACD puppy a month later…but losing Skidder left me with a lingering heartache.

Try not to second guess your decision. You made a choice that was in Kate's best interest, but it left you sad and wondering if you should have hung in there a little longer. Even if Kate had lived a few more years I think you still would wish you could have had a little more time with her. Let's face it, when it comes to love we never get enough time.

I let Skidder go just a few days after her 7th birthday. I knew in my heart that it was the best thing for her, but I spent a lot of time wishing we'd had just a little more time together. For months I found myself muttering things like "Skidder really would have liked ..." this or that. I cried a lot more than usual and found myself gazing down at her grave and rehashing the past. I don't know why it took me so long to realize I was just grieving for her.

A month later I lost my African Gray parrot. We had Mica 24 years. He talked a blue streak. Occasionally he would go on a rip and call all my dogs, including the dogs who had gone to the bridge years before. If I knocked on a window he would holler, "Go lie down!" He got that from us rapping on the window and telling the dogs in the kennel to "go lie down!" He was a piece of work, that bird!

I had to help my 17+ year old cat, Mac, over the bridge just six weeks after Mica was gone and only three months after I lost Skidder. Mac and I were best buddies and Mac and Skidder adored each other. Mac was a feral tomcat who showed up at my barn one spring and knew a good thing when he saw it. I told my husband to go shoot him because we didn't need a stray Tom spraying in and around our barn. But Mac had nine lives and my husband never got a clean shot. After about the third miss it was obvious the cat was meant to stay, and I decided to make him a civil resident.

It took me four months to "tame" Mac so I could touch him with gloves. At that point, he was unceremoniously shoved into a Have-a-Heart trap, tranquilized, and neutered in our basement. Once given the required shots he was turned loose. I knew this traumatic start might mean I'd never see him again, but a week later he reappeared in our barn and was seldom far from my sight for the remaining sixteen years of his life.

Mac was very special. I think he felt he owed us something for giving him a home. A few years later I had to have spinal fusion surgery. I had some serious complications that, over the next four months, resulted in several trips back to the hospital for more surgery. Each time I came home I had to be on an IV pump for massive doses of antibiotics. I had to run the antibiotics through the pump every 12 hours; a process that took the better part of an hour. My last dose began at 11 PM.

Deeply depressed, lonely and in extreme pain, I decided to move into the spare bedroom so my husband could get some much-needed sleep as I followed the procedure.

Mac was not much of a house cat, but he came in one night as I lay there waiting for the IV cycle to finish. I was so very lonely. Mac uncharacteristically hopped up on the bed and hunkered down on my chest, purring. He lay there all night. Now Mac was a seasoned and tough old barn cat who could fend for himself, but he had one very odd quirk: he was scared to death of thunder and lightening. Well, that night as he kept me company I promised he would never weather another thunderstorm alone. It only seemed fair.

I kept my word. For the next eight years, any time there was a thunderstorm, no matter what time of day or night, I would go out and search for Mac until I found him, bring him inside, and hold him until the storm passed. No matter how long the storm, I was his shelter and comfort and we would lie together on the couch and wait for it to pass. Oddly, I was afraid of thunder and lightening too, but my love for Mac helped me conquer my fears.

I knew Mac might make it through another summer, but I also knew there was the risk that he might wander off and die alone. I could not bear that loss. So I helped him over the bridge and laid Mac to rest not far from Skidder. I don't think a heart can break more than mine did that spring. I lost my two best friends.

Grief is a funny thing. You can think you are past it then suddenly it hits you out of nowhere. Last summer we did not have our usual thunderstorm activity, but when we did I would automatically roll out of bed before I realized I didn't have to go find Mac. And Skidder? Well, occasionally I get weepy. Not often, but more than I like to admit. I still talk to her sometimes. Heck, I talk to both of them. I buried them in such a beautiful place that it's hard not to want to sit nearby and reflect on how good life was when we were a team. It doesn't hurt quite so much to reminisce about those times, but sometimes… it's bittersweet.

I hope you can find peace and comfort in your memories. Give it time. Think about the good, and when you feel overwhelmed just try to remember that this too, shall pass.

Under His Wing, Cheryl

Barb (Minnesota) wrote:

Of all the many things I've read on this list that have touched my heart... I can honestly say that you and Kate stand alone. The road the two of you traveled together... and the obvious bond you formed have touched me so deeply. I grieve with and for you, and... thank you for caring so much ... you truly have changed the world with the powers of conviction and love! ... I think you're quite right ...one true hurricane season is enough in anyone's life, but especially in Kate's. I'm happy that her skies are all blue now, too.

Beryl (Minnesota, Lamar-Dixon alum) wrote:

I'm very sorry, Jenny... All I can say is: don't worry, you did good by her. She had a very happy life compared to what it probably would have been, so take comfort in that. We at RAGOM just took in 4 more Katrina dogs from Mississippi, the saga goes on and on. One 6 week old puppy so ill from anemia (from ticks, fleas and ??) that we aren't sure she is going to make it... Keep your chin up and know you did the best you could under trying circumstances, just as we all have.

Laurey (North Carolina) wrote:

I was so sorry to read your post about Kate. What an up and down time you two had together. But so wonderful that she was able to spend the last months of her life with you rather than in the system in the aftermath of Katrina. As I'm finalizing the calendar, I wondered if you might like the chance to change what you wrote about her... Please feel free to revise it if you like... Thinking of you and missing Kate with you, Laurey

Laurey was organizing the 2007 ACD calendars to raise rescue money for cattle dogs. She offered to give Kate the December 2006 page that would be displayed for the whole month. I was glad that Laurey allowed me to update Kate's page now that she was gone, but I struggled with it because words didn't seem to be enough.

Kate's legacy was already at work. In June, I posted information to ACD-L about two ACDs looking for homes. They were both in foster care at Homeward Bound Rescue in Minnesota. One was the blue male that we had brought up from Wisconsin with Chase at the end of May. Both dogs eventually found good homes and I continued to work with Homeward Bound. If not for Kate, I would not have had the connections to be able to help.

On June 10th, Bandit earned his second Novice B Rally leg. I was still wiped out from losing Kate and debated whether to attend the trial. But friends would be there and the entry fee was already paid. So I decided to go, do my best, and not be too hard on myself or Bandit. Our performance went well with a score of 96, and this was only Bandit's second time in the ring.

On June 14th, Nickie wrote:

Hey Jenny ... have you thought about using an animal communicator to see if you can learn more about Kate's life? I've never inquired if some of them feel they can reach an animal that has gone to the bridge, but it seems like a reasonable possibility. And it looks like the message to you is clear enough ... start writing about Kate!

I told Nickie that I had an appointment scheduled with Mary Getten and continued:

I'm dragging even more than I was last week. I always thought Kate was as strong as an ox and thought that she would be around for a while to come. Her blood work was good and as long as her arthritis wasn't too bad and her teeth weren't infected, I thought we had a lot of time left. She looked really nice—her coat was sleek and shiny, and she had muscled out. So, when I suddenly realized that it was probably time to let her go, I was thrown for a loop. Maybe other people saw this coming, but I sure didn't. I thought she was finally getting past the surgeries, was happy and healthy, and that maybe we would be able to finally heal some of her 'issues'. I guess my blind faith in her was a good thing, even if my vision of her healthy, whole, and healed never came true completely. We came a long way since last fall... I've received e-mails from many people who followed her story, even people who I've never heard from before....

Chase and Bandit are doing well. They play rough and tumble together like Bandit and Rainbow did. Chase is a fast little guy and has caught on to playing ball, Bandit's obsession. I have a tough time getting a photo with both of them sitting still!

A couple of weeks after Kate crossed over, I consulted with Mary Getten. I had questions for Kate and was still concerned that she was upset with me for letting her go. The first message that I got from her, which surprised me, *thanked* me for letting her go. She said that she loved me very much, and that she was doing well. She was excited that she had found her people, who had left her during the storm and had been looking for her (they must not have made it…), and she was very happy to be with them. She gave the picture of an older farm couple, probably in their 60's. She was sorry that she couldn't be a normal dog for me. She said that she was stressed after the hurricane. She had tried hard to do well here, but it was difficult. She didn't know how to act around other dogs and they made her very nervous. Sometimes she became upset and fearful and couldn't control herself. She wanted me to know how much she loved me. I made her feel safe, even when she didn't feel safe in the world.

Hearing that Kate's people were already waiting for her at the Bridge, I was struck by the thought that maybe I should have let her go sooner so she could be with them again. Although I had searched the Plaquemines Parish death records, I hadn't found people who appeared to be a match.

I asked Mary what Kate's life was like before and what had happened during the storm. She gave the picture of an older two-story white farmhouse, at the edge of a town in a semi-rural area, with a couple of acres and a few chickens and small barnyard animals. Kate lived outside most of the time and was often chained in the backyard, but sometimes followed the man around the property. She also revealed more about what happened before and after the storm. Her people let her off her chain (a life-saving move) and left before the storm. She was alone at home when the storm hit, and she hid in her backyard. The water got very high and swept her away from the house, which was smashed and destroyed. She swam for a long time and ended up a mile or more away from where she lived. She crawled on top of something and stayed there for days until someone rescued her and took her to a cement block building. There were many dogs, but no kennels. She was so exhausted, out of it, and in shock that she doesn't remember much about this place. This must be the local place where she was taken, or perhaps the LA-SPCA shelter where she was assigned the number 0001-1442 and held until she was taken to Lamar-Dixon. This information is consistent with what I know about her.

Some people worry that animal communicators will tell them what they want to hear. But I was surprised to hear that Kate thanked me for letting her go. This wasn't what I expected and it seemed inconsistent with the struggle she put up when we euthanized her. If she really found her people on the other side, that would help to explain her relief. Perhaps she had lived in Plaquemines Parish and her people had gone inland only to be drowned in the flooded low area of New Orleans when the levees broke. I wondered why they hadn't taken her along. Perhaps they knew that she wouldn't be comfortable leaving home.

Mary had been right-on about so many things that she couldn't have known any other way. She also didn't seem to just try to tell me what I wanted to hear. I became fully convinced that animal communication is possible, even though it's hard to explain and understand. Rainbow and Kate had opened up that world for me.

Through Mary, Kate confirmed that she had recently appeared in my yard in the form of birds and other animals to let me know that she was okay. Mary said that Kate especially liked being a bird and flying. When told of my stories of the birds and animals appearing on the morning walks, Mary agreed that Kate was still very much with me. I could imagine that after the back pain Kate had experienced, it would be very freeing to take the form of a bird and fly.

That night, as I was falling asleep, I dreamt of being engulfed by water and swept away. I was tumbling, head over heels, completely engulfed in water and didn't know which way was up. It felt so real, sudden and overwhelming that I cried out loud and woke myself up. That must have been what the flood was like for Kate.

Brandy (Utah) wrote:

I think Kate's ability to survive the hurricane ordeal so well would point to her being a stray well accustomed to caring for herself. You are not giving yourself and the wonderful joy, love and life you gave Kate enough credit! As I look at the beginning and end pictures I see such a miraculous change! You may not have solved all of the problems but you sure got the important ones!! Kate had a good person in her life—YOU! Kate knew you for what you were, her Angel. I have learned that the second and third week are generally the hardest. We spend the first week in shock not believing that they are really gone, then the pain and emptiness set in. I think everybody worried for you and Kate, you had so many obstacles to get around, but nobody could have seen this coming. I am so glad that Chase and Bandit are keeping you busy. It is wonderful to hear they are getting along... I admire you greatly and feel I have been blessed by having you touch my life.

I replied:

I think you're right about the second and third week. I've been really wiped out this week. The boys play well together and are very entertaining, but I really miss Kate. It's the first time I've had two boys here and the first time... that I haven't had a girl.

I think that Kate and I were angels for each other. She helped me to heal too. I learned so much from Kate and the friends that I've made through her. It's great to correspond with people who understand, since many of the people around me don't understand that well.

I'm planning to write the book about Kate because I don't want her to be forgotten. Many people have e-mailed me that they've been affected by her story.

It seems fitting to remember her that way. I also hope that a book might lead me to someone who can tell me about her life before the storm—perhaps someone who is looking for her or someone who knew her as a stray.

Brandy wrote back:

Kate will be missed by many people. Sadly there are a lot of people who will never understand what a great friend and loss Kate is, or know the feeling of an absolute bond that you can only get from an animal. I feel so bad for those people. They are missing out on a great joy in life. By all means, please write the book on Kate, and yourself. It will open many eyes to the horrors that so many animals faced, how they survived and thrived after such a horrific event. I pray that someone will come forward and fill in the holes that are left in Kate's life (story). I have been lucky enough to know the stories of the animals I have adopted, and it helped to make sense of so many of their behaviors and fears. There are many who have come to love you and Kate through your trials and updates on the list, and we are grieving with you.

Although I believed that Kate's people had died in the storm, I thought that she could have been a stray for part or her life, and there could have been other people who knew her. So I wrote to Laura at PAWS in Plaquemines Parish:

Do you think an old cattle dog could have lived on her own in Plaquemines Parish for a long time without dying or getting picked up? Do you have any thoughts on how I could find out where she came from—anyone who knew of an old cattle dog that hung around a town or something? I'd like to let them know what happened to her and find out about her earlier life.

On June 15th, Dana (Georgia) sent me a notice that the U.S. Senate was considering the Pets Evacuation and Transportation Standards (PETS) Act, which would require that pets and service animals be included in disaster evacuation plans. We were all encouraged to support this law to avoid another Katrina-like disaster in which people were not allowed to take their pets along when they were rescued. I later learned that the bill had passed, but with no funding, which made it ineffective.

Now MuttShack Animal Rescue (www.MuttShack.org) has come forward with the "Katrina Promise", a promise that in future disasters pets will be evacuated along with their families. MuttShack operates under the Department of Transportation and in close collaboration with the Louisiana State Animal Response Team (LSART), the Louisiana Department of Agriculture and Forestry, and the U.S. Department of Agriculture's Animal and Plant Health Inspection Service (USDA's APHIS). In the event of an approaching hurricane or severe tropical storm, MuttShack has committed to mobilizing over 100 temperature-controlled transport vehicles and a nationwide network of trained volunteers. They're preparing to transport animals from parish pick-up points to pre-determined temporary shelters near state-run human shelters so that animals will never be far from their families. But without sufficient government funding, MuttShack needs support from donations to keep this promise (see Appendix for more information on MuttShack's "Katrina Promise" and how you can help).

On June 18th, I received a notice for an upcoming workshop/retreat in New Orleans dedicated to Katrina animal rescuers. We were all keenly aware that hurricane season had begun again, and difficult emotions were resurfacing. Many of us were still experiencing forms of post traumatic stress, and couldn't get the horrible Katrina images out of our heads. People needed to share feelings, and strategies for coping. The retreat was intended to give people that opportunity, continue to build community, and provide some closure.

I wasn't able to attend the retreat, but the notice helped me understand that others shared my troubled feelings. My experience of receiving such heartfelt and personal notes about Kate from people who I had never met was not uncommon either. The Katrina experience and dogs like Kate had brought out the best in many people who empathized and wanted to help. Still, in some ways, we continued to feel helpless.

During June, I sent photos and text to Sarah, along with an outline for Kate's website. I had so much to share. I wanted to include Kate's chronological story, links to the Plaquemines Parish website, Louisiana disaster photos, my Lamar-Dixon photo album that tells the story of how Kate and I met, a page telling how to support rescue in a minute or a lifetime, a list of links to rescue organizations, and links to disaster and hurricane preparedness sites. I also sought permission to add Maura O'Connell's soundtrack of the song "Feet of a Dancer".

For the entire month of June, grief wore heavily on me. I found comfort in networking online about dogs needing rescue. On June 20th, I wrote to ACD-L, asking people to prepare a disaster plan for their family and to do something kind in memory of Kate. I gave them links to disaster preparedness websites and ideas for an "act of kindness" (see Appendix).

On that same June day, Bandit and Chase ran up the hill ahead of me to the "playpen"—the one-acre fenced area where they play ball and blow off steam. The backyard is fenced in chain link and is connected to the field by a channel of field fence with a gate at the bottom. I headed up behind the boys, leaving the gate between the yard and field open. At the top of the hill, I heard a horrible noise and realized the boys were in predator mode. A small fawn sprang up out of the tall grass and headed straight for the east (uphill) side of the fence. Bambi bounced off the fence with both dogs in pursuit. Fortunately for Bambi, he didn't hit the fence head-on or he might have broken his neck. But this was far from over.

I yelled "NO!" "NO!" at the top of my lungs as the three of them headed toward me at the north end of the pen. Bambi was fast and apparently not big enough to jump the fence yet, so he went for the only opening he could find, the channel heading down the hill into the backyard, chain link territory. Meanwhile I screamed "NO! BANDIT NO!" at the top of my lungs, with a few choice four-letter words thrown in. Somehow I knew instinctively not to yell "CHASE!" but I couldn't resist the four-letter words. I'm sure my neighbors loved me, although with "Bandit" thrown in, they probably figured they didn't need to call the sheriff. Mama doe was snorting in the woods on the east side of the field fence. I hoped she wouldn't clear the fence and come after us with her sharp hooves.

Bambi, closely followed by Bandit and Chase (people warned me about this name!), headed down the hill to the backyard, which has an adjacent deck. Since the house is built into the hill, the back of the deck has just three steps up from the yard, but the front of the deck drops off one story to the gravel driveway. As the three headed down the hill, I was still running across the north end of the field. I couldn't see them through the woods. I heard a clatter of hooves on the deck and figured there would be no good way for this to end. Pictures of two dogs playing tug of war with a half-dead fawn flashed in my mind. How would I rescue the fawn? Worse, I wondered if the doe would appear on the scene. As I charged down the hill, I saw the two dogs with their heads through the deck balusters, facing west over the drop-off to the driveway. I was concerned that Chase might fit through the balusters if he pushed hard enough. I hadn't seen him hit them at full speed yet and his head is not nearly as thick as a cattle dog's. This was the same deck that Bandit had taken flight from and landed in the snow the previous winter. I thought I had fixed that, but you never know.

As I came closer, I could see the two dogs standing on the deck, but no fawn. I had heard the fawn's hooves clattering on the deck boards, so figured I would find him splattered on the driveway like one of those chalk lined victims in crime scenes. But before I got there, Bambi charged up the hill outside the fence, heading toward mama doe. The dogs were still crazy, wanting to squeeze through the balusters to get at him. Somehow everything held and the boys stayed on the deck—for the moment. Bambi went up the hill so fast, I thought he was okay, but I couldn't get a good enough look to check for blood or a broken leg.

I realized that I needed to shut the gate to keep the dogs from heading back up the hill. Bandit, the "well-trained" one, realized this just before I did and in spite of my yells, beat me to it. He charged back up the hill while Chase was still trying to push himself through the balusters. I closed the gate after Bandit and before Chase, and shortly thereafter Bandit came back down the hill. As far as I know, Bambi ran up the hill outside the fence and was reunited with mama doe. I hope he didn't have any severe injuries.

A search of the deck and driveway yielded no blood or hoof prints or any sign of the fawn. Unbelievable! From where the dogs were scenting, it appears as though Bambi leapt through the balusters and took flight one story down to the gravel driveway. Both dogs went back to a spot facing the driveway, sniffed at some hair, and pushed their heads through to look down below. Good thing Bambi didn't head toward the chain link fence, or we would have had a messy scene.

Later, after my heart rate slowed down, we went back up the hill. After all, we had just been starting our walk. I took the dogs on leashes to check the field, but the deer were long gone. For the life of me, I don't know why the doe would leave her fawn inside a fenced area where dogs run every day. I wondered if the doe gave birth there and then the fawn couldn't get out. It's a well-protected area, except for the dogs.

Bandit and Chase were tired out, briefly, but were soon back to wrestling. It was more than enough excitement in one day for me.

Bandit and Chase

When I posted this story to ACD-L, Merrill wrote:

*Just as I started reading your post, my mp3 player started playing the Hungarian Rhapsody (think Bugs Bunny and Elmer Fudd). It was ***perfect***. Your dogs come with their own sound track!*

I had to laugh at Merrill's message!

ဆ ♥ os

Kate was still ever-present in my thoughts. I was very curious about where she had come from and wanted to know more about her life before the storm. It was possible that someone still missed her and wondered about her. I also hoped to locate her rescuers.

Ironically, now that she was gone, I had more time to look into her background. In the back of my mind, I was relieved that she wouldn't have to return to hurricane country. I e-mailed her photo to Lori at the Rescue Ranch in Plaquemines Parish, and to my surprise, she e-mailed back that Kate looked like a dog she had seen on posters:

This dog looks like the one that had posters plastered all over Plaquemines Parish. If it is the same dog it was a working dog. I will try to find a poster and send you the owner's info. I'm sure it's still hanging in one of the restaurants down here. God Bless, Lori

I thought about Kate as a working dog. It was possible, I guess, that she had tended one of the herds of cattle in the parish and had not been around other animals much.

Kathleen (California) wrote:

I want to offer my condolences on the loss of Kate. I think the ones that have special problems and need us more give us such incredible gifts. Almost ten years ago my husband and I rescued a mix who had been badly neglected and abused, and it truly broke our hearts when we lost her at a fairly young age to liver/kidney failure. Right up to the end, I think she still bore the emotional scars of her puppyhood...she had always had an intense fear of men. We had worked through that so that she trusted and loved my husband, but there were still some mornings when she would wake up acting terrified of him and other mornings when she would wake up a love bug. I believe she was having nightmares.

I don't want to say the difficult ones are more special, because they all teach us and they're all special. But somehow, the dogs that need us the most just seem to touch our hearts in a unique way. Kate has left a wonderful legacy in the number of people she touched and the joy she brought to you while you were together. And I know that you brought her great joy as well and made her last times on earth wonderful.

I replied to Kathleen (in part):

The difficult ones challenge us to rise to the occasion and become better people. I always thought that Kate would be here much longer. She was such a survivor and looked so strong and sleek as she healed and came out of her shell. She gradually got used to living with Bandit, but was still stressed by having another animal in the house. What I didn't anticipate was that the mental part of it would get to her, that there was a limit to her psychological healing with all the new and stressful things that were thrown at her in such a short time. I think that many of the brave creatures who endured that storm will never be the same. Kate may have been having nightmares too. The seizure came in the middle of the night and my other dog woke me up to let me know.

On June 21st, Dana (from Georgia) wrote to me:

Wow—what an amazing experience you shared with Kate through your animal communicator, not to mention the dream you also had about being engulfed by water. I'm sure it's helpful to have this closure and also to know that she is still with you in spirit. Maybe you can plant a tree or a bush in your yard in her memory—something that will provide rest and sustenance for other animals.

It's funny that you should mention Kate visiting you in the form of a bird. My grandmother always said that she wanted to be reincarnated as a cardinal. She died when I was 16 and I was very close to her, so I took that loss pretty hard. Over the years, both my mother and I have noted times when a cardinal would land in our yard or come to visit in ways that were inconsistent with typical wild bird behavior and we feel very strongly at those times that Grandma is making her presence known. In one case, not long after the headstones were placed at my grandparents' graves (they died 9 months to the day of each other) a cardinal visited the house insistently and my mom felt compelled to check on the gravesites...only to find out the headstones were inadvertently switched. After it was fixed, we did not see the cardinal for a while. Not long ago, I was sitting here at my desk at home and a cardinal appeared outside my window, clung vertically to the brick for what seemed like an unusually long time for a bird of that species and stared at me through the window, then flew away. I was having a difficult time with something emotionally, and that visit felt deliberate.

Dana also told me all about her rescued ACD mix, Jazz, and the work she had done with her.

I replied to Dana:

... I may be delusional, but all of this feels pretty real. I think that Native Americans have traditionally been much more in touch with the animal spirit world, but most of us in this age are so out of touch with nature... I've learned many interesting things in the past year, especially from Rainbow and Kate.

I like your story about the cardinal and think that it's real. I started consulting with Mary Getten last fall after Kate came here and then Rainbow died. Rainbow would get my attention and "be in my face" when I was at work, after she died. She told me that it was an intentional leaving... She did this with two other people who independently got the same message, and then the dog sitter said to me, "I swear sometimes I see Rainbow up on that hill when I'm walking the dogs". Rainbow then told me why she left at that time [she was called to another task]... She had a strong personality and was very high energy.

Dana replied:

Many people are skeptical of things they cannot "see" or confirm in a rational manner. It seems like they are missing out on so much that is around us. My mom's family is Catholic and St. Francis of Assisi was the saint we adopted as our family saint, because he communicated directly with the animals. My mom seems to naturally attract animals too—I think it has a lot to do with her deep intuition. Growing up, I always had a dog... and many birds. I can't imagine not having a pet and the brief times I haven't had one in my life for one reason or another, I missed them a lot.

I wrote back:

Many people have learned not to listen to their intuition, if they had it to start with. I think children are generally much more tuned into this, but don't often know what to do with it.

Dana replied:

Children definitely have strong intuition, but I think they are often discouraged from expressing it further, because we're supposed to be "rational" and "thought-based" rather than "intuitive" and "feeling-based." My stepson is very intuitive about things, and we try to encourage that trait in him. He loves Jazz and delights in her quirkiness... He always tells me that "Jazz is the best dog EVER!"...

Jim wrote from Kansas City, telling me about his latest foster dog, Shadow, a cattle dog mix. He added: *I agree totally with your request to be better to others, people or dogs, just because we can. I'm going to name my next female foster pup Kate. Be well.*

Following Kate's passing, the very personal correspondence that I had with people who I had never met was touching.

At the end of June, Di wrote all the way from Cairns, Australia:

Just wanted to say I am happy to help update the website if you need some assistance. I work in IT and we do websites for people so if you want me to help all you have to do is say what you want done and wait for it to happen :)

Di's offer was timely, and a huge surprise. I had never even heard of Di before. I knew that Sarah was very busy with her animal shelter in Virginia. Plus I found out that Sarah was working with dial-up internet access. They'd had a series of storms that week and her power kept going out. She had made progress on Kate's website, but there was still much to do. My ideas kept expanding and the website was already much bigger than when Sarah had first offered to help.

At the end of June, my friend Ann from obedience school presented me with a beautiful framed drawing of Kate. Ann's brother, who had never met Kate or me, had made the drawing from looking at a photo. He was very talented and captured

Drawing of Kate (by Michael Evans)

Kate's expression well. The drawing shows a depth and liveliness to Kate's eyes that lets her spirit shine through. I was very touched by this beautiful work of art, to know that someone else cared that much and also saw that light in her eyes. Today it sits in a lighted cabinet so that I am continually reminded of Kate.

By the end of June, Laurey and I had updated Kate's December 2006 page for the ACD rescue calendar. This had been difficult for me and I was grateful to Laurey for the extra time she spent to help.

Laurey wrote:

I think it's going to be a wonderful tribute to her. I know you miss her still, and it's easy for us to say how what you did for her should make you feel better... I'm sure it does to some extent, but it doesn't make it any easier for you. You take care and hang in there.

Kate was a very brave survivor and teacher. She was genuine and beautiful, gentle, yet wild. Many of her experiences in Minnesota were so new to her. She grew to trust me completely, but could not trust many other things in this world. It's hard to put into words all that she meant to me. She saved me as much as I saved her because for all the Katrina animals that I felt helpless to rescue, at least I was able to make a difference for this one, for a while.

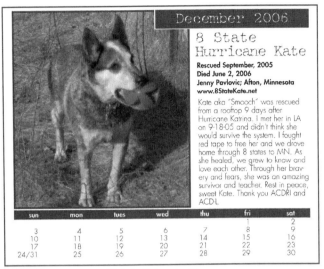

December 2006

8 State
Hurricane Kate

Rescued September, 2005
Died June 2, 2006
Jenny Pavlovic; Afton, Minnesota
www.8StateKate.net

Kate aka "Smooch" was rescued from a rooftop 9 days after Hurricane Katrina. I met her in LA on 9-18-05 and didn't think she would survive the system. I fought red tape to free her and we drove home through 8 states to MN. As she healed, we grew to know and love each other. Through her bravery and fears, she was an amazing survivor and teacher. Rest in peace, sweet Kate. Thank you ACDRI and ACD-L.

sun	mon	tues	wed	thu	fri	sat
					1	2
3	4	5	6	7	8	9
10	11	12	13	14	15	16
17	18	19	20	21	22	23
24/31	25	26	27	28	29	30

Kate's Calendar Page

I remember how Kate sighed and grunted contentedly as she fell asleep at night. How she loved to ride in the truck and panicked if she thought I was leaving without her. How she discovered snow and wiggled on her back in contentment, as though she were making a snow angel. How she played ball for the first time at my house, maybe for the first time ever. How she tore apart every stuffed toy that she found. How intensely she tossed the ball for herself, or chewed on a bone, as though it were part of her therapy. How she smiled and her eyes shone so very warmly with a look of devotion just for me.

I couldn't fix everything for Kate. I wish I could have made it all better and she could still be here enjoying life. But what we had was good, and perhaps the best it could be. The creatures who endured Hurricane Katrina will never recover fully from what they went through. I admire their bravery and dignity in the face of overwhelming odds, and wish them peace.

Rest in Peace Sweet Kate. I'm glad you found your people at the Rainbow Bridge. I hope that you've been made whole. You gave me so much, yet I have a hole in my life where you used to be.

80 ♥ ℭ

"When it comes to love we never get enough time."
Cheryl (Connecticut)

"If there are no dogs in Heaven, then when I die
I want to go where they went."
Will Rogers

Chapter 15

Still Grieving and "Do You Know This Dog"?

In July, I continued to correspond with Lori of Rescue Ranch and Laura of PAWS in Plaquemines Parish. After Katrina, there had only been one road open out of the parish, so they were able to keep track of the animals that were rescued. Lori had seen posters about a missing cattle dog, a working dog. But when she went back to look for the posters, they were gone.

Lori and Laura were both still busy caring for rescued animals and I didn't want to bother them. But I wanted to give someone peace of mind about Kate and I had a hard time letting that go. Laura told me that an ad with a photo in the local paper might help me find out where Kate came from. She sent me the contact information for the Plaquemines Gazette.

She also offered to post Kate's picture at PAWS and wrote, *For your sake I hope Kate's people were looking for her and that this will give them closure knowing she was taken care of until the very last.*

Kate looked different in the various photos and I wanted to capture a view that someone would recognize. In the ad, I included a photo of her just after she was rescued, along with later photos after she had recovered. I took great care to mention that I had information about her. I didn't want to get someone's hopes up that she was still alive, yet I didn't want to announce in the ad that she had died either. Laura helped me with the wording and hung a copy of the ad up at PAWS in case someone who came in would recognize Kate.

A story on the Plaquemines Parish website told about the National Guard's rescue efforts. It showed photos of the guard members with two dogs in a boat. They might not remember individual dogs if they had picked up a lot of animals, but Kate's photo could trigger a memory. Someone might recognize her and remember where she came from. I called the New Mexico National Guard and talked to Lt. Stewart, who had written the animal rescue story. By the time I contacted him, it was almost a year after the hurricane. He didn't remember anything specific about the animals he had rescued.

During July, I was still worn out, but was enjoying my time with Bandit and Chase. During Chase's first two months at our house, they had a few major fights while they worked out their pecking order. When a serious fight occurred, I pulled them apart and held them at arm's length until I could get them into kennels and settle them down. They're both pretty stubborn guys and neither one wanted to give in. Bandit had about ten pounds on Chase and I knew that with his personality he would end up being the top dog (besides me!) Eventually Chase agreed and they became best buddies.

It was fun to watch Chase develop. During July he gained confidence in himself and his life with us. At first he was wary of putting his feet in the dogs' kiddie pool. He finally worked up enough courage to put his front feet in, but it was slippery. One day he put three feet in, but kept the fourth one out on the grass! The next day he finally put all four feet in and started splashing around and having a good time. He got all wet and cooled himself off. He really got into it!

When I introduced Chase to agility obstacles for the first time, he was wary. He watched Bandit run through the obstacles before he tried them. At first he was spooky on the contact obstacles, and then he gained confidence on the dog walk and A-frame. He was also funny about the jumps at first, jumping straight up in the air and coming almost straight down. But his jumping improved with practice. Once he got comfortable with the obstacles, he was very fast, biddable, and agile.

Chase loved to snuggle on my lap and be petted, especially at bedtime. I think he missed somebody. From what I knew, he used to have a mom who loved him, but the man of the household was abusive and threw him away. Chase was more of a snuggler than Bandit, although Bandit's competitive nature was turning him into a *competitive* snuggler. I had two hands and two dogs, so that was okay as long as they didn't get into a fight on my lap!

The large fenced-in "playpen" provided space for the dogs to run. They loved to play chase games, wrestle together, and play ball. Chase is a very smart herding dog who needed a home where he would get enough exercise, and of course love. He just needed to find the right outlets for his energy and intelligence. He now had the opportunity to attend obedience classes and try agility, tracking and (supervised!) herding, along with Bandit, who had already trained in most of these areas. As Chase let his personality out and came into his own, the look of fear left his eyes. He became his handsome self.

I was very excited to learn that Tas, the blue cattle dog that had come up from Wisconsin on Chase's transport, had found his new home at the beginning of July. His new family had lost their other ACD very suddenly to an illness at about the same time that Tas was making the journey north. Perhaps the March to May delay in getting Tas to Minnesota had not been a coincidence, but the right timing for him to find the new family he was meant to be with. I let his former owner know that he had found a good home and she was happy, although she still missed him.

Eileen was very excited for Tas too. I told her that sometimes I felt successful, even though there were still so many dogs in need. Finding out about Tas' new home was one of those times. Eileen wrote: *And FOR SURE you are SUCCESSFUL! Look at all you've done already—placements, transports, adoptions, grants...YOU GO GIRL!!!* Eileen helped me realize how much more involved I was than I had been the year before. She was developing her own network and was very supportive.

Tas' story encouraged me to ask for help more often and was the beginning of a very effective relationship with Homeward Bound Rescue. They came through in a big way for Tas and have fostered and helped find homes for many ACDs and other dogs since then.

In July, I placed Kate's ad in The Plaquemines Gazette and The Plaquemines Watchman with hopes of finding her previous family. The Gazette was a weekly newspaper with a circulation of 3,200. The Watchman was a free newspaper, mailed monthly to all parish residents (about 7,000 addresses in July 2006). The ad read:

Do you know this dog?

If so, please contact Jenny at 555-555-5555 or xxxxxxx@visi.com

I took care of her after Katrina. I'm looking for her people and rescuers. Thank you!

Mary Getten understood my grief and realized why I wanted to find someone who knew Kate. But she encouraged me to quit looking, once she had determined that Kate had found her people at the Rainbow Bridge. She urged me to let it go, but I was compelled to keep looking, at least for a while. I'm a Leo and a researcher, and I don't give up easily. Sometimes my persistence serves me well and sometimes it doesn't!

In July I learned what Sarah was up against in trying to get Kate's website up and running. Her computer had been attacked by a virus, which took a while to fix. Then she still had trouble accessing the website to make additions and changes. I had asked a lot from her and she was trying to work via very slow dial-up access.

Sarah was also up to her eyeballs with rescued horses that needed her help and we were working on a grant application for the ASPCA. So I decided to take Di up on her offer to finish Kate's website. The animals needed Sarah, and Di had the experience and more time to tackle the website. Now that Kate had passed on, it would be a memorial to her.

In late July, Di took over, and that's how Kate's website came to have a true Australian webmaster! I sent Di my outline for the site, including Kate's story and photos, progressing chronologically from September 2005. I wanted to raise people's awareness about what had happened in the storm and how they could prepare their families, including the animals, for a disaster situation. As Di worked on the website, we corresponded and got to know each other.

Di wrote:

I have been tempted on occasion to visit an animal communicator or psychic to speak to my old boy Sparky. He passed four years ago, and a week after he left us, on the very same day and same time, I met a dog that could only have been one of his children (a product of his misspent youth, escaping and impregnating the whole suburb)…It was the spitting image of him, and Carey (hubby) was working at home on the ladder and heard what he swears was Sparky coughing…

Bud was pining dreadfully for Sparky, and wouldn't eat or drink, was vomiting and had diarrhea so we went looking for a companion for Bud…We were uneducated at the time about pet stores and puppy mills and had in fact got Bud from a pet store in a suburb near home, so we went back to the same pet store just 3 days after we lost Sparky… but left empty handed. A week later we went back and lo and behold there was Chip. He was a mere 6 1/2 weeks old and we fell in love with him. Of course we know now that he was far too young but he came home with us and saved both his brother and us… Chip, as he grew up, began to show many of Sparky's habits and behavioral quirks. There are things that Chip does that we had only ever seen Sparky do and it freaks us out on occasion. We nicknamed him SOS (Spirit of Sparky). So, we always reckon Sparky sent Chip to us, to heal us and he came along for the ride. Even though we don't consider Chip to be Sparky reborn, we do think Sparky is in there somewhere influencing him.

I sent Chase's story and photos to be included on the website. Di and I talked about Chase, how he had shown up at my friend Sarah's shelter not long after Rainbow died, and how I felt as though Rainbow had sent him. Bandit had been very sad after Rainbow died. The two of them had been fast friends and playmates ever since Bandit was a puppy. Although Chase has a different build and coat, he has Rainbow's somewhat unusual coloring and markings. He also has a couple of characteristics that I had only ever seen in Rainbow before. Bandit and Chase play the same games that Bandit and Rainbow played, taking on the same roles. So I understood what Di meant about Sparky and Chip.

I'd been interested in communicating with animals for a long time. I told Di about the "Know Your Inner Dog" class that I had taken at obedience school. I had taken the class more than once with different dogs and started to develop some of my own animal communication abilities. I also told Di about my consultations with Mary Getten.

Rainbow was a very high energy girl, probably a hound-cattle dog cross. After she passed on, she had appeared to me at work—in my face and pushing for my attention while I was working on the computer. This was very hard to ignore and I seriously wondered if I had cracked up. But then three other people who knew Rainbow described a similar experience when she appeared to them.

Bandit seemed to be sent to me too. In January of 2004, I had taken my very old dog Rusty to the vet for the last time. Rusty had been a stray, adopted from the local animal shelter. His liver was failing and he was very ill and in pain. It was his time to go. After he left me, I went out to the truck where Rainbow waited. She was his pal, a much younger and higher energy dog. I took Rainbow in to see that Rusty had passed on, then took her back to the truck and was ready to drive home. But I was compelled to go back into the clinic to get her a chew toy. I knew she would be lonely as the only dog and would need something to keep her busy. In the clinic, a blue cattle dog was standing at the counter with an unfamiliar woman. I was surprised because I didn't see cattle dogs often and hadn't seen them before at our vet clinic. I asked the woman if it was okay to pet her dog, and told her that I had just lost my cattle dog mix a few minutes earlier. She encouraged me to pet the blue girl, Opal, and told me that she had a red puppy in the car. He was the last one of the litter and he didn't have a home yet. People on her waiting list had been looking for blues. I told her that I had another red heeler mix in the truck and that we like the reds at our house! I hadn't even had a chance to think about where my next dog would come from. Rusty was very old, but had fallen ill rather suddenly.

Louanne told me that while she was driving over, she had been thinking about finding the red puppy a new home. She offered to get him from the car to show me. I told her that I couldn't make a decision on a new dog right away and that Rainbow was probably upset about Rusty passing on. But Louanne brought the red pup over. He had Rusty's double mask and red ears. He was a very nice, bold, playful puppy and I was taken with him right away. He and Rainbow got along from the beginning. I asked Louanne for references. I would need some time to make a decision. We exchanged information and Rainbow and I went home.

I kept thinking about that puppy. It was clear that Rainbow needed a playmate. I did my homework, checked Louanne's website, and contacted her references, and two weeks later, Bandit joined our family. The amazing thing is that I had made an appointment for the vet to come to my home at the end of the day to put Rusty down. But Rusty was suddenly in so much pain that I didn't want to wait. Louanne lived over an hour away and this was not her regular vet. She was visiting my vet to have an artificial insemination done on Opal, and had brought puppy Bandit along for the ride. If I hadn't gone back in to get Rainbow a chew toy, Opal would not have caught my eye.

Now that I have Bandit, the circumstances that brought us together in that lobby seem to be more than coincidence. We were meant to be together. The only red ACD puppy for miles, Bandit found me just minutes after Rusty died.

80 ♥ 𝒞𝒳

Back to July of 2006...I submitted an ad to the ACD Quarterly, to be published just before the ACD National Specialty at the end of September. It was a memorial to Kate that I hoped would bring people to her website and help them to think about rescue and disaster preparedness. It showed photos of Kate just after I had brought her home, during the time she was with me, and on her last day here.

Di and I continued to correspond about Kate's website. As my ideas evolved, she made them real. Her friendship and her computer expertise were just what I needed.

Finally, Kate's web page was coming together! It included photos of Kate and told her story, "How we met in Louisiana" and "Kate's Journey". We organized the photos and links, edited text, and made other improvements.

Di added a beautiful Rainbow Bridge picture. We encouraged people to look at the disaster preparedness and rescue links, and included links to Sarah's Lost Fantasy Stables and Animal Rescue in Virginia, Australian Cattle Dog Rescue organizations, and other rescue groups.

Di wrote: *I've enjoyed the chance to read Kate's story again and I feel like I know her personally now. It is a very touching story, and made me cry.*

Di told me how to use Audiograbber to extract the song "Feet of a Dancer" from the CD and convert it to MP3 format. Maura O'Connell gave us permission to use the song, and I e-mailed the file to Di for the website. I still cried when I listened to that song. I don't know what the songwriter had in mind, but the song seems to capture the experience of the hurricane animals, and what we hoped for them.

I continued to send updates to Di. I added a link to the new Pets Evacuation and Transportation Standards "PETS" Act and a link to the Shannon Moore memorial website.

Di added a guest book to the website so that people could sign in and write their comments. She also made a front page with photos of Kate and the words "Click to Enter" at the bottom. I felt better already, knowing that Kate would be remembered so nicely.

While working together on the website from halfway around the globe, Di and I chuckled that our boy dogs were all bugging us to go out and play. Some things are the same everywhere!

On August 6th, I sent the link for the draft website to ACDRI. One member replied:

What a great tribute to a brave soul… You have done Kate's memory and short time in Katrina's aftermath a great service. Although she was but one of many, she also had the good fortune to find her way home with you. You made us all feel we were helping in some small way by allowing us to be part of Kate's rescue. Thanks for being a voice for all of the ACDs—those who survived and those that did not during this awful tragedy.

As the Katrina anniversary approached, I wanted to honor the victims. I had Kate's photo put on a T-shirt, to be worn at a local Katrina memorial service on August 29th. The service was at the shelter that I had refused to take Kate to. Hoping that no conflict would arise, I mustered up my courage to go. I invited my Lamar-Dixon friend Beryl to come along and we planned to meet at the shelter.

"So here we are, one year after Hurricane Katrina. Hard to believe — it seems at once as if it was last week and yet a thousand years ago. So much has been done. So much has not."

Laura G.

Chapter 16

Another Year Older...What We Have Become

On August 7th, a woman called in response to Kate's Plaquemines Parish ad. When I listened to her message, my heart was in my throat. With butterflies in my stomach, I called her back. She told me the heartbreaking story of losing her cattle dog in the storm. Kate's ad had given her hope.

Lori and her family had recently moved from Florida to Port Sulphur, Louisiana. When Katrina struck, they were visiting family back in Florida and had left their horses and four dogs in the care of their new neighbors. Port Sulphur was on the 'toe' of the Louisiana 'boot', a very vulnerable part of Plaquemines Parish. It was one of the worst possible places to be as the storm surge of seawater, and the hurricane itself, hit very hard. Later, floodwaters invaded after the levees broke.

Lori's neighbors evacuated without taking the animals. Tragically, her family lost everything in the storm, including their horses and one of their four dogs. Three of their dogs were eventually rescued. Their Rottweiler was found perched on top of a submerged tractor trailer. Their small dog was rescued floating on a sofa bed cushion. Their brown mutt was waiting on their house-less front doorstep. But their Australian Cattle Dog hadn't been found.

Imagine their distress and helplessness knowing that their animals were out there, and not being able to reach the neighbors by phone or to return home right away. It must have been heartbreaking. After they returned, they searched, but couldn't find their cattle dog. Lori told me that he was a red heeler, nine years old at the time of the storm. I knew immediately that Kate wasn't the dog she was looking for because her dog was male and red. Although Kate was blue, she had a red head, so her photos had given Lori hope that perhaps it was her dog Reno.

Before the storm, Reno weighed about 45 pounds and was wearing a faded orange collar with tags with his name and a Florida phone number. The contact information on his tags had not been updated since the move. He was microchipped, but Lori was still searching for the number since their home had been destroyed. She eventually got it from their former vet in Florida. She contacted the microchip company to give them her new contact information and find out if any new information had come in on Reno. Many of the dogs who weathered Katrina came out much thinner and without their collars. But the microchip might help her find him.

Lori found a photo of Reno, but had trouble getting it scanned, so she described him. He was neutered, carried his tail high, had white speckles on half of his face, a shrill bark, and ground-down teeth, and he was a fetch-a-holic.

Since cattle dogs are so tough and at ten years old are usually still very active, Lori had hope for Reno. She thought that if any of her four dogs had survived, it would have been him. I posted his information on the ACD-L and told Lori about the Petfinder Animal Emergency Response Network (see Appendix). I also told her how to find the animal rescue photos that I had seen on the Plaquemines Parish website, along with Lt. Stewart's story. There was a photo of a red dog that might have been Reno in one of the boats. Thanks to my experience with Petfinder and connections with other rescuers, I could show Lori other possible means for finding Reno, if he was still alive.

Later that day, I found a Petfinder entry for a red heeler named Reno in a shelter in New Mexico. He even had white speckles on half of his face, but he appeared to be a younger dog. It was a promising lead since the New Mexico National Guard had been rescuing animals in the Port Sulphur area. Maybe it would be this easy to find Lori's Reno ... but it wasn't. The Reno in New Mexico turned out to be a different dog. Lori found another dog on Petfinder that looked like Reno with a description that was amazingly close, but it wasn't him either. Lori and I continued to correspond about Reno, but did not find him. He may have drowned near home or been washed out to sea.

The Plaquemines Parish ad didn't turn up any information about Kate, but I hope I helped Lori come to terms with Reno's loss.

I still wondered where Kate had come from. On August 9th, I wrote to St. Bernard Parish Animal Control and sent a copy of Kate's ad, thinking that she may have been picked up in that area. A woman replied that she had forwarded the information to the St. Bernard Parish Animal Shelter for their "found pets—lost owners" book.

On August 10th, I received the following message from Di:

The new website is all up and running, including a new guest book... Please let me know if there is anything at all you want to change, or add, or whatever. I have been honoured to do this for you and for Kate!

I was so excited to learn that Kate's website (www.8StateKate.net) was up. August 11th was my birthday and having this website as a memorial to

Kate was a fantastic present. I was the first person to sign the guestbook and I looked forward to reading the entries that would follow.

Di was wonderfully generous to spend so many hours on the website. She hadn't even known that it was my birthday, but her timing was perfect. I announced the new website to ACD-L and other friends, and received many supportive messages.

Sarah (Chase's rescuer in Virginia) wrote in the guest book:

Thank you Jenny for not forgetting Kate or what we all accomplished at Lamar-Dixon and for letting the world know how much one special dog means to the people who love her. You are always in my thoughts and prayers... Much love from your god dog Bruce

Lisa wrote:

I had a great experience getting to know Kate thru Jenny. I am Jenny's dogwalker/petsitter. When Kate came home with Jenny I knew she was a special dog. We became fast friends and had a special bond that only she and I could describe. She went through a lot in the short time Jenny had her. But she was in the best possible hands of her caregiver. Jenny went above and beyond for Kate. I will never forget Kate. She came from a horrible disaster to a loving home, and had a lot of people that cared for her until the end of her life. She will be missed.

Mary (Minnesota) wrote:

What a beautiful memorial and story about Kate. She does live on! And happy birthday to you tomorrow. You have been a teacher to all of us about the special relationship between people and animals, and how we need each other in so many ways. Thank you for sharing Kate's story and your own feelings and experience with all of us. Because of you, Kate lives in all our hearts. Many blessings to you!

Laura (Indiana; Tylertown volunteer) wrote:

Hey! Tomorrow is my baby's birthday too! He'll be three (or, as we like to say, "thwee"). Have a wonderful birthday. I look forward to checking out Kate's website. I planted a memorial garden recently and included her in my meditations... The little rocks around the Buddha each represent an animal that has touched my life in some way and that has passed on. I put one in there for Kate. I wish you peace and many happy memories of her.

Jaye (Missouri) wrote:

When I read Kate's story and looked at the photos, I felt as though I was reliving Gonzales. The scent of dogs, dust, dog food, hot bodies, bleach, feces, human sweat, trash bins, latex gloves, and even the smell of the golf cart carrying the kitties to the cat barn....it all swept over me. This time not in a bad, nightmarish way, but in a way that was healing. To know that Kate represents many of the dogs and cats who got to leave Gonzales and find hope and life again. Thank you Kate and Jenny for helping me heal. Yes, there is always that hole in my heart, but my life has another kind of "whole" that didn't exist before.

Cindy (Virginia) wrote:

...I have Kate's picture sitting up on my entertainment center in a frame so I think of her and you every day.

Cindy also updated me on the progress of her own rescued dogs.

Another friend who had heard Reno's story wrote:

Wow, how sad that people are still looking for their dogs. It's easy to forget about the tragedy when it hasn't been in the news as prominently, but there are still so many dogs out there that were never claimed, or their owners never found the right place to look. Really gives a lot more meaning to disaster preparedness. Great that you have links on the site!

Eileen (Wisconsin) wrote:

Jenny, you can be so very proud of this site. Kate would be too, and I just know that she is happy now at the Bridge, knowing how much she impacted your life, and you hers. I applaud you for all that you do for animal rescue, and though I have never met you in person, please know I am so glad to be your friend!

Di (Cairns, Australia) wrote:

It has been an honour to create this memorial to Kate. Sadly I only became aware of Kate's story towards the very end of her life, when I became a member of

ACD-L. Doing this website, I learned what Kate had suffered and what so many others suffered due to Hurricane Katrina. Although the news in Australia covered the disaster and its after-effects we can have no real understanding of what everyone who lived through it suffered and lost. Jenny has helped to raise my awareness and through that, my gratitude for her work and the work of so many others, in saving the poor animals who lost their families and homes. My heart overflows…

And on it went, making me realize just how much the whole experience had enriched us.

On August 23rd, Laura (Indiana; Tylertown volunteer) wrote to some of us who had helped rescue animals after Hurricane Katrina:

Subject: *Hurricane Katrina, a year later*

My two cents… attached. I hope that anyone who reads this finds pride in their accomplishments and encouragement to go on… With love and gratitude for everything that each of you does…

Hurricane Katrina, one year later…

So here we are, one year after Hurricane Katrina. Hard to believe – it seems at once as if it was last week and yet a thousand years ago. So much has been done. So much has not.

I had been struggling to decide how to mark this day and it came to me to observe the (Korean) Buddhist tradition of performing 108 bows. You begin in a standing position, drop to your knees, touch your forehead to the floor with palms up on either side of your head, stand up, and repeat. The gesture is somewhat akin to lighting a candle in a Catholic church, but the end result is that your ass hurts a whole lot more when you're done.

So I awoke this morning before dawn and shuffled outside to my memorial garden, equipped with my trusty zabuton, some incense, a couple of candles, and a very foggy head.

As I was bowing and standing, bowing and standing, the past year flooded over me. I saw the images, remembered the names, relived the stories, and experienced the intolerable heartbreak anew. Linus, Big Yellow Dog, Mee-Moo,

8 State Kate, Cleo, Leaf, Little Joe, Pasados, Noah's Wish, Camp Katrina, Best Friends, Gonzales, Lamar-Dixon, the Superdome, the Ninth Ward, St. Bernard's Parish...St. Bernard's Parish...St. Bernard's Parish...

Our hearts have broken a thousand times in the last year. And they will break at least a thousand more. But, for many of us, we chose the heartbreak over inaction because inaction would crush our souls. We are each of us climbing an arduous and, at times, forbidding mountain. Day after day, we go on.

Some days, your heart is light and you run on the swift legs of the deer.

Some days, your heart is on fire and you prowl with the powerful legs of the tiger.

But on some days, your heart is drowning, and your legs are like lead.

On those days, stop, for the love of God. Sit down, rest yourself, say a prayer for Shannon Moore and then sit some more. Call a friend, get drunk, go to church, meditate, scream, tell your pets and your family that you love them. Whatever you have to do.

To paraphrase the mighty Ani DiFranco [from "Tiptoe" off the cd Not a Pretty Girl]:

i could wake up screaming sometimes

but i don't

i could step off the end of this pier but

i've got a litter of puppies to bottle feed

and an appointment on tuesday

to have 47 cats neutered

Instead of looking up the mountain to the terrain you have yet to cover, try to see behind you to all of the lives you have saved, the lives you've tried to save, and the innumerable lives you have touched. The number is unknowable, but I assure each of you that it is profound and it is precious beyond words. This is the revolution of Kindness that Michael Mountain [founder and president of Best Friends Animal Sanctuary] talks about. We touch so many lives that we don't even know about.

If you rescue, if you make phone calls, if you transport, if you cross post, if you change someone's mind, if you meditate or light a candle or say a prayer – all of these things change the world. Never underestimate the value of what you do. One step at a time—one dog, one horse, one mind, three dozen cats (come on cat people, that's funny!).

So as I was struggling back to the standing position after my 108th bow, I glanced up at my little Buddha statue and saw something that struck me. A miniscule spider was blithely rapelling down the face of the Buddha. I don't even like spiders, but this one seemed to me as a messenger. As if my little Buddha was winking at me. "Life is here. You are here. All of Life is in this moment. It's OK. Go ahead, girl."

Can I get an AMEN?

"Namaste" represents the belief that there is a Divine spark within each of us. It's an acknowledgment of the soul in one by the soul in another. "Nama" means bow, "as" means I, and "te" means you. Therefore, Namaste literally means "I bow to you."

Namaste. I bow to you all.

Laura

8/23/06

I was blown away by Laura's message, and reminded of how overwhelmed we all were and how overwhelmed we can still get every single day. And yet because we have each other, we are somehow able to keep going and make a difference. One of the most treasured outcomes of my time in Louisiana is the network of amazing friends who I would not have known otherwise.

After reading Laura's message, I went out to walk the dogs. So many thoughts were circling in my brain. I was still grieving over Kate, over Pippi, over Rainbow, over all the devastation and lost animals that I had seen.

I, too, had struggled with how to spend the day. I could not let August 29th, 2006 pass without looking back, without attending the memorial service to remember and honor all of those who had suffered due to

Hurricane Katrina. When we returned from our walk, I replied to Laura:

Thanks for "Spider on the Buddha"... for capturing the past year so well. Katrina has been so much on my mind lately; my heart has been heavy. I got a T-shirt to remember Kate and am wearing it to a Katrina memorial service here on the 29th... My life has changed a great deal since I went down to Louisiana. I have many new friends, am much more connected with people across the country, and am much more involved with rescue. I also am much more aware of how much we're not able to do and how much cruelty there is in the world, and that gets to me sometimes. But it doesn't stop me from trying to make a difference.

Last night I took Chase to the emergency vet twice, once in the evening and once at 1:30 a.m. (he was gagging and choking, but he's OK now). The trip... reminded me of driving up there last October with... Rainbow after she... ran in front of a Buick. I was on the back seat of my friend Eric's car with her and I knew that she was already dead. It was just two weeks after I had returned from Louisiana with Kate, and now I had lost Rainbow. In December I lost Pippi, my 16 year old cat. Then in June I lost Kate. So I was thinking last night that I just can't bear to lose another one. It would just be too much. But now Chase is OK—he's fine.

I placed an ad recently, still trying to find out where Kate came from. I had a strong compulsion to place this ad, and it led me to a woman from Plaquemines Parish who is still looking for her red heeler. I was able to give her some information that might help her find him, if he is still alive. So, maybe that's the reason that I was supposed to place the ad. But I really still want to know where Kate came from, and maybe I never will.

I'm remembering this time last year and how I felt compelled to go down to Gonzales, even though I ended up going alone. I had to choose action for I never could have forgiven myself if I had not gotten out of my chair. And of all the "animal" people that I know here, although none of them could go with me, many of them supported my trip and sent supplies. I knew that I would meet great people down there, and I did. Now I know Sarah, Cindy, Lori, Connie,

Bonnie, Jaye, Beryl, Monica, Veronica, and others. They came from Virginia, Wisconsin, Washington, Missouri, Texas, and even Minnesota, just 10 miles from my own home. And like Kate, many of them seemed to enter my path by luck or by chance—one move this way or that way and it all would have been different...

In May I completed the Noah's Wish training in Wisconsin because next time I want to be with an organized group that knows what they're doing in a disaster situation. I met many wonderful people there. Some of them got involved with transports after I asked them for help.

After I got home last fall, I learned of the cattle dog list, ACD-L. People from that list helped support Kate and me financially and with great advice. Now I am very well networked to cattle dog rescue and... I was able to save at least one dog and find him a new home.

I have stayed in touch with Sarah and helped her get some grant money for her shelter in Virginia. Through Sarah and the generous transport help of folks along the way, I got my new pup Chase. And that's how I 'met' you.

After hearing me talk about all the pets needing homes, my aunt, who had never had a dog, went out and adopted a rescued dog. My aunt and uncle loved him so much that they got a second rescued dog. She told me that if it weren't for me, they wouldn't have dogs. Their daily walks benefit them all. I was so overjoyed to have made a difference just through having a conversation with them and telling them about Petfinder.

I'm still sad a lot of the time, knowing how many animals need good homes and how many are mistreated. But I'm doing a lot more than I was before and I know many pretty fantastic people who I didn't know a year ago. And I met Kate, who really changed my life. Our connection was different than anything I have ever had before. We needed each other to get through the situation. I miss her a lot, but know that she is in a better place now.

The next few months are going to be difficult, thinking about last year. I will finally get going on Kate's book, as I relive the events of a year ago. I needed some space after she died, but I still plan to tell her story since it has meant a lot to so many people. Kate's website has been therapeutic for me and hopefully helps me to communicate important information about disaster preparedness.

This is getting long, but I've had so many random thoughts about the past year. I have wanted to go back down there many times, but was so busy here at home, especially taking care of Kate. I've been corresponding with people down in Plaquemines Parish and would still like to meet them and help them more. I've been reading a book about the river and the wetlands and the levee system, and what went wrong. The knowledge, science and technology to protect New Orleans were there all along, yet the "powers that be" did not build a proper system to protect the city. All of this could have been avoided.

Funny thing, while I was muddling my way through the past year, struggling much of the time, people looked upon me as a leader, as someone with experience, and yet I was making most of it up as I went along.

I'm having some health problems and finally need to take care of myself, something I couldn't do until we figured out what was wrong. But I will continue my own revolution of kindness as best I can. And many of the people who I met through the dog network are now able to give me advice on my own health problems too.

What does all of this mean? I'm not sure how to sum it up coherently, but I will never be the same. I don't think any of us will. Thanks and Peace.

I was rambling, but I had to get this all out. I knew that Laura would understand.

I was excited and apprehensive about attending the Katrina memorial service on August 29th. It would bring up sad and difficult memories. I wore my new Kate T-shirt with her photo and the saying: "Kate...No Act of Kindness is Ever Wasted". Although dogs were invited, I left my dogs at home so that I could focus on the service. Upon arriving, I found a display of photos from Tylertown, Mississippi where many rescued animals were taken for care. The volunteers who went down with this shelter had gone to Waveland, Mississippi along the coast. The animals they rescued had been taken to Tylertown, where Best Friends and the Humane Society of Louisiana ran temporary shelters for the rescued animals. The display was set up to look like Tylertown, with the photos hung on sections of chain link fence. For me, this was a sacred memorial and I was very moved by the display.

A local reporter and her cameraman repeatedly invaded the space to film a segment for the evening news. They did not appear to respect the display at all. They were just there to get a job done and pushed me aside to do it. I, on the other hand, was very moved by the display, which brought back memories of my time in Louisiana. News coverage was a good thing, but it was very sad that the reporter and cameraman didn't show much sensitivity to the subject. After shooting their news piece, they didn't even stay to look at the photos. I was glad to see them go.

I found Beryl and her friend Susan in front of the shelter. They had brought their rescued golden retrievers. We went to join the others outside behind the shelter. It was great to meet other Minnesotans who had gone down to help. The group that had gone with the shelter had bonded as closely as my group of friends from Lamar-Dixon. This group had the advantage of living in the same area and being able to meet to share photos and memories once they returned home.

Beryl, Susan and I met Kim, who was planning to make a film about some of the animal rescuers. We exchanged contact information. A film made by one of the volunteers who had been to the Gulf area would provide an interesting perspective and maybe an as-yet untold story.

We walked past a memorial to the animals that had not survived. One that I recognized was Fawn, who had been fostered by my friend Janna. Fawn was one of many animals who came through the ordeal physically intact, but mentally shattered.

The program included a slide show that would begin after dark, out on the patio behind the shelter. Many of the volunteers had brought photo albums and scrapbooks from the trip. I'd been busy socializing and didn't discover them until darkness was descending, so had time to look at only a couple of albums before the program began.

The second album that I paged through was an impeccable scrapbook. I met Twyla, who told me that a friend had made the book for her. While paging through, I saw a photo that stopped me cold. It appeared to be a picture of Kate on a boat with a few larger dogs. Although Kate had weighed over 50 pounds, the other dogs on the boat made her look small. The photo was taken on September 5, 2005 in Chalmette, Louisiana, just a week after the hurricane.

My heart began racing because I was sure this was Kate. Twyla told me that the photo had been taken by a woman named Christa who survived the hurricane and flood. Twyla had met Christa while distributing pet food in Chalmette (in St. Bernard Parish) after Katrina. Christa was there to check on her house. Christa later sent these photos to Twyla in Minnesota. Twyla gave me her e-mail address and told me that she had Christa's new address at home. The slide show was about to begin, but my heart was pounding wildly and my thoughts kept returning to that photo.

(photo courtesy of C. McCafferty)

Photo of the dogs on the boat

The slide show was a moving record of the shelter volunteers' trip. It highlighted some emotional reunions as some of the rescued animals that were brought to Minnesota were later reunited with their original families. While we watched, we were all in tears over the devastation and the reunions. During the show, Beryl's rescued dog sat by me and comforted me.

The program also addressed puppy mills, which have become an issue in Minnesota. The groups that mobilized to the Gulf Coast gained valuable field experience in very difficult circumstances. The shelter was now organizing rapid response teams to care for animals when large puppy mills are shut down. Similar skills might be needed to care for and transport animals out of these horrible conditions.

During the program, I let my mind contemplate what would have happened if Kate had gone into the shelter system. Kate never would have survived with all the animals that came up from Mississippi. My thoughts that night confirmed that my gut instincts to keep her at my home were right. I'm glad I dug in my heels and stuck by her. Always trust your gut.

After the service, I was anxious to get home to spend time with Bandit and Chase. Being with them comforted me. That night, I e-mailed Twyla to ask for Christa's address and a copy of the photo of the dogs on the boat. Finding the photo was very exciting and I felt sure that it was Kate. The posture and profile looked so much like her, and she was standing apart from the other dogs. I checked my photos of Kate from a similar angle to see whether they matched. As far as I could tell, they matched right down to the speckles.

(photo courtesy of C. McCafferty)

Photo of Kate (left) with the photo of the dogs on the boat

Twyla sent me Christa's address and a copy of the photo. She understood its importance to me. On September 1st, I wrote to Christa and enclosed a copy of the photo. I asked where the photo was taken, whether she knew anything more about the blue heeler and if she had any more photos of her. I also asked if she knew the man on the boat and thought that maybe I could locate him through the boat ID. Was there a place in Chalmette to display Kate's photo and was anyone left there to see it? I closed the letter by saying:

I hope you know that people all over the country care about you. We think about you and pray for you... Best wishes to you and thank you for anything you can do to help me find out more about this dog.

I mailed the letter to Christa in Covington, Louisiana where she had lived since evacuating from Chalmette. I gave her my contact information and hoped that I would hear back from her. I couldn't help but think to myself, *What is the chance that this photo of Kate would make it all the way to me... that people from Minnesota would meet a woman in Louisiana who happened to take this photo and send it to Minnesota... that I would attend a memorial service at a shelter that I had an issue with... that the photo would be included in a scrap book by a woman who brought it to the memorial service... and that it would be in one of the two books that I had time to flip through before the service began?* This didn't seem like mere chance to me.

ଔ ♥ ଜ

Over the summer, my own physical pain had gotten worse and demanded some attention. Doctors had discovered that I had two benign tumors, and I would need surgery soon. Although they were not that large, the tumors felt like I had a bowling ball wedged between my spine and my kidney. By the end of August, I wasn't able to work Bandit in herding. I had signed him up for a weekend clinic and our friend Guy was kind enough to work him for me. Before the pain caught up with me, I had also entered Bandit in a September herding trial and I wanted him to have the opportunity to trial at the ACDCA National Specialty in October.

> *"Never doubt that a small group of thoughtful,*
> *committed citizens can change the world;*
> *indeed, it's the only thing that ever has."*
> Margaret Mead

Chapter 17

Kate's Legacy: Coming Full Circle

At the beginning of September, Bandit and Chase found fallen apples and made up silly games. They raced around with the apples, played with them like balls, then dropped them in the pool and played bobbing for apples. Silly boys! It was good to see them having such a great time. They provided comic relief and brought joy to my life as I struggled with memories of the previous September.

The Katrina memorial service was still fresh in my mind and I wondered about the photo of Kate on the boat. Thinking that Christa must be concerned with many other things, I hoped she would find time to respond to my letter.

Although Kate was gone, I continued to make new friends in dog rescue work, and my network kept growing. I received a message from Melissa (Minnesota, Katrina Winn Dixie volunteer) about a young female cattle dog in trouble. Melissa had been working with a group called Death Row Dog Rescue in Georgia. They tried to find safe alternatives for dogs that, without their help, would be gassed to death on short notice. Melissa wrote:

This dog could still be reclaimed but I wanted to get the ball rolling in case she is not. Approximately 4 months [old], in Georgia at a gas chamber shelter. What do you think? She is available September 7th and will be gassed the 8th.

She looked so forlorn!

I posted the information on ACD-L. There were always too many cattle dogs in need, but I hoped for the best. Rebecca responded from Tennessee. Here is her story:

The Puppy in Georgia

Anyone who knows me knows that I love dogs... the softest spot in my heart is reserved for Australian Cattle Dogs, particularly rescues. I can't help but to want to help those wayward furkids. Kenna was no different.

Having such a love of ACDs, I am on an ACD internet forum. People from all over the world write in about their cattle dogs, whether it be a show dog or an agility dog or just a plain good companion dog. They also write in about cattle dogs that need rescuing. Who can pass up reading those posts? I can't. For the most part, though, I am able to refrain from taking action, as we already have 4 dogs, 2 cats, a foster pigeon, and 6 fish tanks. Do we need another mouth to feed or paws to walk? Sure. Well, no. Not exactly.

Sometimes, though, I can't help myself.

The September 2006 post on ACD-L started out something like this: "4 month-old ACD puppy in GA gas shelter". Well, that can never be good. So I emailed Jenny, a rescuer in MN, who had placed the post on the forum. I asked for some information and a picture. It turns out that the puppy had been turned in as a stray and was being held for three days to see if she would be claimed by her owners. She would then be put up for adoption FOR ONE DAY. The following day she would be gassed. The animal control facility that she was in did not allow puppies to be listed on their web site, so her life was riding on the chance that someone would happen to see her on that one day and adopt her.

Then Jenny sent a picture. If ever a dog looked forlorn, it was this one. She sat hunched in the corner of a cement run with a desperate look on her face. Who could resist? So, after consulting the other members of the household, I wrote back and told them that if they could get her to me, I would foster...

Melissa (who had sent this photo to Jenny) provided the funding and contacted Dawn in Georgia. Dawn (a volunteer for the humane society) and her husband Jason agreed to bust Kenna out of the Animal Control Facility on her one day of adoption. Poor Jason got wetted on by Kenna on their way home! They boarded her overnight and the following day a rescue volunteer (Chrissy of Animal Action Rescue out of Decatur) drove her 4 1/2 hrs one way to the vet clinic in Mt. Juliet, TN, where I work. Tennessee Valley Cattle Dog Rescue agreed to let me post her on their site and foster her under the umbrella of their rescue.

I named her Kenna. The little girl finally had a name. She was no longer just a number at the facility. I bathed her. She was covered in fleas. It was really bad. From there we moved on to the shots and the stool samples. Worms. Lots of them. Finally, I gave her a bowl of kibble and she took a much needed nap. She could rest now.

Over the next few days Kenna began to blossom. Her ears slowly came up. She stopped submissively urinating. She stopped crawling on her belly and whimpering when she so desperately wanted attention. She began to play with our puppy. She learned sit and down and a cute little trick where I would ask her if she was sleepy and she would lay down with her head between her paws.

Kenna was finally safe and loved. I hoped she would find her forever home soon.

On September 3rd, Cindy forwarded an urgent message from Debbie in Lafayette, Louisiana about three cattle dogs at Roicy Duhon Animal Control. I wrote to ACD-L about them. They had been held over from a scheduled death sentence more than once; the next gassing date was September 7th. Gassing is not an easy way to die, if there is one. The problem was that Louisiana was still overloaded with stray Katrina animals and their offspring. The chances of these cattle dogs being pulled or adopted locally were slim to none.

Debbie was a dedicated advocate for the animals. She had a special fondness for cattle dogs and had been watching out for them. She wrote:

My heart belongs to the precious little blue Heeler who has known very little kindness. Someone has not treated her well, and she is scared to death. She has been held over before, and I am making a special plea for her. Please, someone pull her and show her people are not all cruel. Each of these animals is awesome, and deserving of a second chance...

I sent out an inquiry asking if any rescues could pull these dogs and care for them. I mentioned that if we had a rescue plan, Roicy might extend the

The blue girl in Louisiana

deadline until someone could get there. I was very excited to hear from Bazza (Barry) in Florida that he was interested in adopting this pup. He wrote:

Thanks for the heads up, Jenny. I'm interested in helping and would take the female. I think she and Winkipop would be superb together. What's the next step? Any chance we could get her to Florida a little closer drive for me? I'm near Daytona Beach.

I knew Bazza through ACD-L, where he had written many times about his ACD Winkipop. He had been very supportive of Kate and of rescue in general. His website showed photos of Winkipop and their adventures in Florida. I knew they would provide a great home for this girl, if we could get her there. Bazza was the answer to a rescue dog's (and a rescuer's) dream.

I contacted Debbie to let her know that Bazza was interested and asked her if she had any thoughts on transporting the blue girl to Florida. Bazza was willing to take her in as an outright adoption, paying her vet and other bills. He understood the concerns about adopting her to someone in a different state and was happy to answer questions, fill out forms, and provide whatever was needed to ensure a smooth process. However, we had to make sure that animal control would approve of her leaving the state, and that we could get her to Florida.

I put Bazza in contact with the shelter so they could answer his questions and evaluate him as the prospective adopter. Then I started checking into transport options.

Debbie wrote more about the dog:

She is shy but gentle, likely been hit, is getting along fine with her female bigger black Lab kennel mate. I think she is just terrified, likely will be just fine with some tlc...not snappy at all. Problem is, Roicy does not do out of state adoptions unless you come or have someone come and adopt for you. In other words, they will not charge the pet to you over the phone. I believe that they allow others to adopt for an individual. You can pull under a 501 org if you are one or have a friend who has one and would pull for you. Roicy has no problem whatsoever with out of state orgs if the paperwork is correct. Then there will be the problem of where to put her until transport. The vets won't board a dog *out of Roicy most of the time. She is a beautiful little dog, does bark pretty loud when she wants attention. We do not have a foster program per se, have a couple of overnighters. We also have very few volunteers… I think there are a couple of donations on this dog, probably around $100 which would be payable to the vet or boarder of the 501… She is a beautiful little dog, and I fell for her because it is clear she has not been treated well. She seems real healthy.*

We needed someone to pull and care for the dog until we could get her to Bazza, and we didn't have much time to get her to safety. I thought of Nancy, who had looked after Kate with me at Lamar-Dixon. Although Nancy lives about 70 miles from Lafayette, I hoped she could help. Nancy found a friend near Lafayette to pull the blue girl with just a couple of hours to spare on September 7th. Then Nancy picked her up, took her to the vet, and took her home, where she cared for her for over a week. Once Bazza knew the blue girl was safe, he named her Billabong, a true Australian name!

I scrambled to organize Billabong's transport from Louisiana to Florida on Saturday, September 16th. The transport would be done by volunteers, each driving a given distance (or leg), like a relay race. We had volunteers for some of the legs when Nancy offered to drive Billabong all the way to western Florida. Billabong was timid around strangers and Nancy wanted to minimize her stress.

Saturday came and everything went as planned. Nancy and her son drove Billabong from the Baton Rouge area through Mississippi and Alabama, all the way to the Florida panhandle. There Jon took over and drove her to Tallahassee, where Bob and Lynn picked her up. Bazza met Bob and Lynn at their home in Orange Park, Florida. That evening, I received a message from Lynn that Billabong and Winkipop (Bazza's other blue heeler) got along great, and that Bazza was on his way home with the two girls. I was overjoyed that everything had worked out and was very grateful for all the people who had stepped up to help this dog.

The people who saved Billabong were all connected because of Kate. I first learned of Billabong's plight in an e-mail from Cindy (Virginia), who I met at Lamar-Dixon while standing in line to get Kate vetted. Nancy and I met over Kate, who we were both watching out for at Lamar-Dixon. I became acquainted with Bazza and Lynn when they expressed concern for Kate through ACD-L. If not for Kate, I would not have known Cindy, Nancy, Lynn or Bazza.

Once Billabong was safe with Bazza, I realized that it was the one year anniversary of the Saturday that Kate and I each arrived at Lamar-Dixon, where our paths first crossed. Saving Billabong, another homeless Louisiana cattle dog, was a most gratifying way to celebrate that anniversary. During the year, we had come full circle, and Kate was surely smiling down on all of us that night.

One September evening, I received a call from Christa, the woman from Chalmette who had taken the photo of the dogs on the boat. Christa had met the Minnesota rescuers when they were feeding animals in Chalmette, and they'd stayed in touch. She told me the harrowing story of how she and her family had survived in Chalmette (in St. Bernard Parish) after the hurricane and then the flood. She and her children and grandchildren had hidden out with their pets on the second floor of their house to avoid being evacuated by rescuers. The first floor was submerged under floodwaters. They wouldn't leave at that time because they would have been forced to leave their pets behind. They did their best to survive with the food and water that they had.

Christa had taken the photo of the dogs on the boat as she and her family were finally evacuated from Chalmette on September 5th. They were leaving the Bayou Bienvenue Marina on another boat. She didn't know the man or the dogs in the photo. I hoped to use the boat registration number to find the man, but Christa said that the boat might not even belong to him. At that time, people were commandeering any usable boats to survive and to help others. He may have borrowed the boat to rescue the dogs. They might be his dogs, or just dogs that he had plucked from the water.

When Christa's family left Chalmette that day, they took a boat up the river and all the way across Lake Pontchartrain, over 25 miles to Covington, Louisiana. There they went to a fishing camp that they used to visit in the summertime, and had been living there ever since. Christa often visited Chalmette to check on her house and was going there the following weekend. She offered to take the Kate photos that I had sent to find out if anyone recognized her or the boat, but many people had left the area. Chalmette was upriver from Plaquemines Parish, where Nancy said Kate came from. Someone evacuating dogs by boat from Belle Chasse, where dogs rescued in Plaquemines Parish were first taken, may have gone upriver to Chalmette.

Christa gave me the name of the Bayou Bienvenue Marina, where the photo had been taken. I didn't know if anyone was still there or if the mail was being delivered, but I sent them a letter inquiring about the boat and the cattle dog shown in the photo. I gave them my contact information and hoped to receive a reply.

Chapter 18
Taking Stock
and Giving Back

October was a measure of how well we had endured the previous year. At work, I had successfully managed my projects and earned a raise and promotion. Much to my relief, it all came together, in spite of all the other things that had happened in my life.

After a few visits to the Mayo Clinic in Rochester, Minnesota, my surgery to remove the tumors was scheduled for mid-November. Since I wasn't in imminent danger, I opted to have the surgery after the Australian Cattle Dog National Specialty.

I couldn't miss my first ACD specialty. Conveniently, it was also in Rochester, Minnesota that year—only 80 miles from home. Over 200 cattle dogs attended with their people. I met people there who I had only known "virtually" before, saw many wonderful dogs, and had fun socializing with old and new friends.

At the Parade of Rescue Titleholders I enjoyed the inspiring stories of the rescue dogs and handed out their rosettes. I wore my Kate memorial T-shirt and thought I'd be sad that she hadn't lived long enough to attend. But the event was too noisy and crowded for her— she wouldn't have liked it at all! The Parade had been my goal for Kate, but not a desire of hers for sure. That was a big realization for me.

I entered Bandit in the versatility competition, where he competed in obedience, Rally, agility, herding, and conformation for a combined score from all events. Bandit, the overachiever, earned a novice obedience leg, a Rally Novice title, and his first Rally Advanced leg (and 3rd place). I was proud of his agility performance, although he didn't qualify because he knocked a bar off a jump. Melissa and Guy stepped in to handle Bandit in conformation and herding. I didn't have any conformation handling experience and I had not been able to work Bandit in herding since July due to my medical condition. I was ecstatic to see him take 3rd place and 5th place in the two started A sheep herding trials.

Our friend Guy and his dog Zipper won first place in the overall Versatility competition. Amazingly, Bandit placed second, and he wasn't even three years old! It was a proud moment for me. Bandit was very resilient and enjoyed competing in the different activities. He also enjoyed the one-on-one time with me.

ჯ ♥ ღ

Kim, who I met at the Katrina Memorial Service in August, was moving forward with her Katrina animal rescue documentary film (www.LeftBehindKatrinaMovie.com). In October, she wrote:

...I want this film to be the best it possibly can be... The response... has really been overwhelming. I know all the stories are there, waiting to be told. What I've

decided to do is make a short film that will be a "work in progress"…to give a glimpse into what it was like as a volunteer doing Hurricane Katrina Animal Rescue and to inspire people to take action. I can't tell you how exciting that is… to know how many people care about what went on down there and what is currently going on all across the country. I truly believe that by doing my short film, this will turn into something very large and the message will be told to a lot of people.

Kim sent me a questionnaire that prompted me to reflect on the previous year. A few of her questions made me think about why I went to Louisiana and what I had learned:

Kim: Had you ever done disaster rescue before?

Me: No, but I had been on wilderness trips and had attended surgeries and seen blood and dead bodies before.

Kim: What financial implications did your Katrina work have?

Me: I am broke money-wise and rich friend-wise. It was worth it.

Kim: What has changed in your life as a result of Katrina animal rescue?

Me: Many things. My level of awareness. My level of involvement. Also, my level of connectedness with people all over the country. I'm involved with rescue transports, re-homing, and adoptions on a regular basis now. I'm in contact with other Australian Cattle Dog owners through ACD-L. Through the ACD-L list and my contacts from Lamar-Dixon, I've helped to rescue and re-home dogs in Minnesota, Wisconsin, Georgia, Virginia, Pennsylvania, and Louisiana in the past year. I have just been invited to join the board of Australian Cattle Dog Rescue, Inc. (ACDRI), a national breed rescue group. I became a grant application writer for Lost Fantasy Stables and Animal Rescue in Virginia…

I also have a much better understanding of cultural differences in the way people live and care for their pets. I'm still in contact with people in Louisiana and people from all over the country who I volunteered with. We have a special bond based on what we went through, and it's often very difficult for people who were not there to understand.

૪ ♥ ૭

By the end of October, I had joined the board of Australian Cattle Dog Rescue, Inc. (ACDRI), a national ACD rescue organization. I remembered my frantic calls from Louisiana to Deb of ACDRI. When I was invited to join the board, I knew it was time to give something back from the other end of the phone line.

"Be the change you would like to see in the world."

Gandhi

Chapter 19
Healing and Making a Difference

November began with some good news about Kenna. Her foster mom Rebecca reported that a woman named Sheryl had found Kenna's web page. After reading Kenna's story, Sheryl knew that Kenna was just the puppy she had been looking for. Nancy, who had helped rescue Billabong, agreed to do a home visit for Sheryl in the Baton Rouge area. Nancy enthusiastically approved the home, and the adoption was arranged.

Rebecca wrote:

I am so happy that Kenna is going to get such a good home and a chance at a good life. Sheryl and I met in Chattanooga, TN. It was love at first sight for both of them. Sheryl knelt down and Kenna climbed up into her arms. Soon there were wet puppy kisses everywhere. Kenna had found her forever home.

Sheryl wrote me a few days later to tell me that Kenna was wonderful. She and [Sheryl's other dog] Bleu made instant friends and slept curled together…all the way home from the adoption. Sheryl, Kenna, and Bleu could not be happier.

It is amazing to me how many people in how many states were involved in saving this little dog from death. Rescuers in GA asked Melissa for help, Melissa sent the info to Jenny in MN, who posted a plea on ACD-L. I, in TN, answered. Melissa in MN provided funding and organized Kenna's rescue and transport by volunteers Dawn, Jason, and Chrissy in GA. Michael in TN provided the umbrella of his rescue (TVCDR), and Dogster.com hosted her page and allowed Sheryl in LA to find her. What a wonderful group of people.

As if the news about Kenna were not enough, I then heard from Bazza in Florida about Billabong. He wrote: *Winkipop and Billabong had a blast at the tree farm I visited yesterday. They remain best buddies (or sisters)—BB gets healthier everyday—mind, body, and soul.*

Kenna's and Billabong's new lives were part of Kate's legacy. I was overjoyed to hear that they were both doing well.

On November 3rd, I consulted Mary Getten to check on Kate and to help prepare Bandit and Chase for my upcoming surgery. Mary reported that Kate had found her people in the spirit world, but was not with them any more. Kate communicated that nobody here on earth was still looking for her. Mary gave Kate the image of the photo of the dogs on the boat that I had found at the Katrina memorial service. Kate remembered swimming and being on a boat. At the time, she was in shock, exhausted and confused, but she seemed to recognize the picture. Kate liked the idea of me writing a book and thought it was "fun".

I asked about the day that Kate was put down. Kate said that she had always hated going to the vet. Her strong survival instinct made her want to fight the vet no matter what. She thanked me for taking care of her. She had really wanted to find her people.

Next Mary communicated to Bandit and Chase that I would be gone for 3 ½ weeks and that they would stay at Jody's house and then Becky's house. We had not been apart for that long before. Mary told them that I would check in with them mentally and reminded me to do this. The dogs knew that I had not been feeling well. Mary told them that I was going away to get taken care of and that they would need to be gentle with me when I came home.

ॐ ♥ 03

I first heard Levi's story at the end of October. Levi was a young adult male ACD in a kill shelter in Texas. His time was running out. Tammie, a shelter worker, had rescued him as a stray, but she couldn't keep him and took him to the shelter. He had not been claimed and she had been trying to place him for a long time. I kept my eyes and ears open until an opportunity came along.

Homeward Bound agreed to take Levi into a foster home in Minnesota if I could get him there. Trudy was planning a trip to Louisiana to bring a van-load of rescued animals to Wisconsin. I had met Trudy through e-mails when she helped transport Chase. She agreed to bring Levi north if I could arrange for him to meet her in Louisiana.

Levi in Texas

Then Trudy heard about Pirate, a young, sweet-looking blue ACD with a cataract in one eye. Pirate was at Roicy, the gassing shelter that Billabong had come from in Lafayette, Louisiana. Pirate had already been held over a few times and was given until 5:00 p.m. the following day to find rescue or a new home. The website said: *If ever there was a dog at Roicy who needed a miracle then this is the one!* I sent out a general plea to the ACD community, with no response. Then Homeward Bound agreed to take Pirate along with Levi. Trudy had Pirate pulled from Roicy and boarded in advance of the trip to make sure that she would still be alive when Trudy got there.

It took a week of networking to arrange Levi's transport from Texas to Louisiana. The last leg of his transport was filled at the very last minute by Jillian of Boudreaux's Animal Rescue Krewe (B.A.R.K.). LaDonna pulled him near Dallas and started him on his journey, then others drove him to Alexandria, Louisiana. He arrived on Friday night November 10th, not long before Trudy arrived to take the dogs to Wisconsin. Next I arranged transportation for Levi and Pirate from Wisconsin to Minnesota on November 12th.

Pirate in Louisiana

On November 11th, I heard from Trudy that she was on her way north with Levi, Pirate and the others. She would arrive in Wisconsin the following morning, and Levi's and Pirate's transport would continue to Minnesota. On the 12th, I was getting my house and dogs ready for my pending absence. I was mindful to spend extra time with Bandit and Chase since I would be away from them for a long time. That evening, I received the message that Levi and Pirate had arrived safe and sound at Homeward Bound in Minnesota. There they would be fully vetted and cared for in foster homes until approved permanent homes were found.

Trudy made the whole trip from Wisconsin to Louisiana and back with one $100 donation for gas. She paid the rest of the expenses out of her own pocket, and she made the entire drive by herself. Knowing of the extreme need in the Gulf Coast area, she wanted to help the animals on their way to forever homes, and also help some special people she had met after Katrina.

Trudy brought up seven cats from New Orleans to a new rescue group in Wisconsin (This group was started by Emily who had driven Tas' and Chase's transport leg from Madison). Trudy also brought a dog from New Orleans that she had met the previous May and named "Dolly", seven dogs from Roicy that would have been put to sleep, four puppies from Alexandria, and four more dogs from Brookhaven, whose rescuer was desperate to find them forever homes. Trudy wrote: *That is worth all the time and money I spent.* She is a fine example of what one determined person can do to make a difference.

ꝏ ♥ ꝏ

On November 13th, I picked my dad up at the Minneapolis airport. We dropped Bandit and Chase off at my friend Jody's house and headed to Rochester to check in for the surgery. Probably the hardest part about having surgery was leaving the dogs for over three weeks.

Early on Tuesday morning I checked in at the Mayo Clinic. A couple of days later, I was discharged to go home but I wasn't allowed to be around the dogs yet. The following Monday, my dad and I flew to Florida where I spent the next 2 ½ weeks recuperating at my parents' place. With time on my hands and physical limitations, I began putting this book together. I also visited relatives, discovered books by Jon Katz, did Sudoku puzzles, sat in the sun, went for short walks, and enjoyed delicious seafood. In addition, I made good use of the internet, spending hours coordinating rescues.

Meanwhile, Homeward Bound had treated Pirate for heartworm and had her spayed. She recovered quickly and did well in her foster home. On

November 25th, I learned that Pirate had been adopted into "the perfect home". I also heard that Levi was doing well in his foster home. It was great to see both dogs move on to happy endings due to the teamwork and generosity of many people. Those two dogs did not stand much chance to get adopted in their home states.

At the end of November, Melissa sent me the photo of a young female cattle dog mix called "Chicky" cowering in fear at the back of a kennel run. It looked like the same ugly yellow run from Kenna's death row photo. Chicky was at the same place—Spalding in Georgia. At about 5:00 p.m. Melissa wrote: *At Spalding. Last day tomorrow.* We didn't have much time! Chicky looked like a cattle dog-border collie mix. For some reason, she grabbed at me hard. I had the time to try to help this girl, but would we find the means?

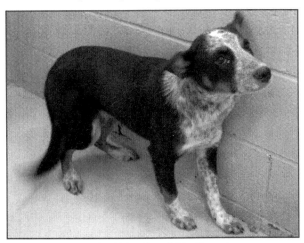

"Chicky" (aka Bonnie) in Georgia

Melissa had a local Georgia contact who could pull and board "Chicky". There was no time to solicit funds, so Melissa and I put up the money. The next morning, the contact (Brenda) went directly to the shelter. Although we had called ahead, "Chicky" was already on her way to the gas chamber when Brenda arrived in the nick of time. The name "Chicky" didn't suit her, so I renamed her Bonnie. People from ACD-L volunteered funds to help pay for her transportation.

Online, we learned that a woman named Rita was driving a transport of dogs up from eastern Kentucky to Chicago the following weekend. She also wanted to rescue another dog from Spalding. Since we had not found a Georgia home or rescue to take Bonnie, Homeward Bound agreed to take her in if we could get her to Minnesota. After much negotiating, we came up with a plan for Bonnie and the other Spalding dog to join Rita's transport.

That week, we learned of an ACD-Corgi mix at Etowah in Georgia. He was short on time and he could come to Homeward Bound with Bonnie. We tried to help him, but we couldn't get through by e-mail or phone. The next day he was gone from the website. It was gassing day at Etowah. I don't have any illusion that I can rescue every dog. But when there is a ride and a rescue available, it's really hard to fail. Losing that Corgi-ACD mix was very difficult and I had too much time to think about him.

While trying to save Bonnie and the other dogs that week, I received encouragement from Eileen. I was especially sad about the ACD-Corgi mix that we had lost. Eileen wrote, in part: *On days when there are, as recently, nine or ten rescue posts on a given day (yikes!), my mind does get tired and my heart gets weary, and I honestly think about taking a break…but then I start thinking that if I do that, just a few more might be lost, and I get right back at it. You have done so much already in such a short time…*

Have you read a book called "The Dreamgiver"? It… is inspirational, and you feel motivated by the time you've finished. It's a fairly short book, and easy reading. Grab a copy if you can. Keeps me going sometimes.

Keep me posted on Chicky/Bonnie. She sounds like a sweetie! I'm glad she grabbed you hard enough to get herself rescued! :)

That week felt like a roller coaster ride. I was much busier connecting people to rescue dogs than I would have been during a work week. I went through the heartbreak of committing to saving a dog and not being successful. I was grateful to Eileen for telling me about The Dreamgiver by Bruce Wilkinson, which has been described as a "practical and innovative guide to achieving your Big Dream." I have since read it more than once. A few days later Eileen wrote:

Jenny, you are doing the VERY BEST YOU CAN. If you save even one, it is worth the effort. You do what you can with the resources you have. It's frustrating, and it's why so many people drop out of rescue after a very short while. You are doing a WONDERFUL JOB.

Eileen always says the right thing at the right time!

Mid-week, I learned of an urgent situation in Kentucky. Three adult cattle dogs, one with seven puppies, were running out of time at a kill shelter. A shelter volunteer, Frieda, had arranged veterinary care for a 1½ year old red male, Kenny; a 3 year old blue female, Sadie, with the litter of young puppies; and an adult red and white female, Punkin. They were all apparently purebreds, except the puppies, whose mother looked purebred. Frieda had been watching out for these dogs and had saved them from death row more than once. She wanted to give them a second chance, but they were running out of time again with no new home or rescue in sight. Frieda told me that she could drive them to Chicago on Saturday, and Homeward Bound agreed to take them into foster homes in Minnesota.

That week, I spent many hours arranging to get Bonnie, Kenny, Punkin, and Sadie and her puppies to safety. The Kentucky dogs would arrive in the Chicago area the following Saturday afternoon. Bonnie would arrive with Rita late that night. Eileen posted a request for help, and two people in the Chicago area offered. Sheree would house the mama and puppies overnight and Gloria would house the other two adults. On Sunday, along with Bonnie, they would all continue to Minnesota.

ଚ ♥ ଓ

As I expanded my work in rescue, I became a target of public criticism. It first came up when I wrote about what I was going through with Kate, and asked for help. Some thought that I advocated rescuing dogs, spending thousands of dollars on them, and keeping them alive no matter what. This was not how I saw my rescue work. So I wrote a message to ACD-L.

I began: *Anyone who has an ACD should be aware of the extreme need for rescue, whether they choose to be involved or not.*

I explained that Kate's story was visible because she was a Katrina survivor and I had asked for advice and posted updates on ACD-L. Many people knew her story, but most didn't know about the legal issues tied to Katrina survivors like Kate. Nancy, who lived in Louisiana had offered to foster Kate, but couldn't. Why? Because a shelter was required to sponsor each dog, and all the shelters in Louisiana were overflowing. So, that's why I got the Minnesota shelter to sponsor Kate and drove her over 1,200 miles to my home.

I explained that Lamar-Dixon was being evacuated because Hurricane Rita was coming. Kate's only other option then was to be flown somewhere to another shelter. A flight might have killed her. After I got home with Kate, the Minnesota shelter didn't return my calls for over a week. By then I knew that she wouldn't do well in the shelter environment, and I continued to foster her in my home.

Few outsiders knew about the legal agreement allowing the original owners to reclaim their pets. Kate had to be fostered and listed on Petfinder, and could not be adopted until October. Then the date was extended to December, then March 1st. In the meantime, she had veterinary needs and behavioral issues that had to be addressed, so I sought advice on ACD-L. I was caring for her while she was still the legal property of "lost" owners.

As I cared for this dog who was not officially mine, the financial burden built up. It took Eileen and Nickie a while to convince me to let others know that Kate and I needed financial help. Overall, ACD-L people had been wonderfully supportive, and I appreciated that.

I explained that my experience with Kate had led some people to think that I was a rescue expert. I had a lot of visibility and became very well networked across the country.

The need for rescue in the south had skyrocketed since Hurricane Katrina, with an ongoing population explosion of stray animals and an exodus of people. I began receiving requests for help and learned of groups that transport dogs from southern states to rescue groups in Wisconsin and Minnesota. This is a general trend happening for many breeds – a symptom of a changing world.

I wanted people to understand that I wasn't always an advocate of shipping rescued dogs across the country. The 'supply' of dogs needing rescue tends to be in the southern part of the country, and there is more 'demand' for these dogs up north. We don't generally see many ACDs in shelters in Minnesota.

I described how I first came in contact with Homeward Bound in January of 2006, and how they fostered and placed Tas later that year. Since then we've worked together and Homeward Bound has fostered and placed ACDs from kill shelters in Indiana, Kentucky, Texas, Louisiana, Tennessee, Georgia, and other states when the dogs had a small window of time to escape the gas chamber, and local volunteers acted quickly. Although there was risk involved with rescuing these dogs without much information, most of them turned out to be very nice dogs when given a second chance. Their happy endings are posted at www.8StateKate.net.

We had rescued over twenty dogs between May and December of 2006. People had offered to help pull, foster, and transport dogs, recruit other volunteers, and donate funds—usually without being asked. I was very grateful for this support. I was glad that dogs were getting rescued and placed, however it happened.

Ending my public explanation, I hoped that I had set the record straight.

Not long afterward, Di, Linda, Eileen and others launched the AuCaDo Rescue Forum (www.aucado.us/forums), which provided a bulletin board with more timely and dedicated communication about ACDs needing rescue. It provided another way for us to communicate, to help prevent more dogs from slipping through the cracks.

ༀ ♥ ༃

> *"What is man without the beasts? If all the beasts were gone, man would die from great loneliness of spirit, for whatever happens to the beasts also happens to man. All things are connected. Whatever befalls the Earth befalls the sons of Earth."*
> Chief Seattle

> *"It made a difference for that one."*
> The Starfish Man

Chapter 20

My Starfish Story and Where Do We Go From Here?

The day before I flew home from Florida, I asked Mary Getten to check in with Bonnie, the rescued ACD mix in Georgia. Mary said that Bonnie was scared and nervous, wary and confused. She was not playing or making waves, trying to keep a low profile around the other dogs in the home. Mary told her about the long journey she would take, that she would find a new home at the end, and that everything would be okay.

Next Mary told Bandit and Chase that I would be coming home soon, and they would have to be gentle with me. She told them that Becky would take them to our house first and I would arrive with Lisa later that evening. Without an explanation, I thought they would be distressed to go home and not find me there. Mary said they had done well but thought that I had been gone too long.

Next I asked Mary to contact Kate, who felt much farther away emotionally than before. Mary found her spirit playing, having a good time running around outside with people in their 20's or 30's, younger people than she had been with before. I was surprised that she wasn't with the elderly couple. Perhaps she'd had more than one other family in her lifetime.

Mary told Kate that I was working on her book and that many people were interested in her story. She was pleased to hear this. I had Mary ask Kate what she was called before the storm. She gave a name that sounded like "Chula", not a name that Mary would have thought of. I asked again about what Kate remembered from the storm. She said that her people drowned, that they had let her off her chain and left, but weren't that far away. She didn't want to think about being here on earth. She appreciated all that I had done for her, but Katrina was a very difficult time in her life and she didn't like to think about it. She was much farther away now. I told her that I was sorry that I had taken her to the vet so many times. She said there was no blame, that she knew I was trying to help her.

I asked Mary to tell Kate that I still love her and miss her, but I'm glad that she's happy and in a better place. She wanted me to know that she's grateful for what I did for her and she was sorry that she couldn't pull it together better after the storm. I told her it was okay. I realized, finally, that even though I still wanted to be close to Kate, it was very difficult for her to think about her life here. And again, painfully, I had to let her go.

I had stayed with my parents in Florida for over two weeks, and had been away from Bandit and Chase for over three weeks. I missed them a lot. I was excited to get back to them, but was concerned about my ability to take care of all of us. I had come a long way during my recuperation period in Florida, but was still in pain.

For the coming weeks of recuperation, I was prohibited from lifting more than ten pounds, vacuuming, shoveling snow, or doing heavy laundry. There was no snow in Minnesota yet, but I wondered how I would get along alone with two dogs in our small house. I also wondered how I would fare on the trip back home.

In addition, I had the latest rescue efforts on my mind. If all went well, the rescued Kentucky and Georgia dogs would be transported to Minnesota the following weekend. It was a huge effort, involving people from different states who had never met before.

During the previous week, I had walked the beach each day. Walking had been prescribed to help me heal, and visiting the beach made me feel more alive than anything else. Bending over to collect shells had been too painful at first, but now I was able to bend over and pick them up.

In past years, I had collected sand dollars on this beach. This year, even at low tide I had only found a few broken shards. I was searching for a whole sand dollar as a sign that everything would be okay, maybe as a message from Kate that she was watching over me. During these early days of recovery from my surgery, I was concerned about what lay ahead.

On my last beach walk before returning to Minnesota, the conditions were not right for finding sand dollars. I had reached the beach too late for low tide, and had almost come to the end of my walk without finding that sign I had searched for.

As I walked at the water's edge, a man approached me and held out his hand. He said, "This morning we had our best day. We found over a hundred shells. I want you to have these." Then he placed four perfectly formed sand dollars in my hand. I was completely stunned. This man had no idea what he had done to reassure me that everything would be okay. He invited me over to the small beach camp where his two friends were sitting and offered me my choice of the shells they had collected.

As I looked through the beautiful shells, he told me that the best shelling of the season would be at about 8:00 a.m. the following morning. It was full moon, and low tide would be much lower than usual. He encouraged me to return.

My flight wasn't until afternoon, so I went back the following morning at 8:00. I couldn't resist the chance to walk on that beach one more time. I was amazed to see how low the water was and how much more of the beach was exposed. Walking at the water's edge, I found one sand dollar after another. It was truly amazing! I also found many other beautiful shells and was enchanted by this magical morning at the beach, my last morning in Florida.

Nearing the end of my walk, I encountered the sand dollar man. I felt truly blessed, and thanked him for inviting me back to the beach that morning. Although he didn't know it, he had come to represent faith, reassurance, and perhaps a bit of magic. He wished me well, then bent over and reached into the water. He fished around and then raised his hand, holding a small starfish in the palm.

"It's alive, isn't it?" I asked.

"Yes, and it has five points. Isn't it beautiful?" he replied.

"Yes," I said. "I have never seen a starfish on this beach. I've seen many of them in other places, but not here".

"This is rare," he replied. "He's out of his element here." I noticed that the starfish was starting to curl up the ends of its legs. My new friend said, "He's starting to dry up. He needs to get back out to sea". And with that, the man turned, waded farther out to sea and gently placed the starfish back in deeper water.

I was mesmerized, you see, because I knew the starfish story* as a powerful testament to the value of one person doing what they can to make a difference. This story is often quoted among animal rescuers and was first told to me by my friend Eileen. I had just met a man who returned a starfish to the sea at a time when I needed to meet him the most.

Once I was on my way home, I realized that his original gift to me was four sand dollars and we were trying to rescue four adult dogs. I had been looking for one whole sand dollar as a sign and I had been given four. I had my sign, and more. I made it home to Minnesota safely, and soon the dogs would be safe too. I had helped make a difference, at least for those four.

Here's the version of the starfish story that I first heard from my friend Eileen:

*The Starfish Story

Adapted from *The Star Thrower*,
by Loren Eiseley

Once upon a time, there was a wise man who used to go to the ocean to do his writing. He had a habit of walking on the beach before he began his work.

One day, as he was walking along the shore, he looked down the beach and saw a human figure moving like a dancer. He smiled to himself at the thought of someone who would dance to the day, and he walked faster to catch up.

As he got closer, he noticed that the figure was that of a young man, and that what he was doing was not dancing at all. The young man was reaching down to the shore, picking up small objects, and throwing them into the ocean.

He came closer still and called out "Good morning! May I ask what it is that you are doing?"

The young man paused, looked up, and replied "Throwing starfish into the ocean."

"I must ask, then, why are you throwing starfish into the ocean?" asked the somewhat startled wise man.

To this, the young man replied, "The sun is up and the tide is going out. If I don't throw them in, they'll die."

Upon hearing this, the wise man commented, "But, young man, do you not realize that there are miles and miles of beach and there are starfish all along every mile? You can't possibly make a difference!"

At this, the young man bent down, picked up yet another starfish, and threw it into the ocean. As it met the water, he said, "It made a difference for that one."

When I arrived home on December 7th, I was overjoyed to see Bandit and Chase. Taking care of myself, my home and the dogs again wasn't easy, but I was glad to be back. My new ACD desk calendar displayed Kate's page for the whole month of December. I hoped that many other people were remembering her along with me.

On Saturday, December 9th, I received the message that the dogs from Kentucky had arrived safely in Illinois. Unfortunately, some of the dogs had coughs. Sheree called me with concerns about the puppies. Since the dogs were now under the umbrella of Homeward Bound rescue, I called Katie in Minnesota.

Although Sheree gave them the best of care, one of the seven puppies died while at her home. He was much smaller than the others and probably would have died anyway. But he wouldn't have had a chance at all if we hadn't brought them north. We rushed to get all the dogs into rescue and to the vet. On December 10th, the four adults and six remaining puppies arrived in Minnesota. They were treated by the vet and settled into their new foster homes.

Bonnie was spayed and after a couple of weeks started to come out of her shell. I felt very strongly about her and considered adopting her myself, but this was not the time for me to get another dog.

At the end of December, Bonnie met her new family at a Petco adoption event! Kenny recovered well from his cough and was neutered. A family that was pre-approved for another dog noticed Kenny and their son was drawn to him. They went home, learned about the breed, and came back for him. He went to his new home on December 30th.

Punkin was adopted on January 7th to a home with another dog from Homeward Bound. She settled in like she had been there forever. Sadie and her puppies were cared for until the puppies were weaned. The puppies recovered from the cough and all six survived. Sadie was spayed and they all eventually went to good homes.

ଔ ♥ ଔ

I never went back to life the way it was before my trip to Louisiana. The experience changed me. I now look through the eyes of determination and possibility. I made friends with the same convictions, and the guts to do something about them. For all of my grief and despair over the things that I couldn't do in Louisiana, I'm very grateful for these friends and for the journey.

I'm also grateful that I could make a difference in the life of this one dog, Kate. You see, Kate saved me as much as I saved her. Although I'm not much good at asking for help for myself, I had to ask for help for Kate. I cared deeply about her and I couldn't take care of her needs all by myself.

Kate led me to many wonderful friends who I never would have known otherwise. Together we continue to help save the lives of many other dogs... and even though I have seen tragedy and despair, I still believe in magic, hope, possibility, faith, and love.

This is real life. I can't tie Kate's story up with a beautiful bow and tell you that everything came out fine. I wish she were still here, enjoying this beautiful day, playing with the other dogs, but she's not. She's in a better place, and I like to think that she's smiling down on us. I'm grateful to have known her and for all that she inspired from me and from others. We did our best and even though it wasn't perfect, somehow we made a difference.

My life is different now, because I knew I wouldn't have forgiven myself if I hadn't gotten off my butt and gone down to Louisiana. What is waiting out there for you? When will you begin to follow your heart, to do your part? What would the animals tell you if you were truly listening?

To some people, Kate may have just looked like an ordinary dog. But to me, she was a very brave survivor and teacher. Her legacy is a pack of survivors: Tas, Chase, Kenna, Billabong, Levi, Pirate, Kenny, Punkin, Bonnie, Sadie and her pups, Vixen, Maddie, Spin, Sophie (Kat), Brie, Pepper, Maggie (Suzy), Graduate, Lucy, Friday, Chance, Nudge, Cassie, Wolfie (Speed), Atlas, Rosie, Raven, Derby, and Miner, Sally, Gypsy, Silver, Bandit, Katya, Waylon, Dawson... and many more. The "Happy Endings" page on Kate's website is growing, with the faces of these dogs who have been rescued through the efforts of many volunteers.

This is the end of the book, but not the end of the story. Kate's legacy lives on in the rescue efforts of many people, in the lives of the dogs who have been saved, and in simple acts of kindness everywhere. Her legacy lives on every time someone gets out of her chair and steps up to make a difference, not knowing where that first step will take her.

I hope this book will lead me to the rest of Kate's story, of her life in Louisiana before Hurricane Katrina, and give peace to anyone who wonders what became of her. She may be gone from this earth, but she is not forgotten.

80 ♥ 03

ชช ชช

*At least 50% of the profits from this book will be used to establish the **8 State Kate Fund**, to provide financial relief for animals in desperate situations.*

ชช ชช

Afterword

December 2007

While working on this book, I came across the photo of the dogs on the boat again. I tried to trace the boat's license number to its owner, but was told that the information was confidential. I tried one more time by e-mailing a copy of the photo to the Louisiana Department of Wildlife and Fisheries. Amazingly, the boat owner's information was e-mailed back to me.

The man in the photo is Jace, a shrimp fisherman from Chalmette. When I searched his name online, I learned that Jace rode out fourteen foot Katrina waters at a friend's house. His boat was one of the few that survived the storm. All of his friends' boats are gone and many of his friends have left the area. His wife and children moved inland for a while, fearing hurricane season. He was going to move too, but fishing is his living. What else would he do? Recently, his family moved back to Chalmette to join him.

I wrote a letter to Jace and included the photo of the dogs on his boat. About a week later, he called me and left a message, telling me that the cattle dog in the photo belonged to his mom. My heart was in my throat. Could I be that close to finding out Kate's origin? But the dog in the photo is still with Jace's mom in Louisiana. It wasn't Kate after all!

I'm grateful that Kate came into my life, for our journey together, and for her legacy of rescued animals and true friends. I know our paths were meant to cross, and I cherish all that she gave me. I didn't go down there to get a dog, but a dog got to me. I wonder where the next journey will take me.

80 ♥ CR

April 2008

A new foster dog joined our family this week … a red heeler mix who was rescued by a kind woman after being abandoned with her littermates in the Tennessee wilderness. Unlike Kate, this girl gets along well with other dogs, but is afraid of people. I was asked to help because she needs a home where she can learn to bond with a person. I've missed having a girl here, but I was hesitant to open my heart this way again. It still hurts. She's been here for just three days and our journey is only beginning. But she's starting to warm up to me already.

Lisa was right when she said "… *every act of kindness you do from here on will directly relate to Kate…*" I know in my broken heart that I can do this.

Appendix

What You Can Do Now to Prevent Your Dog from Getting Lost, And to Help You Find a Lost Dog

The pain and panic of losing a dog can be made a little easier, and maybe avoided completely, by taking some steps now.

Collar and ID: Make sure your dog wears a secure collar with current ID tags. Include a phone number where you can be reached, and a back-up phone number for a second person who can easily be reached by phone.

Microchip: Have an identifying chip implanted at a vet clinic or a humane society. Attach a tag with the microchip number to the dog's collar. Register the chip and keep your current contact information updated with the microchip company. Keep a record of the microchip number in a safe place (like your wallet) and add it to your dog's file at the veterinary clinic.

Photos: Take clear, up-to-date photos of your dog from several angles, in good lighting. Digital photos are easiest to distribute quickly by e-mail. Give copies to a friend or family member who can access the photos on short notice.

Written description: Describe your dog as if writing for a person who doesn't know dog breeds very well. Include coloring, approximate weight, unusual markings or scars, etc. For example, my dog Bandit has a unique cowlick down the middle of his face, a black triangle marking on his tail, and a toenail that sticks out sideways from an old injury.

Info Package: Keep an information package for each dog in a file in your vehicle's glove compartment. Include photos, a written description, microchip information and ID number, contact information and a copy of recent vet records.

Contact person: Ask a friend or family member to be a contact person —someone who could easily be reached by phone while you were out searching for your dog. The dog could be lost in an area without cell phone reception, and you wouldn't want to be sitting at home waiting for phone calls if your dog was lost.

Train the Recall: Teach your dog to know its name and come to you when called. Reward the dog with great treats when she comes to you and never scold a dog you have called, even if she takes forever to reach you. Always make "come" a good thing.

Socialize and Train: Get your dog accustomed to different situations, including people and loud noises. A dog that isn't terrified may be less likely to hide and thus easier to find. Teach your dog a "drop" on command, so that the dog can be prevented from running into the street and might be stopped by your voice if running away.

For more information, including examples of effective "Lost Dog" posters, search "how to find a lost dog" on the internet.

The St. Bernard Parish website has a wealth of information for those who are still looking for pets lost during Katrina at http://sbpanimal. homestead.com/katrina.html.

*"What you do makes a difference,
and you have to decide what
kind of difference you want to make."*

Jane Goodall

Ways That You Can Help: How to Support Animal Rescue in a Minute or a Lifetime from the Comfort of Your Home/Community

After returning from Louisiana, I looked for ways that I could continue to support animal rescue from home. I came up with this list. Many of these opportunities don't cost you anything, but can make a big difference when added to the efforts of others. Once you start noticing and trying ways to help, more ideas will come to you.

Australian Cattle Dogs

(Note: Other breeds have similar resources. Ask around to find what's available for your breed.)

🐾 Use the rescue section of the online AuCaDo Forum (www.aucado.us/forums/) to network about Australian Cattle Dogs needing rescue. This network has also been effective at fundraising and helping to arrange transport for rescued dogs. There are other similar groups for other breeds, mixed breeds, and other species.

🐾 Subscribe to ACD-L (the Australian Cattle Dog List, which can be joined through the "cattledog chat" link on www.cattledog.com) to network with other ACD owners. This group can be very helpful to people who are new to the breed. There are other similar groups for other breeds, mixed breeds, and other species.

All Dogs (and Cats, and Other Animals…)

🐾 Click daily for free food donations to shelters at www.theanimalrescuesite.com.

🐾 When ordering online, go through www.dollarback.com or www.igive.org to shop from many online stores and give a percentage of purchases to support a shelter. Search on Dollarback or igive to find the organization that you want to support.

🐾 When searching online, try www.goodsearch.com. This search engine donates a penny to the charity of your choice every time you search the internet.

🐾 Use a credit card that benefits animal organizations

🐾 Purchase items from companies that donate a portion of the proceeds to rescue. Two examples are www.helpinggudders.com and www.petwearusa.com.

🐾 Purchase shirts, pet toys, cookbooks, holiday cards and ornaments, and other items that support animal rescue organizations. Many of the rescue organizations listed in this appendix sell their own products.

🐾 Join and participate in a regional online rescue list. Many lists, such as WisconsinAnimalRescue and MinnesotaAnimalRescue, can be found on YahooGroups. Look for a list in your area.

🐾 As part of your annual United Way contribution at work, write in an animal rescue organization to receive part of your monthly donation. Make sure the organization of your choice is eligible for United Way funds.

🐾 Apply for matching grants through the corporation you work for. I received matching grants for my volunteer rescue and grant writing hours to give $250 each to two animal rescue organizations.

🐾 Help write grant applications for a rescue organization. Sarah (of Lost Fantasy Stables and Animal Rescue in Virginia) and I have successfully obtained grant money to support the animals in the care of this 501(c)(3) rescue.

🐾 Support local shelters and rescue groups with donations and volunteer time, especially around the holidays when they need extra help. Help walk and play with the dogs. Help care for and play with the cats.

🐾 Collect donated "gently used" animal items for your local shelter or another shelter that needs help. Be sure to first ask the shelter what items they need and will accept.

🐾 Help transport rescued animals from shelters to new homes or foster homes via a transport network that travels through your area. If you are unable to drive a leg of the trip, you can donate gas money for someone who can drive but can't afford the gas. These transport networks literally save lives. Look online for a transport group in your area, such as MidwestRapidTransit@yahoogroups.com.

🐾 Volunteer to perform home visits in your area to check out prospective homes for rescue groups. Usually there are specific instructions and forms for you to fill out.

🐾 Donate frequent flyer miles to rescue organizations that travel to disaster sites.

🐾 Support legislation for changing the way animals are handled and prioritized in disasters. Help your local community develop a disaster response plan that includes a plan for animals. Join your local Community Emergency Response Team (CERT).

🐾 Follow and support (or oppose, depending on the situation) other animal-related legislation regarding puppy mills, breed-specific legislation, dog fighting, and other animal laws. Stay aware of the animal-related issues and legislation in your community.

🐾 Think about your talents and skills and how they could be applied to help animal rescue groups

🐾 Stay networked. After Katrina, I stayed in contact with new friends from Lamar-Dixon for mutual support and networking. One of the good outcomes of our experience in Louisiana is that we now have new friends all over the country.

🐾 Add your own ideas here (and please submit them at www.8StateKate. net):

_____

_____

_____

_____

_____

_____

_____

_____

_____

_____

_____

_____

_____

_____

_____

_____

ℬ 💚 ℭ

Animal Rescue Organizations to Support

Grass roots animal rescue organizations need your help, and spend the majority of their funds directly on animals. When donating, check charity ratings to make sure that your donation will really go to help the animals. This information is available at www.GuideStar.org or the attorney general's office for the state where the organization is incorporated. Some organizations publish their financial information on their website. If this information is not readily available, ask what percent of their expenses is spent on program activities and on administrative expenses. Also, ask what percent of their annual donations is spent on program activities. Be wary of groups that do not share their financial information, and groups that do not put the majority of their expenses into program activities.

The following is a list of groups that I've interacted with and can recommend, based on what I know at this time. This is *not* a complete list of rescue groups! Many other valuable rescue organizations exist that I haven't worked with yet. Due to my own attachment to Australian Cattle Dogs, I often work with rescues specializing in this breed and they're highly represented in this list. Every other dog breed has its own dedicated rescue groups. An internet search will lead you to rescue organizations that work with your breed of interest.

Most rescue organizations have fine animals available for adoption and would welcome your financial and/or volunteer support. In addition, most rescue groups desperately need more knowledgeable people who can foster animals needing help.

Please check the website at www.8StateKate.net/WordPress. Click on 8 State Kate Fund to see the evolving list of groups that have been supported by the fund.

Key:
⚡ = Australian Cattle Dog Rescue (lightning bolt Bentley)
🐕 = Has helped rescue Australian Cattle Dogs
🐕 = Dogs
🐈 = Cats
🐎 = Horses
🐄 = Hoofed animals (other than horses)
☆ = Other animals and/or birds, not mentioned above

Abused Animal Rescue & Rehabilitation Farm & Foundation (AARRFF)
Accepts donations and has applied for 501(c)(3) status
Location: Scio, Oregon
Serves: Specialize in Australian Cattle Dog rescue and large animal/ livestock rescue. Also take in other breeds of dogs and cats. AARRFF is dedicated to the rescue of all animals.
Contact: Diana Moffat
Website: www.aarrff.org
E-mail: LadyLawOr@hotmail.com
Mission: *We provide rescue for shelter animals, foster care for animals in search of their "forever" home, assistance in the re-homing of currently homed animals, networking with other rescue organizations, education on spay/neuter and life-long sanctuary for others. ~Saving Animals one life at a time~*

All Cattle Dogs Rescue (ACDR)
Accepts donations and has applied for 501(c)(3) status
Location: Nashville, Tennessee
Serves: Australian Cattle Dogs, primarily; concentrates on herding breeds, but will rescue any dog if there is room
Contact: Anna Wilson
Website: www.cattledogrescue.org
E-mail: blueydogrescue@comcast.net
Phone: 615-278-9323 (voice mail) or 615-598-1940
Mission: *Our focus is to aid stray, abandoned or otherwise unwanted dogs, mostly ACDs. We primarily pull from shelters, but will occasionally assist a family to re-home a misplaced dog before it ends up in a shelter. We also try*

to stay involved in situations where an individual has found a dog with the intention of placing him/her.

Animal Action Rescue (AAR)

Accepts donations and is a 501(c)(3) organization
Location: Decatur, Georgia
Serves: All breeds of dogs and cats
Contact: Chrissy
Website: www.animalactionrescue.org
E-mail: GTigger719@aol.com
Mission: *AAR is a licensed, non-breed specific rescue organization based in Decatur, Georgia. We are dedicated to rescuing dogs and cats from high-kill shelters and neglectful homes, promoting spay/neuter programs, and educating the community about responsible pet ownership.*

AuCaDo Australian Cattle Dog Rescue of Michigan

Accepts donations and is a 501(c)(3) organization
Location: Remus, Michigan
Serves: Australian Cattle Dogs only
Contact: Monica R. Larner
Website: www.cowdogrescue.com
E-mail: cowdogrescue@gmail.com
Phone: 989-330-5147
Mission: *Rescuing homeless heelers and helping them find their forever homes.*

AuCaDo Australian Cattle Dog Rescue of Illinois—Chapter of AuCaDo of Michigan

Accepts donations through AuCaDo Rescue of Michigan, a 501(c)(3) organization
Location: Southern Illinois
Serves: Australian Cattle Dogs only
Contact: Sue Christianson
Website: www.petfinder.com/shelters/IL438.html
E-mail: blueysacds@americonnect.net

Mission: *To rescue cattle dogs in need, to place them in responsible homes and to educate the public about these wonderful dogs.*

AuCaDo Australian Cattle Dog Rescue of Ohio—Chapter of AuCaDo of Michigan
Accepts donations through AuCaDo Rescue of Michigan, a 501(c)(3) organization
Location: Northern Ohio
Serves: Australian Cattle Dogs only
Contact: Corene Glessner
Website: www.petfinder.com/shelters/OH715.html
E-mail: acd2rsq@yahoo.com
Mission: *To rescue cattle dogs in need, to place them in responsible homes and to educate the public about these wonderful dogs.*

Australian Cattle Dog Rescue Association (ACDRA)
Accepts donations and is a 501(c)(3) organization
Location: Covers the Eastern Seaboard states from Maine to North Carolina
Serves: Australian Cattle Dogs and ACD mixes
Contact: Melinda Wood
Website: www.acdra.org
E-mail: president@acdra.org
Mission: *We are a network of volunteers whose goal is to match displaced ACDs with suitable homes while also educating the public about these highly energetic and intelligent dogs. We provide a web presence for the shelters that have happened upon these unique dogs as well as a resource for the foster homes that socialize them in a family setting.*

Best Friends Animal Society
Accepts donations and is a 501(c)(3) organization
Location: Kanab, Utah
Serves: The sanctuary is home to about 2,000 dogs, cats, horses, rabbits, birds and other animals.
Website: www.bestfriends.org

E-mail: <u>donations@bestfriends.org</u>, <u>animalhelp@bestfriends.org</u>
Phone: 435-644-2001
Mission: *Best Friends operates the nation's largest sanctuary for homeless animals; provides adoption, spay/neuter, and educational programs around the country; and publishes Best Friends, the nation's largest general-interest animal magazine. Best Friends is working with shelters, rescue groups and our members nationwide to bring about a time when there will be no more homeless pets.*

Blue Crush Australian Cattle Dog Rescue
Accepts donations
Location: Asheville, NC
Serves: Western North Carolina and South Carolina
Website: <u>www.bluecrushrescue.com</u>
E-mail: <u>bluecrushrescue@bellsouth.net</u>
Mission: *Our goal is to find, place, and transport abandoned or endangered purebred Australian Cattle Dogs and place them in loving and safe homes. We believe that when you adopt an Australian Cattle Dog you do so for the life of that dog. Our dogs come from shelters and abusive situations throughout NC and SC. We place them in volunteer foster homes until they can be placed in permanent homes. All dogs going into the rescue must be evaluated as having a good temperament and show no aggressiveness towards dogs or people. Our rescue is funded solely by donations that go to ACD care and placement, and education of the public on rescue and ACD-related issues.*

Boudreaux's Animal Rescue Krewe (B.A.R.K.)
Accepts donations and is a 501(c)(3) organization
Location: Alexandria, Louisiana
Serves: All dogs regardless of their breed
Contact: Jillian Donaghey
Website: <u>www.petfinder.com/shelters/LA185.html</u>
E-mail: <u>LongJ1003@aol.com</u>
Mission: *Our journey began several years ago when we went to a local city-run shelter to look at a problem that we had heard about. There we saw first-hand the "Death Row Dogs". Ten beautiful pets lined up to be euthanized. Ten beautiful pets that looked into our eyes and we knew that they had done nothing to deserve "Death Row". We pardoned them and gave them a second*

chance at life. We have continued our mission to pardon as many "Death Row Dogs" as we can and have found that each and every one of them has never let us down. We know these pets are grateful for their forever homes, but we are grateful for all of the wonderful lessons that they teach us each and every day that we work with them. Our goal will continue to be rescuing "Death Row Dogs" and making sure that they get the much-deserved second chance of life in a forever home.

Carolina Australian Cattle Dog Rescue & Rebound

Accepts donations and is a 501(c)(3) organization
Location: North and South Carolina
Serves: Australian Cattle Dogs only
Contact: Melissa Tooley
Website: www.carolinarescue.com
E-mail: carolinarescue@yahoo.com
Mission: *We are dedicated to helping Australian Cattle Dogs in need of rescue from kill shelters, neglect and abandonment in both North and South Carolina. Through our foster/ adoption program, these dogs receive routine veterinary care, training and lots of TLC while we search for their new forever homes. Through our website, adoption flyers, and public events we strive to educate the public about this breed and prevent other cattle dogs from becoming another dog in need.*

Flying K9s Herd Dog Rescue

Accepts donations
Location: Cincinnati-Dayton, Ohio and Indianapolis, Indiana areas
Serves: Australian Cattle Dogs (primarily), Border Collies, Australian Shepherds and mixes of these three breeds
Contact: Sjoukje Janssen
Website: http://flyingk9s.petfinder.com
E-mail: flyingk9s@hotmail.com
Phone: 937-602-0323
Mission: *We specialize in placing the herding breeds noted above. Most of our foster dogs are rescued from local shelters when they are out of time; all are temperament tested. We will not accept aggressive dogs or dogs with serious behavioral issues. We are a small operation, and only take in one to three dogs*

at a time. They live in our homes with us and our own dogs, learning the basics of house life. Occasionally, when a dog shows great potential, we begin their training as a disc dog!

Friends of Mansfield Animal Shelter

Accepts donations and is a 501(c)(3) organization
Location: Eastern Connecticut
Serves: Dogs—specialize in Australian Cattle Dogs and Kelpies, but we help all we can
Contact: Cheryl Hutchings
Website: www.fomas.petfinder.com
E-mail: fomas2001@yahoo.com
Mission: *A small volunteer organization, based out of the town shelter in Mansfield, CT, helping to fund expenses for the shelter animals and offering a small foster network for less fortunate animals in high kill shelters. Our goal is to raise enough money to build an eco-friendly state-of-the-art shelter in our area.*

Homeward Bound Rescue (Minnesota)

Accepts donations and is a 501(c)(3) organization
Location: Minneapolis-St. Paul area
Serves: All dog breeds and mixed breeds
Website: www.homewardboundrescue.com
E-mail: homewardboundrescue@yahoo.com
Phone: 763-295-3116
Mission: *We specialize in making great use of foster homes to match families with the appropriate dog for their home. When we have open foster slots, we also specialize in harder to adopt dogs with medical and social needs.*

Homeward Bound Animal Rescue (Texas)

Accepts donations and is a 501(c)(3) organization
Location: Dallas-Fort Worth area
Serves: Dogs
Website: www.petfinder.com/shelters/TX122.html
E-mail: srich@flash.net
Phone: 817-792-5122

Mission: *We are an all volunteer non-profit no-kill organization dedicated to rescuing companion animals and placing them into foster homes until they can be permanently adopted.*

The Humane Society of Louisiana

Accepts donations and is a 501(c)(3) organization
Location: PO Box 740321, New Orleans, LA 70174
Serves: The Humane Society of Louisiana leads the fight against cruelty to animals statewide
Website: www.HumaneLA.org
E-mail: info@humanela.org
Phone: General Info: 1-888-6HUMANE, Tylertown shelter: 601-876-2781
Mission: *Humane-LA has rescued, rehabilitated and adopted out more than 9,000 abused and neglected animals. While we are not a public animal shelter, we take animals directly from overburdened shelters and rescue groups as we have funding, foster homes and space available. Our programs include Cruelty Investigation and Abuse Prevention, Community Chapters and Outreach, Animal Care Services and Programs, and Advocacy and Education. As a licensed private detective agency, we work with law enforcement and animal control officers to accept custody of animals seized in criminal cases of abuse. We also accept animals from such cases from public and private animal shelters, to the extent funding permits. If you would like to sponsor or foster an individual animal in need, we'd deeply appreciate your support.*

Indy Pit Crew

Accepts donations and is a 501(c)(3) organization
Location: Indianapolis, Indiana
Serves: The American Pit Bull Terrier and all bully breed dogs
Contact: Stacey Coleman (President)
Website: www.indypitcrew.org
E-mail: info@indypitcrew.org
Phone: 317-592-9614
Mission: *The Indy Pit Crew evolved from a desire to address the difficult issues facing the misunderstood American Pit Bull Terrier and other bully breeds in and around Indianapolis. Through education and community*

outreach, we combat dog fighting, strive to eliminate pit bull over-population, and encourage responsible ownership, while inspiring a better understanding and appreciation for the American Pit Bull Terrier and all Bully Breed dogs.

Lost Fantasy Rescue
Accepts donations and is a 501(c)(3) organization
Location: Ceres, VA
Serves: Horses and companion animals, also licensed for wildlife and some exotics
Contact: Sarah Dutton
Website: www.lostfantasystables.org
E-mail: lostfantasystables@yahoo.com
Mission: *We provide rescue, sanctuary, and adoptive homes for horses and companion animals in need. We speak for those who have no voice and give hope to those who no longer have any.*

Louisiana Society for the Prevention of Cruelty to Animals
Accepts donations and is a 501(c)(3) organization
Location: 1700 Mardi Gras Blvd., New Orleans, Louisiana 70114
Serves: We're chartered to conduct business statewide, but focus on Orleans Parish.
Website: www.la-spca.org
E-mail: info@la-spca.org
Phone: 504-368-5191
Mission: *The Louisiana SPCA is devoted to improving the lives of animals and eliminating the homelessness, neglect, and abuse that signal animal suffering. Chartered in 1888, our history has been paved with an understanding that only through an improved human-animal ethic can we better the lives of companion animals and of our community. Our programs and services are infused with the highest standards of care and compassion.*

Meet the Pack Australian Cattle Dog Rescue
Accepts donations
Location: Lyndhurst, Ontario, Canada
Serves: Australian Cattle Dogs and ACD mixes

Contact: Sue Cameron-Day.
Website: www.west.petfinder.com/shelters/ON279.html
E-mail: meetthepack@hotmail.com
Mission: *I rescue ACDs and ACD mixes from high kill shelters/pounds. I help owners who need to re-home their dogs by educating them and screening for the best and safest homes.*

MuttShack Animal Rescue Foundation
Accepts donations and is a 501(c)(3) organization
Locations: Los Angeles, CA; New Orleans, LA; Monroe, WA; New York, NY
Serves: All pets, wildlife, horses, farm animals
Contact: Amanda St. John
Website: www.MuttShack.org (Support the Katrina Promise)
E-mail: info@MuttShack.org
Phone: 866-718-1001
Mission: *MuttShack Animal Rescue and Disaster Response is volunteer driven. We respond to animals in disasters and effect ongoing shelter rescue. We provide free online FEMA volunteer training, and support local communities in mass animal evacuation transport and sheltering. Local Chapters exist all over the United States. Please support animals in your area.*

NE/CO K9's
Accepts donations
Location: Lamar, Nebraska
Serves: Australian Cattle Dogs, Dachshunds
Contact: Kelly Denbo
Website: www.necok9s.org
E-mail: necok9s@gpcom.net
Mission: *We are a small rescue in Western Nebraska, helping to find homes for Cattle Dogs and Dachshunds in Nebraska, Colorado, Kansas, and Wyoming.*

New Hope Australian Cattle Dog Rescue
Accepts donations and is a 501(c)(3) organization

Location: Arizona and Colorado
Serves: Australian Cattle Dogs only
Contact: Shannon Stevens (AZ), PJ (CO)
Website: www.newhopecattledogs.com (AZ), www.nhcdrescuecolorado.com (CO)
E-mail: shannon@newhopecattledogs.com (AZ), PJ@nhcdrescuecolorado.com (CO)
Phone: 602-690-8374 (AZ), 720-201-5241 or 303-717-7695 (CO)
Mission: *To help discarded, stray and unwanted Australian Cattle Dogs that need a second chance at finding a forever home and provide education and training to the public.*

Pasado's Safe Haven
Accepts donations and is a 501(c)(3) organization
Location: Sultan, Washington
Serves: Dogs, cats, all farm animals: goats, llamas, cows, horses, donkeys, pigs, chickens, geese, ducks, turkeys, sheep
Contact: Amber Chenoweth
Website: www.pasadosafehaven.org
E-mail: amberc@pasadosafehaven.org
Phone: 360-793-9393, ext. 109
Mission: *Pasado's Safe Haven is a non-profit animal rescue and rehabilitation organization. Our mission is to provide programs and services that fill the voids left unanswered by other animal welfare agencies in Washington State. Our goal is to provide services to those animals who "fall through the cracks" and who are not served by other shelters or existing programs.*

P.A.W.S.—Plaquemines Animal Welfare Society
Accepts donations and is a 501(c)(3) organization
Location: Belle Chasse, Louisiana
Serves: Dogs and cats. The first priority is taking animals from the local pound. Owner surrenders are accepted when there is room.
Contact: Laura Hutcheson
Website: www.paws-site.petfinder.com
E-mail: paws2003@bellsouth.net

Mission: *P.A.W.S. is a non profit group. We are no-kill and have 100 plus animals in our rescue adoption center at all times. We depend on donations as the biggest part of our survival.*

Rescue Ranch
Accepts donations and is a 501(c)(3) organization
Location: Belle Chasse, Louisiana
Serves: Horses and other hoofed animals
Contact: Lori Wilson, Director
Website: www.rescueranch.net
E-Mail: lori@rescueranch.net
Phone: 504-393-8485
Mission: *The mission of Rescue Ranch is to provide the necessary resources to rescue, restore, retrain, and relocate at-risk and abused horses and other hoofed animals. Rescue Ranch also works with disadvantaged and at-risk children using horses and other resources to foster outreach, education and personal growth through activities and volunteer opportunities.*

Rocky Mountain Cattle Dog Rescue
Accepts donations and is a 501(c)(3) organization licensed by the State of Colorado
Location: Denver, Colorado
Serves: A foster based rescue serving Australian Cattle Dogs in the greater Rocky Mountain region
Website: www.rmcdr.com
E-mail: rescue@rmcdr.com
Mission: *To educate the public about the Australian Cattle Dog and to rehabilitate and rehome great dogs into good homes. Foster homes are always needed.*

St. Bernard Parish Animal Shelter
Accepts donations and is a 501(c)(3) organization
Location: Chalmette, Louisiana
Serves: The people and animals in St. Bernard Parish
Website: www.sbpanimal.homestead.com

E-Mail: sbpanimal@aol.com
Phone: 504-278-1534 or 504-228-1093
Mission: *To balance the health, safety and welfare needs of people and animals by protecting the rights of people from dangers/nuisances caused by uncontrolled animals; insuring the legal protection of animals from mistreatment; promoting, motivating and encouraging responsible pet ownership; providing a quality adoption program. To work with other groups to insure there are NO MORE HOMELESS PETS in our parish by developing programs to find pets responsible new homes; addressing the root problems of pet overpopulation and abuse; providing resident seniors with the health benefits of pet ownership while giving a second chance to adult pets at little or no cost to the senior; providing free humane educational materials to elementary school classes with the goal of breaking the cycle of animal, spouse and/or child abuse; providing low cost or free sterilization of dogs and cats owned by parish residents to stop the births of unwanted litters, preventing the tragic deaths of healthy companion animals in our shelter.*

Saving Georgia Dogs, Inc.
Accepts donations and is a 501(c)(3) organization
Location: Barnesville, GA (south of Atlanta)
Serves: All breeds of dogs
Contact: Suzy Bailey, Director
Website: www.savinggeorgiadogs.org
E-mail: info@savinggeorgiadogs.org
Mission: *We are an all-volunteer animal welfare organization and licensed rescue. We save dogs every day from death row in high-kill shelters throughout Georgia with an emphasis on shelters using the gas chamber to euthanize. We also are trying to implement spay/neuter programs to help reduce the number of unwanted pets in the state.*

Saving Paws Animal Rescue, Inc.
Accepts donations and is a 501(c)(3) organization
Location: Appleton, Wisconsin
Serves: Cats and dogs
Contact: Michelle McRae, Director
Website: www.savingpaws.com

E-mail: info@savingpaws.com
Phone: 920-830-2392
Mission: *We are a newly formed organization dedicated to rescuing homeless, abandoned and special needs animals in Northeast Wisconsin and finding them new adoptive homes or providing them lifelong sanctuary. We also seek to decrease the number of unwanted animals and the amount of animal cruelty in our community through outreach and education. Our no-kill shelter is completely volunteer-run and 100% of donations go directly to the care of the animals. Our philosophy is that ALL pets are worth saving, even if they have behavioral or health problems. Our future plans include building separate shelter areas for a variety of special needs pets.*

Southern Indiana Cattle Dog Rescue
Accepts donations
Location: Austin, Indiana
Serves: Australian Cattle Dogs only
Contact: Robyn Adair
Website: www.sicdr.petfinder.com
E-mail: rescuebluedogs@hotmail.com
Phone: 502-663-1118
Mission: *We are a privately run rescue group dedicated to saving Australian Cattle Dogs and Australian Cattle Dog mixes from euthanasia in government animal control facilities. We fully vet and temperament test all animals in our care before adopting them out.*

Tennessee Valley Cattle Dog Rescue (TVCDR)
Accepts donations and is a 501(c)(3) organization
Location: Georgetown, Tennessee
Serves: Australian Cattle Dogs only
Contact: Michael Stumpff
Website: www.tvcattledogrescue.org
E-mail: acdresq@gmail.com
Mission: *We focus on rescuing stray, abandoned, and unwanted Australian Cattle Dogs. We primarily rescue from municipal and county shelters in Tennessee, but occasionally assist with dogs from bordering states.*

8 ♥ CR

Disaster Preparedness Resources

🐾 Emergency Animal Rescue Service (EARS, of United Animal Nations)

www.UAN.org

At the website, select "Our Programs" then select "Emergency Animal Rescue Service." There you will find information on Volunteer Training Workshops, Disaster Preparedness, and Related Legislation. I completed the EARS one-day training workshop in Minnesota in 2007. This is a relatively inexpensive, yet complete course.

🐾 MuttShack Animal Rescue Foundation

www.MuttShack.org

Visit the website to learn more about MuttShack, see a video about the Katrina Promise, learn about Animal Rescue Certification (basic certification is now required for all disaster responders), and fill out the MuttShack Volunteer Application.

www.MuttShack.org/Animal_Rescue_Certification_Prospectus.htm

This prospectus provides a list and link to free online Emergency Management Institute (EMI) and independent study courses that are required for MuttShack First Responder Basic Rescue Technician Certification and for volunteering with LSART—the Louisiana State Animal Response Team. When you complete this training you will be issued a certificate from FEMA. MuttShack also offers online training at the Intermediate and Advanced Rescue Technician (Professional Development Series) levels.

❧ Noah's Wish

www.NoahsWish.org

At the website, select "Disaster Preparedness" or "Disaster Planning and Emergency Management."

Noah's Wish was founded for the purpose of caring for animals in disasters. I highly recommend the Noah's Wish Volunteer In-Field Training Program that is given in different areas of the country throughout the year. I took their training course in 2006 because I was impressed with how they operated after Hurricane Katrina. They also offer a training course on how to provide administrative support during disaster response. Organizational skills are in great demand during and following disasters.

❧ Book: <u>Out of Harm's Way: The Extraordinary True Story of One Woman's Lifelong Devotion to Animal Rescue</u>

by Terri Crisp and Samantha Glen

Includes a very thorough appendix entitled "Basic Tips for Safeguarding Your Dog and Cat During Disasters." Terri Crisp was a founder of EARS and Noah's Wish.

❧ Petfinder Animal Emergency Response Network

http://disaster.petfinder.com/emergency/

Internet location for nationwide lost and found pet listings during and following disasters.

❧ ♥ ❧

❧ Recommended Reading ❧

1 Dead in Attic: After Katrina, by Chris Rose

Beyond Words: Talking with Animals and Nature, by Marta Williams

Blessing the Bridge: What Animals Teach Us About Death, Dying, and Beyond, by Rita M. Reynolds

Communicating with Orcas: The Whales' Perspective, by Mary J. Getten

Conversations with Animals, by Lydia Hiby

The Culture Clash: A Revolutionary New Way of Understanding the Relationship Between Humans and Domestic Dogs, by Jean Donaldson

Dancer on the Grass: True Stories about Horses and People, by Teresa tsimmu Martino

Dog Days: Dispatches from Bedlam Farm, by Jon Katz

The Dogs of Bedlam Farm: An Adventure with Sixteen Sheep, Three Dogs, Two Donkeys, and Me, by Jon Katz

Dogs of Dreamtime: A Story About Second Chances and the Power of Love, by Karen Shanley

❧ Recommended Reading ❧

The Dogs Who Found Me: What I've Learned from Pets Who Were Left Behind, by Ken Foster

The Dream Giver, by Bruce Wilkinson

Emergency Animal Rescue Stories: One Woman's Dedication to Saving Animals from Disasters, by Terri Crisp

Feisty Fido: Help for the Leash-Aggressive Dog, by Patricia McConnell

Fifteen Legs: When All That Stands Between Death and Freedom is a Ride, by Bonnie Silva

Fight!—A Practical Guide to the Treatment of Dog-Dog Aggression, by Jean Donaldson

Getting in TTouch with Your Dog: A Gentle Approach to Influencing Behavior, Health, and Performance, by Linda Tellington-Jones

The Great Deluge: Hurricane Katrina, New Orleans, and the Mississippi Gulf Coast, by Douglas Brinkley

How to be the Leader of the Pack and Have Your Dog Love You for It!, by Patricia McConnell

Hurricane Katrina: Aftermath of Disaster, by Barb Palser

❧ Recommended Reading ❧

Java: The True Story of a Shelter Dog Who Rescued a Woman,
by Stacy J. Lewis

Katrina and the Forgotten Gulf Coast, by Betty Plombon

The Language of Animals: 7 Steps to Communicating with Animals,
by Carol Gurney

The Language of Miracles, by Amelia Kinkade

Learning Their Language: Intuitive Communication with Animals and
Nature, by Marta Williams

Lessons from a Stock Dog: A Training Guide, by Bruce Fogt

Mine! A Practical Guide to Resource Guarding in Dogs,
by Jean Donaldson

The New Work of Dogs: Tending to Life, Love and Family, by Jon Katz

On Talking Terms with Dogs: Calming Signals, by Turid Rugaas

Out of Harm's Way: The Extraordinary True Story of One Woman's
Lifelong Devotion to Animal Rescue, by Terri Crisp and Samantha Glen

❧ Recommended Reading ❧

Rescued: Saving Animals from Disaster, by Allen Anderson, Linda Anderson, and John Ensign

Rescuing Sprite: A Dog Lover's Story of Joy and Anguish, by Mark R. Levin

Seeing Eye to Eye With Your Dog: Solving the Canine Puzzle, by Debra Schneider

Sightings: The Gray Whales' Mysterious Journey, by Brenda Peterson and Linda Hogan

The Storm: What Went Wrong and Why During Hurricane Katrina— The Inside Story from One Louisiana Scientist, by Ivor van Heerden and Mike Bryan

Three Cats, Two Dogs: One Journey Through Multiple Pet Loss, by David Congalton

Unforgettable Mutts: Pure of Heart, Not of Breed, by Karen Derrico

The Wolf, the Woman, and the Wilderness: A True Story of Returning Home, by Teresa tsimmu Martino

Please visit www.8StateKate.net, where you can...

...See more **photos** of Kate's journey

...See the **Happy Endings**—read the stories of the dogs we have helped, and learn about dogs that are looking for homes

... Read the **blog**, including my return trip to Louisiana in 2008, rescue activities, and life with Bandit, Chase, and Cayenne **www.8StateKate.net/WordPress**

...Learn more about the **8 State Kate Fund**, providing financial relief for animals in desperate situations

...Purchase other **Kate products** to benefit animal rescue!

...Sign the **guest book** and share your ideas

Order *8 State Hurricane Kate: The Journey and Legacy of a Katrina Cattle Dog* at www.8StateKate.net

5350817R0

Made in the USA
Charleston, SC
02 June 2010